TOTALLY CHARMED

OTHER TITLES IN THE SMART POP SERIES

Taking the Red Pill
Science, Philosophy and Religion in The Matrix

Seven Seasons of Buffy
Science Fiction and Fantasy Writers Discuss Their Favorite Television Show

Five Seasons of Angel
Science Fiction and Fantasy Writers Discuss Their Favorite Vampire

What Would Sipowicz Do?
Race, Rights and Redemption in NYPD Blue

Stepping through the Stargate
Science, Archaeology and the Military in Stargate SG-1

The Anthology at the End of the Universe
Leading Science Fiction Authors on Douglas Adams' Hitchhiker's Guide to the Galaxy

Finding Serenity
Anti-heroes, Lost Shepherds and Space Hookers in Joss Whedon's Firefly

The War of the Worlds
Fresh Perspectives on the H. G. Wells Classic

Alias Assumed
Sex, Lies and SD-6

Navigating the Golden Compass
Religion, Science and Dæmonology in Philip Pullman's His Dark Materials

Farscape Forever!
Sex, Drugs and Killer Muppets

Flirting with Pride and Prejudice
Fresh Perspectives on the Original Chick-Lit Masterpiece

Revisiting Narnia
Fantasy, Myth and Religion in C. S. Lewis' Chronicles

TOTALLY

DEMONS, WHITELIGHTERS AND THE POWER OF THREE

CHARMED

EDITED BY
Jennifer Crusie

with Leah Wilson

BENBELLA BOOKS, INC.
Dallas, Texas

This publication has not been prepared, approved or licensed by any entity that created or produced the well-known television program *Charmed*.

"Confessions of a *Charmed* Addict"
 © 2005 by Jennifer Crusie
"'They killed Prue! YOU BASTARDS!'"
 © 2005 by Evelyn Vaughn
"The Ultimate Witch"
 © 2005 by Robert A. Metzger
"Will the Real Phoebe Please Stand Up?"
 © 2005 by Jennifer Dunne
"How Paige Matthews Saved *Charmed*"
 © 2005 by Leah Wilson
"*Charmed*: A Modern Fairy Tale"
 © 2005 by Debbie Viguié
"A Stake in the Future" © 2005 by Ruth Glick
"Enchanté…Not" © 2005 by Peg Aloi
"Three Is a Magic Number"
 © 2005 by John G. Hemry
"Charmed into Goodness" © 2005 by Anne Perry
"Why Are the Elders Such Jerks?"
 © 2005 by Richard Garfinkle
"Evil: Can't Live With It, Can't Quite Vanquish It"
 © 2005 by Kate Donovan
"What *Is* She Wearing?" © 2005 by Tanya Huff

"Sitting on the Dock of the Bay, Casting Spells"
 © 2005 by Nick Mamatas
"Talent and the Socialism of Fear"
 © 2005 by Jody Lynn Nye
"Why Can't This Witch Get Hitched?"
 © 2005 by Maggie Shayne
"Home Improvement in Magic Land"
 © 2005 by Vera Nazarian
"Good Witches Need Love, Too!"
 © 2005 by Alison Kent
"'Witch-Lit'—A Season of Romance"
 © 2005 by Catherine Spangler
"Charming the Tweener"
 © 2005 by Valerie Taylor
"The Charm of *Charmed*"
 © 2005 by Laura Resnick
"Seducing the *Charmed* Virgin"
 © 2005 by C. J. Barry
Cast Biographies
 © 2005 by BenBella Books, Inc.
Additional Materials © 2005 by Jennifer Crusie

All rights reserved. No part of this book may be used or reproduced in any manner whatsoever without written permission except in the case of brief quotations embodied in critical articles or reviews.

BenBella Books, Inc.
6440 N. Central Expy, Suite 617
Dallas, TX 75206
www.benbellabooks.com
Send feedback to feedback@benbellabooks.com

Printed in the United States of America
10 9 8 7 6 5 4 3 2

Library of Congress Cataloging-in-Publication Data

Totally Charmed : demons, whitelighters and the power of three / edited by Jennifer Crusie with Leah Wilson.
  p. cm.
 ISBN 1-932100-60-1
 1. Charmed (Television program) I. Crusie, Jennifer. II. Wilson, Leah.
PN1992.77.C47T68 2005
791.45'72—dc22

2005021159

Proofreading by Jessica Keet and Stacia Seaman
Printed by Victor Graphics, Inc.
Cover design by Laura Watkins
All photos copyright © Albert L. Ortega
Text design and composition by John Reinhardt Book Design

Distributed by Independent Publishers Group
To order call (800) 888-4741 • www.ipgbook.com

For media inquiries and special sales contact Yara Abuata at yara@benbellabooks.com

CONTENTS

Introduction: **Confessions of a *Charmed* Addict** JENNIFER CRUSIE	1

The Sisters

"They killed Prue! YOU BASTARDS!" EVELYN VAUGHN	7
The Ultimate Witch ROBERT A. METZGER	15
Will the Real Phoebe Please Stand Up? JENNIFER DUNNE	25
How Paige Matthews Saved *Charmed* LEIGH ADAMS WRIGHT	35

Their Roots

***Charmed*: A Modern Fairy Tale** DEBBIE VIGUIÉ	43
A Stake in the Future REBECCA YORK	49
Enchanté . . . Not PEG ALOI	59

Their Moral and Magical World

Three Is a Magic Number JOHN G. HEMRY	71

Charmed into Goodness ANNE PERRY	81
Why Are the Elders Such Jerks? RICHARD GARFINKLE	91
Evil: Can't Live With It, Can't Quite Vanquish It KATE DONOVAN	103

Their Material World

What *Is* She Wearing? TANYA HUFF	117
Sitting on the Dock of the Bay, Casting Spells NICK MAMATAS	123
Talent and the Socialism of Fear JODY LYNN NYE	129

Their Men

Why Can't This Witch Get Hitched? MAGGIE SHAYNE	139
Home Improvement in Magic Land VERA NAZARIAN	151
Good Witches Need Love, Too! ALISON KENT	159
"Witch-Lit"—A Season of Romance CATHERINE SPANGLER	171

Their Viewers

Charming the Tweener VALERIE TAYLOR	183
The Charm of *Charmed* LAURA RESNICK	191
Seducing the *Charmed* Virgin C. J. BARRY	199
Cast Biographies	211

CONFESSIONS OF A CHARMED ADDICT

WHY I KEEP GOING BACK TO HALLIWELL MANOR

JENNIFER CRUSIE

SEVERAL YEARS AGO, I posted to a pop culture internet loop, "I am totally hooked on the cheese that is *Charmed*." That was a lie; while *Charmed* does have its Velveeta moments, the things that make me watch the series aren't cheesy at all. For every unbearably twee episode about leprechauns and unicorns, there are stories that deal honestly with sisterhood, love, longing and loss. Seven seasons have passed, and *Charmed* is still worth watching for the things that got me the first time I tuned in, the things that charmed me, if you will.

The aspect that grabbed me first was all that *power*. The magic itself is fun in a nose-twitching kind of way, and it's very nice that the sisters are Helping Others, but what I really love is the way they fry everybody who tries to hurt them. Prue when she was angry was poetic justice in motion, and once Piper learned to blow things up, it just got better. I'm addicted to that sense of wrongs righted—not only bad guys foiled, but gloating, rude, obnoxious, snotty bad guys, demons that act like every rotten human being I've ever met. It was fun that Prue could move things with her mind, but it was *satisfying* when she moved something right into the middle of a jerk's sneer. Oh, yeah, I love the power.

But there's also the sisterhood. *Charmed*'s premise is inherently sentimental: three sisters reunited by discovering their destinies, forced to work together because their power is much greater when they cooperate, putting aside their differences and becoming a team. Go team. But in the early episodes, it wasn't hokey because *Charmed* was still taking itself seriously enough to show the Halliwells as real people with real flaws. In those shows, Shannen Doherty, Holly Marie Combs and Alyssa Milano made their characters so sympathetic and their relationships with each other so emotionally true that they went beyond the Bewitched Brady Bunch into honestly cathartic connection. (The only sour notes from this period were the treacle-soaked appearances of Grams and Dead Mom, especially Dead Mom, who it seemed never had an impious thought in her life until she was outed in the fourth season as an adulterer. *That* appearance I enjoyed.) The outcome of all of that emotional growth was a family of three strong women working together and supporting each other. That alone would have kept me tuning in every Sunday.

And then there are the love stories. I'm a sucker for a good romance, and there have been some great ones on *Charmed*, three of the best from the guys with staying power. Ted King's Andy tried to make things work with Prue for all of season one and then died protecting her, a hero to the end. Brian Krause's Leo has a doofus personality that meshed sweetly with Piper's spineless nice girl in the early seasons, but it's Julian McMahon's Cole who gets the prize for Best Boyfriend Ever. Part human, part demon and all Phoebe's, Cole may have been the Source of all Evil, but he was also charming, funny and desperately in love.

The problem is that it's hard for a series to maintain emotional intensity throughout a long run. Thus, in the early seasons, when the sisters loved and lost, it hurt. Andy's death mattered. Prue's death mattered. Cole's death mattered (all three times). But as the years have passed, Leo has become unbearably pious and dorky, and miscellaneous other boyfriends have come and gone without making enough of an impression for the viewer to care. This emotional attrition wasn't helped when the show's writers began to trade drama for campy comedy, which made for either amazing television or cover-your-eyes disaster. The entire romantic arc of Phoebe Queen of Evil (as the vamping wife of Cole's Source) was brilliant; lecherous leprechauns were just wince-inducing. There's been some great kitsch—the "Y Tu Mummy Tambien" episode stands out for me here—and abysmal misfires—I'm not getting over that leprechaun disaster anytime soon. In these later seasons, the scenes that featured weak guest actors tended toward mugging and melodrama; those that featured good supporting casts—Adrian Paul as the mummy-lover, Billy Zane's all too short run as the doomed ex-demon Drake, Oded Fehr's nicely calibrated evil as Zankou—soared as the actors found the energy and the emotion in the camp and stepped on the "melo" to heighten the drama.

One episode in particular showed *Charmed* at both its best and worst. In 2005's "The Seven Year Witch," long-suffering and incredibly dull Leo was once again taken away from Piper by the Elders, those heavenly storm troopers in choir gowns. Piper was mortally wounded, and only Leo could save her, but the Elders had taken Leo's memory.... I'd go on, but it's too painful, truly one of the worst plots in *Charmed* history. (And that's saying something. Did I mention the leprechaun episode? It was called "Lucky Charmed." No, I'm not kidding.) In one particularly abysmal scene, Leo chose his life with Piper over his heavenly duties and fell off the Golden Gate Bridge, after which an Elder moonlighting as the Exposition Fairy explained, "He has fallen from grace." If Paige and Phoebe were truly against evil, they'd have shoved him after Leo.

So why was this episode also great? Because Julian McMahon came back and sparred with Holly Marie Combs, giving Combs somebody to act with for a change. It was a dark day for *Charmed* when McMahon left to nip and tuck, and his guest appearance here only underscored the loss. The dialogue in their scenes would have been cringe inducing, except that nobody can sell undying love like McMahon or furious pain like Combs, and their rematch was fast and clean and emotionally true. (My *Charmed* fantasy: Cole comes back from the dead again, realizes he loves Piper and seduces her. Cole and Piper are such rich characters and McMahon and Combs are so good together that I'd watch that one play out forever. And it's not like Cole is easy to kill or tends to stay dead. I'm just saying, it could happen.) Meanwhile, over on the couch, a maniacally chipper Billy Zane was holding his own against Alyssa Milano's blinding smile and tragedy-tinged perkiness, both of them hopelessly happy to be with each other even though he was doomed to die at sundown. The dialogue in this episode may have been over the top, but the energy was real.

And that's where *Charmed* is at its best: when it generates that manic energy in service to honest emotion, an unabashed focus on love—of sisters, significant others and humanity—that refuses to be cynical or blasé. There are very few shows on television that spit in the eyes of the critics and follow their own too-warm-to-be-cool, too-hokey-to-be-hip paths, but *Charmed* goes blithely on its way, turning its stars into Lady Godiva and Red Riding Hood, dressing the pious in white robes and the bad in black leather, putting the cheese in its cheesecake and the ho in "Holy cow, what is she wearing?" Like the little girl with the curl, when *Charmed* is good, it is very, very good, and when it's bad, it's, well, Dead Mom and leprechauns, but even then I keep coming back for more. This is a show that's having a damn good time and inviting the viewer to have one with it.

Of course my reasons for watching *Charmed* aren't the only ones. The essays in this book will give you twenty-one more viewpoints on the sisters, their roots, their morals and magic, their material world, their lovers and their viewers. And beyond these writers, many more voices weigh in, from the breathless adoration of the Internet fan boards to the snarky loathing of the Television Without Pity critic who is still mourning the loss of Andy and Cole, particularly the shirtless episodes. They and millions like them tune in every Sunday night to see what Piper, Phoebe and Paige are doing (and wearing), drawn by the magic, the sisterhood and the love.

And I'm there, too, because even with leprechauns, even with Leo, even without Cole, I am still hopelessly hooked on the cheese that is *Charmed*.

THE SISTERS
THE POWER OF THREE...UH, FOUR

The core of *Charmed* is the sisterhood of the Halliwell women, but what takes that sisterhood beyond those mushy "very special moments"—please, somebody, put stakes through the hearts of Grams and Dead Mom so they will *stay dead*—is the beautifully developed arcs the characters experience and the equally well-developed arc their sisterhood has achieved over the past seven seasons. Their sacrifices for the greater good and for each other are heart-wrenching and real, and the maturity they find is hard-earned.

"THEY KILLED PRUE! YOU BASTARDS!"

(A.K.A. DEATH REALLY TAKES A HALLIWELL)

EVELYN VAUGHN

As the kick-ass older sister, Prue Halliwell was first among equals, so when the actress who played her departed the show, the writers had a real problem on their hands. Evelyn Vaughn thinks they solved it just fine by remembering that some characters are so indelible, they're irreplaceable.

TO FULLY UNDERSTAND what happened to Prue Halliwell, and how *Charmed* turned her tragedy into a qualified triumph, we must first grasp one salient point:

Characters are not the actors who portray them.

Oh, suuure. We like to *think* we know that. Every time we hear about some obsessed fan snarking at Susan Lucci because Erica Kane does something bitchy, we shake our heads in condescending superiority. And yet, how often is Keri Russell greeted with shouts of, "Hey, Felicity!" How often do we let our perception of an actor color our memory of the character? Captain Kirk was not William Shatner, people! Captain Kirk was sexy as hell, but he had nowhere near the sense of humor Shatner does. As Leonard Nimoy wrote in his 1975 autobiography *I Am Not Spock*, "I am not Spock."

And the real test? How often do fans mourn the marriage of a popular actor?

Please. Like you really would have had a chance with Russell Crowe if only it weren't for her? Be glad for the nice folks, for heaven's sake!

True, actors are intricately connected to their characters. Actors *look* like their characters—or vice versa, if you want to get into a chicken/egg debate. Often actors seem to merge their energies with those of the character, creating a being that we, the audience, cannot experience through any other means. (As Leonard Nimoy wrote in his 1995 autobiography *I Am Spock*, "I am Spock." A complex guy, that Nimoy).

The actor is by no means trivial. The actor is the channel through which we get our weekly character fix. But *the actor is not the character.*

And this is a problem.

Because of this, actors can get pregnant when it's less than logical for their character to. This forces the writers of their show to either film very creatively around the character (Carrie Bradshaw, B'Elanna Torres) or write an out-of-character pregnancy (Maddie Hayes? Phoebe Buffay?? *Xena*???) Actors who dislike each other can get in the way of characters who are madly in love (I'm talking about you, *Moonlighting*). Actors quit (like David Caruso in *NYPD Blue*) or are fired (like Suzanne Somers in *Three's Company*) or become ill (like Kate Jackson in *The Scarecrow and Mrs. King*).

In more tragic circumstances, actors die. That deprives the world not only of the great spirits that were Jerry Orbach, John Ritter and Jon-Erik Hexum, but of the pleasures of Detective Lenny Briscoe from the *Law & Order* franchise, Paul Hennessy from *8 Simple Rules*...and Mac Harper of *Cover Up*. Maybe it seems trivial, to mourn the loss of a character when a real human has been taken. But really, most of us *didn't know* the human. We don't know if he was a morning person or a night owl; we don't know if he was scared of heights or spiders; we don't know if he liked ketchup. Our sympathy for the person and his family, while quite real, has a distance to it. Or it should. But we do mourn, because we knew of that person what he put into his character, and we've lost that. We had a seasonal, weekly date with an imaginary friend, and we *miss* it.

Thankfully, the death that struck the Charmed Ones at the end of their show's third season was far less tragic. It was a make-believe death. But on a television series, when a show can rise or fall on the popularity of its characters, losing a major star can spell catastrophe. The popular Web site jumptheshark.com lists not one, not two, but *three* different ways a show can ruin itself through the loss of a star.

When *Charmed* faced (some would say "brought about") the loss of Shannen Doherty, a lot was put on the line. Not only was Doherty one of the most visible and well-known of the show's stars—she played one of three sisters who, together, formed the unbeatable Charmed Ones, wielding the Power of Three. The cover of the Book of Shadows; the opening credits; Kit's collar tag: they all show the Celtic triangle knot, people. Threes!

And yet the producers ditched one third of their trio. This was a huge risk! It was like the Beatles breaking up...except without the great music and probably nowhere near as important on a cultural level.

And nobody blamed Yoko Ono.

Well...hardly anybody.

"Why?" you might ask—especially if you weren't reading the trades during the spring/summer of 2001. "Why did they have to kill Prue?"

As you might expect, several versions of the story are floating around. The official one reports a "mutual decision." The more common story, and the particular curse of female colleagues, is that the gals just didn't get along. Some sources say that Alyssa Milano, who plays younger sister Phoebe, issued the producers an ultimatum: her or Doherty. She has denied it. Some sources say that Doherty first asked to leave and was refused, but later was fired. Over the phone. One has to wonder how things would have been different if Milano herself hadn't replaced Lori Rom in the pilot episode as the "youngest" Halliwell sister.

In any case, the past is past—unless you have your own Book of Shadows and can try out one of those cool Reverse Time spells, although almost anyone well-versed in pop culture knows they rarely turn out well...except maybe for Marty McFly. The point is, we don't really know the actresses and our interest in their career ups and downs could be seen as fairly tacky.

But *we knew Prue*. We *lost* Prue. And the writers/producers were faced with some pretty dire choices.

Think about how it could have gone....

SOLUTION 1

Prue Just Leaves Town

This solution has had mixed success with TV series in the past. Sometimes, the character leaves for a decent but annoying reason, like when Doug Ross quit County General—and, worse, his lover Carol!—after one of his worst days ever on *ER*. To his credit, George Clooney had given the series five years before leaving for what he'd already built into a successful movie career. And the show had been building his character's dissatisfaction with authority from the start. But surely I wasn't the only one yelling at the screen, "You've been up for days, threatened with a lawsuit, fired...get a good night's sleep, *then* make a major life decision!" Annoying.

Sometimes the reason is disgustingly contrived, like back on *Cheers* when Diane Chambers couldn't marry Sam Malone because...she had to write a book instead? Me, I know plenty of novelists who are also married. But Shelley Long was determined to move on and, like Clooney, she'd given the series five years, so that was that. I don't blame her. I blame Diane, and the writers. *To write a book?* Sheesh.

Occasionally the departure actually makes sense, no matter how we protest the plot twist, like when *Law & Order*'s Detective Mike Logan lost his notorious temper, slugged a politician and got demoted to Staten Island so that Chris Noth could move on to sexier pastures, or when Sam Seaborn left the West Wing in order to keep a promise by running for state office, freeing Rob Lowe up for *The Lyon's Den* and *Dr. Vegas*. (Rob, Rob, why must you hurt us so?)

And sometimes characters just mysteriously vanish in a puff of misplaced continuity, like Richie Cunningham's brother Chuck on *Happy Days* or Ellenor Frutt's baby on *The Practice*.

The problem for *Charmed* was that Prue would not have left. Remember, we're talking the character, not the actress. Prue Halliwell was the oldest sister; she was the strongest witch. There was no way in hell the writers could have sold us on the idea that she suddenly decided to elope, or to pursue a new career off somewhere that didn't have telephones or transatlantic flights. If she even tried it, surely her sisters would have assumed she was under an evil demon's spell and done everything in their Book of Shadows to return her to her right mind.

In a bad situation, this was one minor triumph for the show. They did *not* attempt to have Prue simply move away.

SOLUTION 2
Someone Else Can Play Prue

I'm surprised that *Charmed* didn't go this route. True, it's become something of a self-referential joke, such as when the characters on *Roseanne*—including a new version of Becky—complained loudly about the way *Bewitched* swapped Darrins midstream. And it's hard to pull off, because it strains our willing suspension of disbelief. After Richard Thomas left *The Waltons*, the writers made a mistake in trying to bring in a new John Boy, because not even the Baldwin sisters' medicine could have kept his close-knit family, much less the audience, from noticing the difference. No amount of plastic surgery could explain the changes in the new Fallon Carrington Colby (who went from a Pamela Sue Martin to an Emma Samms) on *Dynasty*. And although *Alias Smith and Jones*' Hannibal Heyes and Kid Curry were under cover as Joshua Smith and Thaddeas Jones, old west outlaws didn't have the power of disguise to convince us that a Heyes who used to look like the talented but tormented Pete Duel suddenly looked like narrator Roger Davis.

But that said? *Alias Smith and Jones* supposedly took place in the American West, *Dynasty* in Denver and *The Waltons* in Virginia. In a supposedly ordinary West, Denver and Virginia. *Charmed*, on the other hand, is a show about magic. Yes, it's set in San Francisco, but it's a magical, overrun-with-demons San Francisco.

With the kinds of powers the Charmed Ones had, the writers could have switched actors for Prue and made it marginally believable. Prue could have woken up one morning looking completely different, stared at herself in the mirror and murmured a classic Sam Beckett "Oh boy" from *Quantum Leap*. She could have switched bodies with someone else, like Buffy and Faith did for two episodes of *Buffy the Vampire Slayer*, or Xena and Callisto did on *Xena: Warrior Princess*. A new actress could have carried Prue around in her head like Dr. McCoy carried Spock throughout most of *Star Trek III: The Search for Spock* after the mindmeld in *Star Trek II: The Wrath of Khan*.

And the thing is, *they could have made this work*. The Charmed Ones would have looked a little different, but they otherwise would have remained intact. This would have, in fact, been the easy way out. It would have left us with Prue, albeit a Prue who might not have lived up to the original.

Which is the second triumph of how the show handled Doherty's unfortunate absence. They didn't take the easy route. They went with....

SOLUTION 3
Prue Really Dies

Mind you, I'm not a big fan of death within TV shows. In fact, I usually hate it. I'm one of those people who believes that we see more than enough death in our real lives without tuning in and sitting through commercials in order to get an extra helping in our entertainment. I only tried one episode of *CSI*—its pilot with its "fooled you!" ending that killed the apparent lead—before rejecting it for just that reason and didn't learn what a good show it was until three seasons later. Even without regularly watching *NYPD Blue*, I hated losing Jimmy Smits' Detective Bobby Simone. And do not even get me started on the final episodes of *Forever Knight* and *Xena*, or the let's-kill-Catherine episode of *Beauty and the Beast* (the series, people; the series).

I mean—yes, the characters may not *belong* to the viewers. But the only reason the characters' shows are produced is because viewers commit themselves enough to tune in week after week. This is how you reward their devotion?

Really. *Don't* get me started.

And yet somehow, despite all that, Prue's death worked. It worked on so many levels that what could have been *Charmed*'s biggest tragedy became *Charmed*'s greatest triumph. And why is that?

It's because the writers and producers remembered the audience. And they remembered the truth: *that the characters are not the actors.* Maybe they didn't like Shannen Doherty; only she and they know for sure. But the love they felt for Prue was tangible.

Here's what they did that made Prue's death work:

GOOD THING 1

It Was Significant

It's bad enough when characters die. But for the love of heaven, at least let them go out with style. I can think of a certain Enterprise security chief who wasn't given that dignity on *Star Trek: The Next Generation*. (People will argue that a senseless death like Tasha Yar's is "realistic," but again I counter: TV isn't about realism but verisimilitude. I don't tune in for reality. Thanks anyway.) Then there was Paul McCrane's Dr. Robert Romano on *ER*, who survived a special-episode amputation only to have a helicopter fall on him. Characters didn't even learn of his death on-camera. Anticlimax, much?

At least Prue died valiantly. She threw herself between a demon bolt and an innocent. It's how she would have wanted it...other than the being dead part, that is.

GOOD THING 2

Other Characters Mourned Her

Generally, when a character is killed off, writers use that opportunity to show us the resulting grief, usually at the graveside. The characters on *21 Jump Street* looked appropriately grim as we learned via an expository eulogy that Captain Richard Jenko had been killed by a drunk driver (read: Frederic Forrest just didn't work out). Johnny Depp and

Michael DeLuise with clenched jaws, mmm! When *ER*'s Mark Greene finally died, even a few departed characters like Peter Benton showed up at the funeral. (Not, sadly, Doug Ross. And Doug would have been there.) But unless the funeral scene is the final shot of the episode, the episode usually then veers off into business-as-usual, and within a week the character is forgotten.

Less time than that, if someone dies on *Smallville*.

On *Charmed*, Prue got her mourning period. She died in the last episode of the third season. The first episode in the fourth season was all about her funeral, including the presence of a mysterious young woman whose name starts with a coincidental P. Two episodes later, despite the remaining Halliwells having learned they've got a half-sister named Paige, Piper was still furious enough at the loss of her sister to cause all kinds of problems. Okay, so that's only three episodes, but it's better than most television characters get, and besides, after that Cole started going evil again. Priorities are priorities.

The sisters still haven't forgotten Prue. Paige sometimes mourns her inability to ever live up to her dead older sister's powerful reputation. Phoebe and Piper sometimes mention missing her. If the Powers That Be hadn't so thoroughly burned bridges, I wouldn't be surprised by a special guest spot via flashback or ghostly visitation, a la George Clooney's Doug Ross doing a cameo on *ER* (I will always love him for that) or, more to the topic, Julian McMahon bringing Cole back, however briefly, to *Charmed*.

If *we* haven't forgotten Prue, it would suck for her sisters to have done so. They haven't. Well played.

GOOD THING 3

They Didn't Try to Replicate Her

True, the producers did replace Prue. The remaining Halliwells found a long-lost half-sister of whom they'd been hitherto ignorant—a stretch, yes, but no more of a stretch than some of those clothes they wear, or the number of men they go through. But the character of Paige, competently played by Rose McGowan, is no carbon copy of Prue. Paige is the youngest, while Prue was the oldest. Perhaps because of this, Paige has a better sense of humor than Prue had. Paige is easygoing, while Prue was take-charge. And Paige has certain skills inherited from her Whitelighter father, which Prue did not. In other words, the writers brought in another sister to complete the triad, but they deliberately did not try to recreate the character of Prue when they did so.

This is less common than you'd think. When the blond, smiling, tanned Farrah Fawcett left *Charlie's Angels*, taking the character of Jill Munroe with her, who replaced her? The blond, smiling, tanned Cheryl Ladd, as Kris Munroe, Jill's younger sister. When Suzanne Somers proved to be ahead of her time (that would be the time of *Friends*) by demanding too large a raise on *Three's Company*, her character, Chrissy Snow, was replaced by—wait for it!—her cousin Cindy Snow, played by Jenilee Harrison doing a Suzanne Somers impression, right down to the snort. When the writers of *The Andy Griffith Show* decided to spin the popular character of Gomer Pyle off into his own show (*Gomer Pyle, U.S.M.C.*), who should show up to take his place but his cousin, Goober Pyle. Both brunettes. Both goofy. Both with thick accents.

Too often it's a case of second verse, pale imitation of the first.

But *Charmed* dared to be different. If nothing else, Prue had black hair, while Paige is a redhead—most of the time.

In other words, it could have been worse. Much, much worse. As long as characters are portrayed by actors (and who can tell what computer animation will bring), television shows like *Charmed* will face crises such as these. And when they do, they will have a choice. They can discard the characters as quickly and thoroughly as they discard the actors who played them. Or they can keep the viewers in mind—you remember, those people who help bring in ratings?—and remember that, imaginary or not, characters deserve respect. They aren't just pawns to move around the playing field of a series. They are the reason we tune in. And a wrong step (such as Cindy Snow) is reason enough to tune out.

As for the way the writers disposed of Cole...?

That's another essay.

> Evelyn Vaughn believes in the magic of stories. The author of a dozen published romance/adventure novels and as many fantasy short stories (written as Von Jocks), she is perhaps best known for her paranormal books with Silhouette Shadows and Silhouette Bombshell. As Yvonne Jocks, she edited two anthologies about witches for Berkley Books. When not weaving words, she teaches English at Tarrant County College SE in Arlington, Texas.
>
> Evelyn is an unapologetic TV addict. She's still trying to figure out how to time travel or meet up with some of her favorite characters. Check out her Web site at www.evelynvaughn.com.

THE ULTIMATE WITCH

ROBERT A. METZGER

Piper Halliwell isn't just the levelheaded, bra-wearing, heir-bearing sister, Robert A. Metzger says. She's also the one with the most power, real and potential. And the scientist in him can't help building a better Piper—nuclear capability and all.

MAGIC AND SCIENCE DON'T MIX.
Most folks might believe that—but most scientists don't.
What is not often appreciated is that the goal of scientists is not in the deriving of new equations, the building of a better eight-sliced toaster or the discovery of a new species of an Amazonian tri-horned beetle. No. The goal of scientists is to perform magic. No one has articulated this better than Arthur C. Clarke, a scientist of great renown (he invented the concept of the geosynchronous satellite) as well as one of the major science fiction writers of the twentieth century, having written *2001: A Space Odyssey*. Clarke created three laws that distilled the core of how science and scientists work. They are:

> LAW 1: When a distinguished but elderly scientist states that something is possible he is almost certainly right. When he states that something is impossible, he is very probably wrong.
> LAW 2: The only possible way of discovering the limits of the possible is to venture a little way past them into the impossible.
> LAW 3: Any sufficiently advanced technology is indistinguishable from magic.

So why should you care?

You're interested in the Halliwell sisters—in witches, Whitelighters, demons and the various powers they wield. Digging into the nuances of Arthur C. Clarke's three laws is not why you're reading this book about the Charmed Ones. But there is a connection.

Science can show us how to build a better witch.

And when we're talking about *better*, we're talking about *powers*. Might it be possible to take a look at what powers the Charmed Ones possess, analyze them from the perspective of a scientist and then come up with a better witch? I think so. Let's first take a look at just what powers the witches of *Charmed* manifest:

PRUE: Telekinesis and Astral Projection
PIPER: Molecular Inhibition and Molecular Combustion
PHOEBE: Premonitions and Levitation
PAIGE: Orbing and Telekinetic Orbing

All these powers are certainly magical and quite complementary (the better to fight demons with). However, there is one witch whose powers have a decided *physics* bent to them—still magical of course, but powers that your average physicist-on-the-street might take a moment to consider. That witch is Piper, whose powers center around the manipulation of molecules. Scientists just love molecules, having spent centuries in not only figuring out just what they are, but also in figuring out how to control them and how to harness their powers. So Piper will be the template upon which we'll build a better witch through science.

Imagine for a moment that you are a young scientist and you've had a startling breakthrough in the lab where, instead of running the standard experiments on blending frog DNA with a Pentium 4, you'd spent the last week watching the first seven seasons of *Charmed*. You run to the office of your mentor, Dr. Ancient One (Clarke defined an old scientist as one over the age of thirty), and tell this master of the equation and test tube that after having downloaded every episode of *Charmed* ever produced into your neocortex, you experienced a genuine eureka moment and realized that it would be possible to analyze the powers of the Charmed Ones, discern the underlying scientific principles of those powers and apply your broad depth of scientific insight to figure out how to enhance their magical abilities, pushing them into realms of witchdom never before imagined.

This is the working hypothesis that you present to Dr. Ancient One.

Dr. Ancient One has of course never seen a single episode of *Charmed*, so does not have a clue as to what your sleep-deprived ramble is referring to. However, he is able to ascertain that you've claimed you can improve the magical ability of a witch by applying scientific insights.

"Impossible!" he wheezes.

Hearing that makes you smile, because you know Clarke's first law: if an ancient scientist tells you something is impossible, then he is probably wrong.

"Impossible!" he wheezes for a second time.

And now your confidence grows even greater, because you know Clarke's second law: it is only while exploring the realm of the impossible that you will discover something truly new. Dr. Ancient One has confirmed your suspicions that you are in fact operating in the realm of the impossible. Excellent!

"Magic?" Dr. Ancient One finally croaks.

And with that you know you're on the verge of major discoveries because, as Clarke's third law tells you, any sufficiently advanced technology is indistinguishable from magic. If Dr. Ancient One believes you're operating in the realm of magic, then you're undoubtedly knocking on the door of an earth-shattering breakthrough. And quite possibly, if you can successfully apply scientific principles to the creation of the ultimate witch, perhaps the *Charmed* production staff will hire you as a technical consultant. Then your knees go weak and you break out in a cold sweat. You realize that if you can pull this off, perhaps they might even ask you for a script treatment.

Just before you faint, you manage to use all your scientific powers to pull yourself together (you start mumbling the value of pi out to 200 significant digits—a very powerful, mind-numbing spell, that works on both mortals and witches), regain some small amount of composure, shake Dr. Ancient One's gnarled, old hand and run back to your lab, stopping only at the vending machine to stock up on salt-laden snacks and hyper-caffeinated sodas, knowing it will be another all-nighter in the pursuit of scientific truths. You barricade yourself in your lab, plop yourself down at your desk and open up your notebook. The entry you put down is:

How to Build the Ultimate Witch

Where to start? Like any good scientist, you know that it is best to consider those avenues of research for which you feel passion, with which your persona resonates. You think of all the experiments you've run, and ask yourself what have been the most exciting moments of your scientific career.

Invariably you recall those moments in which you blew something up.

Nothing quite says science like an explosion.

You smile as you think of Piper and her dual powers of Molecular Combustion and Molecular Inhibition. Fire and Ice. This is a sort of yin and yang thing, and as a scientist you resonate with that. One of the most fundamental premises of physics is that for every action there is an equal and opposite reaction. This is what drives a rocket ship: the hot, explosive gasses blowing off in one direction, the rocket then thrusting off in the opposite direction. You first consider Piper's power of Molecular Combustion. As a scientist, this one is easy for you to understand. Heat is nothing but enhanced molecular motion.

Take a balloon full of gas. What keeps the skin of the balloon taut are the gas molecules inside of it, bouncing about, ricocheting not only off one another, but against the sides of the balloon as they smash into them. Each time one hits the inside of the balloon and bounces back, the "for every action there is an equal and opposite reaction" credo comes into play. As the molecule bounces away, the side of the balloon recoils just a microscopic bit. Because these gas molecules are striking the balloon evenly on all sides, the balloon does not go scooting away like a rocket, but all that bouncing does apply a uniform pressure to the inside of the balloon, keeping it inflated and its skin taut.

Then Piper's power is applied.

Molecular motion is increased, so that the molecules in the balloon start moving around faster, and as a consequence, when they collide with the inside of the balloon they impart a greater force.

So what happens then?

The balloon grows bigger, of course. And the more that molecular motion is increased, the bigger the balloon gets. If this continues, eventually the balloon pops and the hot molecules go spilling out into the room. What works for a balloon will work for any object, including the demons that Piper typically focuses her power on.

So Molecular Combustion makes scientific sense. This is the yin of her powers. Now for the yang: Molecular Inhibition. This one makes you scratch your head a bit. Molecular Inhibition you certainly understand from a physics perspective. If you took that same balloon and decreased the motion of the molecules within it, the punch with which they'd hit the inside wall of the balloon would decrease, and the balloon would start to shrink as the gas inside cooled. The problem is that when Piper employs this power it is not in order to slow down or stop the motion of molecules but rather, seemingly, to stop time. When Piper unleashes Molecular Inhibition, the fragments of an exploding object suddenly hang still in midair. Your physics training tells you that this is not really a case of Molecular Inhibition, but of Temporal Inhibition, in which *time* is slowed or stopped, and that is a whole different ballgame.

If you take an object, freeze it to a temperature of absolute zero, what happens is that the molecules within it stop buzzing about and are in fact locked in place. But if you take that object and knock it off a table, it still falls to the floor regardless of what the molecules inside of it are doing. So something else is at play in the case of what the Charmed Ones refer to as Molecular Inhibition.

So where is the true yang of the yin's Molecular Combustion?

Then you see it and realize once again that it pays to do your research. Since you just reviewed every episode of *Charmed*, the episode "Bride and Gloom" is still fresh in your sleep-deprived brain. In that episode Prue was forced into marrying an evil warlock in a ceremony that, in turn, made the other sisters evil. This also had the effect of twisting the sister's powers. What had erroneously been called Molecular Inhibition now truly became Molecular Inhibition, when this ability was transformed into what was then called cryokinesis. Piper could literally freeze objects, encasing them in ice.

Now this is more like it.

And it suddenly all makes sense from a scientific perspective. When Piper is a good witch, she can explode objects by increasing molecular motion, but when she is a bad witch, she can freeze objects by decreasing their molecular motion. There is none of the confusing aspect of time slowing and stopping involved in this—it is a pure case of equal and opposite reactions, in this case manifesting itself differently depending on whether Piper is good or evil.

And it is at that point that you have your eureka moment of scientific bliss.

What you just realized is that your insight is nothing new. In fact, the scientific basis for this magical ability to speed up or slow down molecular motion is more than a century old, developed by one of the greatest scientists of the nineteenth century—James Clerk Maxwell.

Never heard of him?

Well, you should thank him.

More than a century and a half ago Maxwell came up with a set of equations that unified electricity and magnetism, and with the aid of these electromagnetic equations, such developments as radio and television became possible. Whenever you talk on your cell phone, your voice is transformed into electromagnetic waves that obey Maxwell's equations.

But there was also something else he did in another area of research, that of thermodynamics. He created what is now called *Maxwell's Demon*. That's right—one of the greatest scientists of all time created a Demon.

And this is what his Demon did.

Maxwell imagined a sealed box full of gas (much like our balloon) that is divided into two compartments connected by a very small door. Sitting next to the door is a demon with the power to see individual molecules. Whenever the demon sees a molecule zipping about at great speed (high-energy molecules are what make things feel hot) about to hit the door, he opens the door and lets the molecule pass into the other compartment. In a similar fashion, whenever he sees a molecule dragging by, barely moving (low-energy molecules are what make things feel cold) in the compartment that he just let the hot molecule zip into, he opens the door and lets it into the other compartment. After a while one compartment holds all the slow-moving molecules, while the other compartment holds all the fast-moving molecules.

Wait a few moments and something magical happens.

One side of the box starts to grow icicles, while the other side of the box glows red from heat. Has this behavior ever been observed? Have you ever watched a box grow icicles from one side and burst into flames on the other?

I doubt it.

And the reason should be obvious—you don't have access to a Maxwell's Demon. They are tough to control, no doubt about it. Scientists have been trying to build one of these little beasts for the last century and a half without much luck, though in the last few years they have had some success building them to operate in very small boxes, such as you might find in the microscopic corners of integrated circuits.

But in this case you don't need to build one.

Because one already exists—Piper's powers obviously flow from a Maxwell's Demon over which she has control. Now while Piper can use her Maxwell's Demon to explode some evil demon, or encase a witch in ice, to the scientific mind it is obvious that Piper has not even scratched the surface of the inherent powers of a Maxwell's Demon.

But a scientist can show her the way.

Consider first the classical operation of Maxwell's Demon. He works best when shoving hot molecules in one direction and pushing cold molecules in the opposite direction. Think about Piper as she faces down a demon, attempting to use Molecular Combustion to blow it up. She could get so much more bang for her buck if she played to the strength of Maxwell's Demon. Rather than having it just try to stuff fast-moving molecules in the vicinity of her target, she should also have it remove slow-moving molecules and direct them toward a second target.

Two for the price of one.

Take a standard demon, and have Piper's Maxwell's Demon concentrate every fast-moving molecule in its head and every slow-moving molecule in its chest. Faster than you can say presto, its head will explode, and its frozen chest will shatter into infinite pieces from the shock of the exploding head. Or, if facing two demons, one can be made to explode and the other frozen and then shattered. Yin and yang. For every action there is an opposite and equal reaction. This is science pure and simple. Such an approach would be so much more efficient, requiring far less strain on Piper and probably allowing her to use her powers over much greater areas.

But that is just the tip of the iceberg.

The essence of Maxwell's Demon is that it can control the positioning of individual molecules. Here is a fun trick: Air is a gas. Like any gas, if you get it cold enough it will turn to a liquid, and if you get it even colder it will turn into a solid. Now, levitation is a handy thing and Phoebe has the power to use it. But Piper could make her own sort of levitation. She could use her Maxwell's Demon to place the most frigid air molecules right in front of her, actually freezing the air to assemble a solid staircase. Piper could then literally walk on air. Might not be levitation in the conventional witch sense, but it would certainly get the job done.

The positioning of molecules does not have to be restricted to selectively moving only the hot and cold ones about. Maxwell's Demon could also target the *type* of air molecules he is using. Air is composed primarily of nitrogen and oxygen molecules, but also traces of carbon dioxide, neon, argon, water vapor and a whole host of various polluting gases (like carbon monoxide, nitrogen oxide and ozone). If you assemble these different molecules in to thin sheets and shine a light at it, the light can be bent as it passes through or even reflected (all described through the use of Maxwell's equations) depending on the thickness of the sheets of molecules and the distance between each stack. The ability to bend and reflect light would allow Piper to wrap herself in a cloak of specially aligned air molecules, making her invisible or even transferring her image to a different location. Now that would be a mighty handy ability to have when trying to sneak up on a demon.

Further consideration of Maxwell's Demon would lead one to believe that, if the Demon can manipulate a gas molecule, then it should be able to grab on to that molecule and have some fun and games with it. An oxygen molecule actually consists of two oxygen atoms tied together with a chemical bond. This bond can be broken by adding a dab of energy. Now we know that Maxwell's Demon is a master of moving energy about, so it should have no problem breaking a bond between atoms.

This opens up a whole new range of powers.

Everything is constructed of atoms, and the atoms in a particular object are held in place and locked together because of the bonds between them. Piper should be able to command Maxwell's Demon to sever any bond between atoms she desires. Imagine a speeding car is hurtling down the street at Piper. While she could apply the powers of Maxwell's Demon in a conventional manner, turning the left half of the car into an exploding fireball and the right half into a chunk of frozen steel and plastic, she might still be crushed by the oncoming debris. So why not just use Maxwell's Demon to sever all the bonds down the center of the car, causing it to collapse in half—with the two halves then falling to either side, missing Piper as they rush by?

With a wave of her hands, she could cut anything. And in a similar fashion she could use Maxwell's Demon to bond atoms together. Fighting a horde of rampaging vampires? No problem. Simply attach atomic bonds between their feet and the street and they'd be stuck, literally glued there, unable to escape and waiting for the sun to rise.

The ability to break or attach bonds would also open up another whole realm of possibilities in the area of health. Diseases generally fall into two categories: those caused by bacteria or viruses, and those that come about because of a genetic defect in DNA. A well-trained Maxwell's Demon could eradicate diseases occurring under both of those conditions. In the case of a viral or bacterial invader, it would be a trivial thing for a Maxwell's Demon to locate the bugs (they're so much larger than gas molecules) and snip a few key bonds within them—they'd be dead, and the patient cured. In the case of genetically based diseases, it would be a bit more challenging, requiring the demon to manipulate the patient at the genetic level, correcting defects in DNA by snipping out defective genes (nothing but long chains of twisted molecules), and then through molecular manipulation assemble a healthy gene to replace it. No easy task to be sure, and it might require a witch with a detailed knowledge of genomics and molecular biology to take full advantage of a Maxwell's Demon with the ability to manipulate DNA. But once you've trained your Maxwell's Demon to fool with DNA, then a person's entire DNA could be rewritten, resulting in subtle transformations such as turning someone's brown eyes to blue, or more major modifications such as giving someone a tail, another person's face, enhanced mental powers or a speedier metabolism to quickly burn off those unwanted pounds.

Maxwell's Demon could handle all of this.

But with a little training it could do even more.

Piper could train her Maxwell's Demon to go nuclear.

Now, because Maxwell's Demon can access molecules and atoms, it would be no problem for it to seek out some very specific atoms—say those especially heavy varieties such as uranium atoms. While these atoms are relatively rare, the demon wouldn't have much problem flitting about over great distances, gathering an atom here and there before returning and placing all of them in a pile.

Take a uranium atom with just the right number of neutrons and protons in its nucleus (called uranium-235 for this application), and these atoms will on occasion spontaneously decay into two smaller atoms, spit out a few neutrons and give off a big burst of energy. Those neutrons are really energetic and, if they collide with another uranium atom, can cause it to spontaneously split, throwing off more fast-moving neutrons in the process. If you can keep these uranium atoms packed together in a tight enough volume (not easy since the heat they are giving off wants to blast them apart—just like when Piper uses her thermal combustion powers to blow something up), this chain reaction of splitting atoms will result in a nuclear explosion.

Piper should be able to teach her Maxwell's Demon to do this.

With Piper's current limited understanding of the science behind her powers, she can at best explode a demon's head and freeze a few objects. But if she were able to get in intimate contact with her inner Maxwell's Demon and learn just what the possibilities are when you can control individual molecules and atoms, Piper's powers would be almost infinite, including invisibility and pseudo-levitation, as well as the ability to tear anything apart or attach anything together, simultaneously freeze and vaporize any object, cure all diseases, alter anyone at the DNA level and, for those extreme emergencies (possibly when facing the Source of all Evil), even unleash a nuclear reaction.

This would be one powerful witch.

And then there is the final step. While atoms and molecules are small, on the order of one-billionth the size of the tip of your finger, there are objects much much smaller. Theoretical physicists believe that the fabric of the universe, what is called space-time, while over most distances (even atomic) shows no structure or texture, does in fact eventually show structure at distances that are a billion-billion-billion times smaller than that of an atom. At those dimensions space-time is a churning froth of tortured geometry. It is at those distances that wormholes are born, connecting different points in the universe together—shortcuts across normal space-time. For a witch who had mastered all the capabilities of a conventional Maxwell's Demon, the final frontier would be to train that Demon to access the very fabric of space-time, to touch reality at those distances a billion-billion-billion times smaller than that of an atom. To be able to generate wormholes from the froth of space-time would allow a witch to open up portals between any two points in space, time or both.

Teleportation becomes trivial.

Time travel is a snap.

And for the witch and Maxwell's Demon who really wish to impress friends and throw a scare into evildoers, the application of just the right jolt of energy over those infinitesimal distances could initiate another Big Bang, the event responsible for the creation of our entire universe. Yes, such a witch could create an entirely new universe.

That would be the ultimate witch.

And it really would not take much. All that is required is an understanding of the scientific basis of magical abilities and a bit of extrapolation, plus a solid background in science, and you have the ultimate witch, one in whom magic and science have been melded together to create something that neither could have spawned alone. The key of course is for Piper to comprehend the underlying basis of her own magic, as she will only be able to fully exploit her inner Maxwell's Demon once she understands the physics behind the manipulation of molecules, atoms and the fabric of space-time. If Piper could master the science that truly underpins her magic, then she'd find herself not only on the path of becoming the ultimate witch, but also in fulfilling the prophesy of Clarke's third law: Any sufficiently advanced technology is indistinguishable from magic.

> Robert A. Metzger is a research scientist and a science fiction and science writer. His research focuses on the technique of Molecular Beam Epitaxy, used to grow epitaxial films for high-speed electronics applications. His short fiction has appeared in most major SF magazines including: *Asimov's*, *Fantasy & Science Fiction* and *SF Age*, while his 2002 novel *Picoverse* was a Nebula finalist, and his most recent novel *Cusp* was released by Ace in 2005. His science writing has appeared in *Wired* and *Analog*, and he is a contributing editor to the Science Fiction Writers of America's *Bulletin*.

WILL THE REAL PHOEBE PLEASE STAND UP?

JENNIFER DUNNE

In the first season, Phoebe was the Halliwell Flake, a kooky, reckless, sex-crazed spirit in need of a higher goal and some foundation garments. But as Jennifer Dunne traces her evolution over the years, she finds that Phoebe is the most complex of the sisters, the true visionary among them.

I STARTED WATCHING *CHARMED* midway through the Phoebe-and-Cole doomed love story arc and was immediately captivated. The show's focus on the characters' relationships, both romantic and familial, as the basis for each episode was dramatically different from the "monster of the week" format common to other series. As a paranormal romance writer, I couldn't resist. I wanted to know who these people were and how they'd gotten to this point in their lives. I wasn't able to watch it regularly, however, and trying to pick up missed episodes out of order in late-night syndication only added to my confusion.

I quickly devised a series of questions that would place any episode I watched into the story landscape I was building in my mind. The answers to most of these questions—was Prue working for Bucklands or as a photographer?—did not change the essential nature of the characters (either way, Prue was a bit of an overachieving workaholic) and had no impact on my ability to enjoy the show. Even Cole's flip-flopping between good and evil, one of the most extreme changes, didn't alter his essential obsession with Phoebe, only the manner in which he pursued it.

The one character I could never pin down, however, was Phoebe. She went from a slacker with a series of dead-end jobs, to a "housewife" who looked after the Manor while her sisters were at work, to a diligent college student, to an advice columnist, to a student once more. In her personal life, she went from a flirtatious sex kitten to a woman consumed by a single overwhelming passion. She was the impetus for the sisters receiving their powers and becoming the Charmed Ones, as well as, in both past and future lives, the cause of witch hunts that ended in her execution. Unlike the other characters, her various incarnations seemed to lack any unifying basis.

Then I realized that her continual reinvention of herself *was* the constant to her character. Her sisters might have focused on success and achieving a normal life, but Phoebe's focus was on discovering her own identity. Her efforts to modify her self-image have made her an agent of change for not only her sisters, but all the characters on the show.

From the very beginning, her search for identity has fueled the sisters' development as the Charmed Ones. The spirit board revealed the Halliwell secret by spelling out A-T-T-I-C to Phoebe. While Prue and Piper were content with the status quo and saw no reason to follow the spirit board's prompting, Phoebe readily answered its call. Her faith and willingness to embark upon the quest of discovery opened the attic door that had remained locked to her sisters. She was the one to find and read the Book of Shadows, invoking the spell that released the sisters' powers and united them in the Power of Three.

Her search for identity continued to pull her sisters along for the ride. Phoebe was the first to define their new existence, stating, "We're the protectors of the innocent. We're known as the Charmed Ones" in the very first episode ("Something Wicca This Way Comes"). She was the first to experience her power, the first to seek out someone to save rather than merely reacting to a demon or warlock attack, the first to expand her use of the Book of Shadows to find spells for more than vanquishing and the first to write her own spell. And where her sisters worried that their powers would forever doom them to a life of isolation, never able to have families and children due to the risk of freezing them or accidentally moving them to another zip code, Phoebe set their feet firmly on the path of destiny when she reassured them that even if such a thing did happen, she would use her power of premonition to "see them, find them and bring them back safely" ("Wedding From Hell," 1-6).

Her search for self-knowledge sometimes put her life at risk, as when she switched places with her past or future selves, or threatened the lives of her sisters, as when her desire to learn about the mother she never knew interfered with her ability to stop the warlock Nicholas from gaining immunity to the Charmed Ones' powers. But it also saved her life, as when her admission of her true nature as a loving person instead of a cold fish transformed her back from being a mermaid, allowing Leo to heal her.

The single question she most frequently asked in her quest to understand herself was whether or not she had a weakness that made her more prone to evil than her sisters. First raised in "Is There a Woogy In The House?" (1-15), Piper speculated that being born in the house simply meant Phoebe was more attuned to the forces within it, but Phoebe was not willing to take such a simplistic view of her own nature, responding, "That's exactly my point. I could go either way. Good or evil. Kind of freaky." She revisited the question in "Pardon My Past" (2-14), when she learned that her previous incarnation joined forces with a warlock lover, and told her sisters, "Being in my past life, that powerful, evil feeling, it was...it was seductive. And that's what scares me. I mean, what if that's who I really am?" She first tried to distance herself from Cole not because she feared that he could not control his demonic powers, but because she was afraid she would not be able to resist their evil allure. The question assumed far more urgency when, after trying a series of compromises between her innate goodness and growing evil powers, Phoebe had to decide whether she would take a stand with the forces of evil, and destroy the Charmed Ones, or with the forces of good, and vanquish her husband, the Source of all Evil.

So what good has all of Phoebe's self-analysis been? Is she any closer to understanding just who she really is?

One of the most common methods of analysis used today is called the Myers-Briggs Type Indicator™.[1] Unlike psychological tests, which must be administered and graded by trained professionals and which exist mainly to determine how far from "normal" a person is and in what way their psyche is damaged or deficient, the Myers-Briggs method of personality typing is easily understood by lay people and results in sixteen different personality profiles, none of which is inherently better than the others.

Key to this profiling simplicity is the belief that you do not need to know the depths of someone's mental processes to understand their overall personality, but rather merely judge their observable behavior on four sliding scales between mutually exclusive extremes. The four

---

[1] Myers-Briggs Type Indicator is a registered trademark of Consulting Psychologists Press, Palo Alto, California.

scales are Introverted-Extroverted (inward-looking or outward-looking), Sensor-iNtuitive (gathering information through specific details or as part of relationships and theoretical frameworks), Thinker-Feeler (making decisions based on facts or subjective values) and Judger-Perceiver (preferring to make decisions or gather information). The dominant extreme for each scale is selected to create a four-letter abbreviation, such as ISTJ or ENFP, indicating one of sixteen possible personality types to which a person's behavior most conforms.

Phoebe might never have analyzed herself with the Myers-Briggs profiles, but we have plenty of examples of her behavior that will allow us to identify her type. By knowing how Phoebe behaved in the past—sometimes in the *way* past!—we can determine how she views her place in the world and how she is likely to behave in the future.

Clearly, Phoebe is a people person. She enjoys parties, makes new friends in all varieties of situations and never lacks for companionship. This makes her extroverted. Her power of premonition is obviously intuitive in nature, and even without using her power, she demonstrates an ability to understand what people mean as opposed to what they say. Unlike her sister Prue's rigid adherence to procedure and analysis based on the bottom line, Phoebe is swayed by emotion. She does things because they feel good and helps others because she feels their pain—quite literally, while she had the gift of empathy. Finally, she is perceptive, taking in and relating back information without making value judgments about the nature of what she is seeing.

This would make Phoebe's type an Extroverted iNtuitive Feeling Perceiver (ENFP), sometimes known as a Visionary or Champion. The defining traits of this personality type are an uncanny understanding of others' motives and likely behavior, a vision of life as being fraught with possibilities for great good or great evil and a desire for authenticity in all that they do.

The high-level sketch of this personality type certainly seems to match the main thrust of Phoebe's character. But that might just be a coincidence. We need to delve deeper, uncovering the inner Phoebe, to determine if this is an accurate representation.

Visionaries often go through many different jobs and careers, approaching fields of study through obscure back doors and taking roundabout ways to get where they're going. They may seem directionless or lacking in purpose to others, but Visionaries know that everything they learn will eventually find an application and tend to resist limiting their options by choosing a career until they feel they have adequately explored the possibilities—usually some time in their mid or late twenties.

Once they find an idea-oriented career focusing on human possibilities, especially one that offers plenty of variety, challenge and independence, they will become enthusiastic to the point of telling the entire world about what they do.

Phoebe bounced around a variety of jobs: hostess at a restaurant, lounge psychic at a hotel, assistant at an auction house, real estate agent and consultant for the police. She even boosted her intelligence briefly to try and get a job at a dot-com company. When she finally enrolled in college again, she started off with only two core classes and seven electives, unwilling to commit to a course of study too quickly. And taking on the role of an advice columnist because she's the innocent you're protecting was certainly an unusual approach to landing a job. Billboards, radio and TV ads, as well as syndication of her column, certainly tell the entire world what she does.

Another aspect of Visionaries is that they live their lives in accord with their values and strive always to achieve inner peace. When giving testimony about the Guardian demon's attack on Darryl, Phoebe was the one who protested that it was wrong to lie in a courtroom, even though her lie protected the sisters' secret. Her rage at a restaurant's mistreatment of breast-feeding Piper prompted her Lady Godiva–inspired ride through the streets of San Francisco to raise public awareness of the situation and force a change. And while her desire for inner peace helped her share a house with her sisters and mediate the initial conflicts between Paige and Piper, it more often prompted a need to escape scenes of conflict. Even before the show began, she'd run away from Prue's belief that Phoebe slept with her fiancé and nearly ended the Power of Three when she ran away from her painful situation with Cole by embracing the life of a mermaid. Most drastically, her longing for the vision of a world at complete and total peace made her crusade for the Avatars' plan to create a utopia until she convinced her sisters to go along with the plan.

Finally, most Visionaries are enthusiastic, loving people who are almost constantly in love with someone or some new idea. Overcome with the possibilities of the new relationship or idea, they see only the positive aspects. They tend to throw caution to the wind, overlooking details about their love interest that would give a more cautious person pause, romanticizing and idealizing their partners and making superhuman efforts to rationalize discrepancies between reality and their imagined ideal. When flaws in the relationship become too obvious to ignore any longer, Visionaries feel betrayed out of proportion to the situation because of all the energy they have invested in perfecting the relationship. Swinging to the opposite extreme, they overgeneralize their partners' faults and failings, so that a loved one who once was considered incapable of doing any wrong becomes incapable of doing anything right.

The parallels between that description and Phoebe's relationship with Cole are obvious: in the beginning, Phoebe rationalized away all signs of Cole's demonic nature and, after their divorce, in "Happily Ever After" she swung to the other extreme, insisting that Cole was to blame for everything the evil witch did and refusing to listen to his warnings about Adam. However, you can see the same trends with regard to ideas. Phoebe embraced her witchcraft powers with abandon, seeing only the positive opportunities while her sisters pointed out all of the possible drawbacks to lives filled with magic. And her overwhelming dedication to her new role as aunt after Wyatt was born nearly cost her everything she'd worked so hard to achieve in her career.

But the point of a personality analysis is not simply to understand who a person is. An accurate understanding does more than explain what someone has done in the past; it allows you to predict a person's future behavior. Given that *Charmed* is a character-driven show, what troubles can we expect Phoebe's personality to create in future episodes? More importantly, what pitfalls could Phoebe avoid, or at least minimize the pain from, if she had a better understanding of her personality type?

Visionaries are prone to overextending themselves, making too many commitments and starting too many projects because they fear missing something exciting. This results in a need to take time out and relax before they burn out. We saw this in season seven, when Phoebe took a hiatus from her advice column. This struggle is likely to become more pronounced, resulting in dropped commitments at work or failed or near-disastrous demon encounters, until she finds a new means of relaxing.

Visionaries also tend to attract an entourage of followers who look to them for guidance and leadership. We saw a brief preview of this when the Vortex demon sent Phoebe into an alternate reality where she was wildly famous. In that reality, she faced both an obsessed fan and a reader who blamed her for destroying his marriage when his wife took her advice. We may see something similar again, but in reality this time. Either outcome would shake Phoebe's confidence that writing the advice column was what she was meant to do and precipitate a crisis of conscience.

Another common trait of Visionaries is a low boredom threshold and a dislike of repetition. They appreciate change for change's sake, often finding new and novel ways to improve on processes. However, they're equally prone to breaking processes that were running smoothly. This trait may manifest itself in Phoebe as a series of amusing or intriguing side effects when she tries new combinations of magic. She also may be in for trouble at work if she changes the format, structure or content of her column too drastically for Elise's taste.

Because they perceive the world intuitively, Visionaries often assign symbolic meanings to events and circumstances. Under stress, these symbolic meanings tend to turn dark and foreboding and lead to crippling feelings of being an impostor. The Visionary often blames a scapegoat for their loss of identity. This sounds like a perfect scenario for the fear demon Barbas to return, possibly tricking Phoebe into attacking an innocent, one of her sisters or even one of her nephews.

Visionaries are often procrastinators and care more about the people and feelings involved in projects than with the facts and figures. This could lead to trouble for Phoebe if she waits until the last minute to hand in a column, allowing key information to be printed that is incorrect. The *Bay Mirror* could be sued for libel, or readers acting on her column's information could cause injury to themselves or others, again prompting guilt and a feeling that she is a fraud or unworthy of her column. Phoebe can address these feelings of fraud by gaining credentials that are publicly recognized as giving her the right and ability to offer advice, such as the doctorate in psychology she chose to pursue in late season seven.

Since all Visionaries share a hatred for the pointless rules and time-wasting processes of bureaucracies, Phoebe will no doubt find herself facing off against at least one faceless corporate machine. It's possible that the giant media conglomerate owned by Jason Dean will take a more active role in managing the *Bay Mirror*, forcing Phoebe to conform to corporate dictates—or else. She may also uncover corporate or governmental injustice and take a vocal, visible stand against it.

Finally, Phoebe will find another romance. It's possible that, with Piper and Leo working on their marriage and adjusting to Leo's newly human status, and Paige mourning Kyle, Phoebe will be the one whose active dating introduces new men and their resulting difficulties into each week's episode. After all, I have to make some allowances for the dramatic needs of a weekly series. If that is the case, she will most likely follow the Visionary tendencies of either under-committing, holding back while she waits to see if someone better comes along, or over-committing, rushing full-throttle into every new relationship seeing only the positive possibilities. Given her past history, under-committing is much more likely. Phoebe can experience the thrill of romance without the commitment by choosing entanglements with no possible future, such as her affair with her ghostwriter Leslie, who was scheduled to leave San Francisco when his assignment ended, or the ex-demon Drake, who had a limited time to live as a human.

What I'd prefer to see, though, is Phoebe finally finding the ideal man. Her relationship with Cole was full of passion and excitement, but ultimately doomed. Even Jason had non-magical power and fire. She's always been attracted to intense relationships, but given her personality, those types of relationships are destined to fail, requiring more and more energy to maintain until at last they explode. A Visionary's perfect mate, on the other hand, is a solid and steady man who can become the center of her wild orbit. Someone who dots his i's and crosses his t's, who keeps things on a steady course and an even keel. She could easily meet a man like this when, due to the Visionary's dislike of details and following instructions, she runs into tax trouble and needs help sorting out her finances. Her confusion over what she always thought she wanted—excitement, intensity and novelty—versus the unexpected appeal of a staid, solid individual would take a long time to resolve, cutting as it does to the heart of her self-image.

Another choice for a perfect partner is the absent-minded scientist, lost in his own world and relying on the Visionary's connectedness to tell him who and what he needs to pay attention to in the greater world outside his lab. Perhaps someone other than the original scientists who were killed in the first season's "The Truth Is Out There...and It Hurts" will develop the anti-demon vaccine. The Charmed Ones could be asked to take the key scientist under protective custody, or to help him with his work.

Whatever new twists and turns are in store for Phoebe and the rest of the Halliwell clan, we can rest assured that some things will never change. As in the past seasons, Phoebe's search for self-knowledge will be the wild card that drives the sisters' stories forward. She will continue to question who she is and what her life is all about.

Unlike her sisters, who can face all manner of Hell-spawned demons without fear, Phoebe has taken a harder role. Week after week, she faces down her inner demons, fearlessly confronting the best and worst within herself. Would this be easier if she was pre-armed with the knowledge of her personality type's strengths and weaknesses, or would it only lead to even more second-guessing and worry about succumbing to a weakness her sisters do not have?

Most of us will never come face to face with a supernatural evil creature, but all of us have to face the potential for darkness within ourselves. I love Phoebe because she meets this challenge head-on, without shirking. And week after week, I will continue to tune in to see what she discovers inside herself, and how those discoveries change her world.

Jennifer Dunne writes erotic romance novels and novellas for Ellora's Cave—including "Dancing in the Dark" in the anthology *Party Favors*, featuring a heroine obsessed with Julian McMahon's portrayal of Cole Turner—and fantasy and science fiction novels for Cerridwen Press. She is a three-time EPPIE award winner and has been nominated for the PRISM, Sapphire, Pearl and many other awards not named after sparkly jewels. Visit her Web site at www.jenniferdunne.com.

HOW PAIGE MATTHEWS SAVED CHARMED

LEIGH ADAMS WRIGHT

Paige came late to the magic game, a pinch hitter for the lost Prue. Leigh Adams Wright makes the case for the newest Halliwell sister by arguing that her appearance in the fourth season revitalized the show by reinventing it, and that the character of Paige was integral to the success of the following seasons.

I CAME TO *CHARMED* LATE. My mother had been watching for years, but my mother, I regret to say, while in possession of many good qualities, does not always have the best taste in television. But I was home visiting one Sunday and I didn't have anything else to do, so I settled in to give it a shot. It was that or risk not getting any popcorn; a girl's got to have priorities.

Mom gave me a rundown, but I was still starting my *Charmed* experience at a disadvantage. It was the beginning of the fourth season, and I hadn't seen the first three. I'd gotten the gist—they're witches—from the media buzz surrounding the show, but I didn't know how their magic worked, or where it came from. Everybody was pretty upset about Prue being dead, but I didn't really know who Prue was—though I felt for Piper and Phoebe and sympathized with their grief. These characters were as much a mystery to me as their magic was, and so it was a little hard to keep up. The one thing I remember having a handle on, though, was Paige.

It's difficult to be a first-time viewer. You can't tell the characters apart, you've got no idea what's going on in their lives and, in the case of a supernatural show like *Charmed*, there are rules they have to follow that you don't know about. The show isn't doing a thing to help you, either—you have to catch on yourself, and on the fly. With a show like *Charmed*, one that has a rich family history and men who have a tendency to go a little evil on short notice, it's even harder.

It was lucky that I came in on that first episode of season four. Because Prue had just died. Because the show was in a period of upheaval, still trying to determine what it was going to become, and so my newbie status was less of a handicap. But most of all, because that was the episode where we met Paige.

There seems to be a pretty fundamental split among *Charmed* fans: those who like Paige's addition to the show, and those who don't. Paige is a breath of fresh air, a big improvement on the uptight Prue, and lets the show and its characters develop in ways Prue's presence never would have allowed, or she's obnoxious, and whiny, and *really* badly dressed, and needs to get *over* herself already. But love her or hate her, her character might have been the smartest thing *Charmed* has ever done. Her introduction not only served to unequivocally usher in a new, Prue-less era, one with a lot fewer practical concerns and a lot campier style, but also created a golden opportunity for the show to successfully attract and keep new viewers.

For the *Charmed* neophyte, Paige was like a guide, but better—Paige was a sister in bewilderment. She was new to *Charmed*, too. She knew no more about these people and the world they lived in than I did, and that made her easy to identify with. She acted out my confusion for me: freaked out at the appropriate times, asked the questions I wanted to ask. Plus, everything I was supposed to know about her, I did. Where Paige was concerned, I could be totally confident that I knew exactly as much about what was going on as anyone else in the viewing audience.

More importantly, though, the other characters *explained things* to, and through, Paige—things *I* needed explained. Look at season four, episode three—"Hell Hath No Fury"—Paige's first episode as a fully vested Charmed One. After a negligible opener in which we saw Piper, Phoebe and Cole careening about town, demon-hunting in dearly departed Prue's SUV, we cut to Paige, at work... reading about witches. It's a quick scene, a throwaway moment, but her single read-aloud line—"Throughout history, witches have been misunderstood, persecuted and destroyed; the public hanging, drowning and burning of women suspected of witchcraft is a far more recent chapter of our history than most people realize"—established an air of vague menace as well as the Halliwells' need for secrecy.

This episode, too, briefed both Paige and the new viewer on the dangers of using magic for personal gain: comic though her sudden increase in cup size may have been, it was also effective. For Piper or Phoebe to "forget" that hard-learned lesson in order to educate me would have lost the show's integrity; for Paige to do so made sense.

As a device, she worked beautifully. Her presence was a way to rationalize clueing new viewers in to things they needed to know *without* alienating *Charmed* first adopters: anvil-free (or at least anvil-light) exposition. Information could be imparted to the new viewer without having to sacrifice the integrity of the characters. Instead of explanatory monologues existing solely for the purpose of transmitting information, expository dialogue could also illuminate the interpersonal dynamics developing between the members of the newly formed trio. The scene in "Hell Hath No Fury" where Paige was first introduced to the Book of Shadows not only told us newbies that "It is a book of spells, right?" but that Piper *really* wasn't handling Prue's death well and that Phoebe was embracing her new role as Paige's big sister. Compare this to shows whose networks have decided they need to be more friendly to new viewers, and therefore the characters spend a few minutes at the beginning of each episode reestablishing their situations and relationships by telling each other things all of them already know.

But overall, the most important thing Paige's presence did for me as a new viewer was keep me from feeling like an outsider. There's a reason excluding people is the emotional fighting tactic of choice in middle-school cafeterias everywhere: it works. And where I could have felt excluded by the references to events in previous episodes, by the intensity and the details of Piper and Phoebe's mourning for Prue—excluded enough to stop watching the show—Paige's presence, and her own sense of exclusion, kept me involved. She might have felt out of place, unworthy of filling Prue's shoes and not yet comfortable with the family dynamics, but we as viewers (new *and* old) knew she belonged—that she was a Charmed One, and that even if she couldn't see it now, her destiny was with them. That knowledge promised me a place as a viewer too: as Paige would be integrated into the show, so would I.

Of course, any new lead character could have done most of those things: provided a point of identification through his or her newness, kept the explanations for new viewers less heavy-handed. What exactly is it about Paige herself, youngest half-sister and daughter of a White-lighter, that made her such an effective and necessary addition?

Part of it was Paige's role as newly discovered sister—as an outsider who was expected to, in time, become an insider, her situation was an easy and satisfying parallel to my own. But the ways her newness, her difference from her sisters, was defined made the difference between Paige simply being a useful tool for acclimating new viewers and being an asset to the show itself.

Paige was introduced at a point where many veteran shows start to lag. These days in particular, a show is lucky to get past its first four episodes, let alone a whole first season; after three of those seasons, whatever initial situation the show's creator set up has pretty much run its course. The interpersonal relationships have been played out, any secrets have been revealed and the show's premise is starting to feel a little tight across the shoulders. To survive, a show has to move beyond its original incarnation and become something new. *Buffy the Vampire Slayer* was a perfect example of this: the central metaphor it employed for its first three seasons, "high school is hell," could only be considered new and inventive for so long, but even more crucially, the relationships between the characters would have become stagnant. The show survived by reinventing itself, notably by sending its core characters to college and into new, separate relationships in the fourth season, and again by forcing Buffy's "rebirth" into hellish adulthood from the idyllic, "heavenly" existence of her youth at the beginning of the sixth. Each time the metaphor shifted subtly—"high school is hell" eventually became "adulthood is hell"—and the characters grew, largely thanks to their relationships with the supporting cast, but the characters themselves and the rules of the world remained familiar and satisfying to (most) loyal viewers.

The key word here when applying this concept to *Charmed*—really, when applying this concept, period—is *reinvention*. Shannen Doherty's departure could not have come at a better time as far as the narrative was concerned. And the *Charmed* team could not have packed any more potential for reinvention into her replacement than they did into the character of Paige Matthews.

The first and most obvious benefit of Paige's introduction was the emotional challenge it presented to Piper and Phoebe. All three of the original Charmed Ones were defined by their place in the birth order, but Paige's integration into the family changed that—with Prue dead, Piper had to move from peacemaker to sister-in-charge, and irrepressibly irresponsible Phoebe had to learn to mediate between her surviving sisters. Prue's absence made character growth necessary, but Paige's presence, as youngest sister and witchcraft novice, solidified the direction of that growth.

More, Paige was *different* from her new sisters. The only child of adoptive parents, she had a different personal history and a different last name. Where the Charmed Ones were previously confined to their own family life, Paige provided a whole new set of stories for the writers to tell. She was connected to the other two, but she was fundamentally separate as well, in a way Prue was not. Her beliefs could credibly clash with those of the other two, creating conflict and providing perspective where the previous, more homogenous trio of Halliwell sisters could not have.

In addition, she wasn't just a witch—she was half-Whitelighter, too. Though her powers filled the same niche Prue's did in the Charmed Ones' predestined bag of tricks, they were fundamentally different. They came from a different source and worked in different ways. Instead of using straight telekinesis, she orbed. With subtly different powers, too, come subtly different responsibilities—and subtly different stories. Recently, this has come to particular fruition as, late in the seventh season, Paige began to tentatively embrace her Whitelighter heritage and take on witch and future Whitelighter charges of her own.

Not only did her half-breed status generate storylines for her, but as the child of a witch and her Whitelighter, Paige's very existence set the precedent for Piper's pregnancies by Leo—a story move which let the show reinvent itself yet again, changing *Charmed* from a show about three barely grown sisters and their search for love to a show about three fully adult sisters and their quest to make the world a safer place for their families. On a less conceptual level, it also set the stage for the overarching plot for the show's sixth season.

But the most radical, most brilliant part of Paige's character is how her addition turned everything regular viewers thought they knew about the Halliwell family history on its head. Everything that seemed self-evident was suddenly open to re-evaluation; what previously seemed to be set in stone suddenly became suspect. Thought there were only three Halliwell sisters? Guess again. The Halliwell family regained a sense of mystery, of *potential*, that most shows only get during their first season. Even unused, that potential breathed new life into the show.

Sure, part of Paige's effect on the show grew out of Rose McGowan's energy, and the chemistry between the new trio playing the Charmed Ones. But there are also very particular attributes of Paige's character that not only provided new viewers with a way into the show, but the show itself with a way out of the corner it had painted itself into. If Prue had remained, the show would have petered out seasons ago. Instead, it's on its eighth season, with the promise of more—and we have Paige to thank.

Leigh Adams Wright, who would like to apologize to her mother for defaming her for narrative purposes, is a proud supporter of popular culture in all its many and varied forms. Her previous work includes essays in *Finding Serenity: Anti-heroes, Lost Shepherds and Space Hookers in Joss Whedon's Firefly* and *Alias Assumed: Sex, Lies and SD-6*.

THEIR ROOTS
HISTORY AND THE HALLIWELLS

If Cole was the Source of all Evil, then what's the Source of all Halliwell? The *Charmed* stories have drawn on myths, legends, fairy tales and history, but in spite of the pilot title, not much Wiccan this way comes when you're looking at the sisters' lineage.

CHARMED: A MODERN FAIRY TALE

DEBBIE VIGUIÉ

While each of the Halliwells has her own distinct personality, Debbie Viguié argues that they're all descended from the same source. Their staying power comes from the fact that they're all fairy tale heroines.

MUCH OF MODERN STORYTELLING is based on ancient stories and parables that we call fairy tales. In some cases these fairy tales serve as more than just superficial references and leave their mark more visibly in the content and structure of the modern story. Everyone who watches *Charmed* knows that they have often used elements of fairy tales in their episodes. But a closer comparison of individual fairy tales to the characters and events in *Charmed* leads to a view of the larger picture, namely a comparison of themes in fairy tales with themes in *Charmed* and ultimately the structure of the genre as it impacts the television show.

Four fairy tale themes that help shape the overarching story of *Charmed* are the power of love, the importance of innocence, the battle between good and evil and characters disguising themselves. These themes can be seen in broad strokes throughout the show: Love plays a predominant role, from the love of one's sister to the love of one's mate, to the love of humanity in general. Innocence is celebrated, both in individual characters and in the larger population as a whole: the normal humans the Charmed Ones protect are always referred to as "innocents." The battle between good and evil is at the heart of the show: good witches fighting evil warlocks and demons. The element of disguise is prevalent as well, from every creature and person who has masqueraded as something other than they are to the sisters themselves, as they both hide their identity from others and, previous to the show's start, had their identity hidden from them. To really understand the complexity with which these themes have been woven through the series, though, requires a closer examination of the sisters and the fairy tale characters they have taken on.

The power of love for both good and evil is a theme played out in many fairy tales. In *Charmed*, this theme is most strongly reflected in Phoebe. Piper may be the romantic of the family, but Phoebe has always been the most romantically adventurous, tending toward dramatic, passionate love affairs with men who embrace their bad-boy side. The most recent example was reformed-demon Drake, but as far as bad boys go, no one can hold a candle to Cole. While Phoebe and Cole were dating, Phoebe played the role of Beauty to Cole's Beast, and their story, like Beauty and the Beast's, was all about the ability of love to change the heart and conquer all.

While the details change across tellings, the crux of the story is always the same: Beauty, a good, deeply caring woman with a strong sense of family responsibility, is thrust into a relationship with a creature that is not what he appears. The Beast tries to woo Beauty, despite the fact that she can tell he is a hideous monster, needing Beauty to fall in love with him so that he can return to his human form. In a similar manner, Cole wooed Phoebe in an attempt to make her fall in love with him. Cole's motives, though, were much darker than the Beast's: Cole wanted Phoebe to fall in love with him so that he could use her trust to destroy her and her sisters. Also unlike the Beast, Cole was able to hide the demon in him, presenting only his human face to Phoebe for a long time. When Phoebe found out that Cole was half-demon, she struggled just as Beauty did to see only the humanity and the goodness in the man she loved. Eventually Cole won Phoebe's heart and her love transformed him, turning him into a better person, just as the Beast won Beauty's love and was transformed from a monster to a prince. Like the Beast's transformation, Cole's transformation began as an internal one but ended in a physical change as well: his demon half was vanquished, leaving him fully human. Love tamed the monster and conquered all.

Had everything ended there, Phoebe would have forever remained Beauty, who changed her prince through the power of her love. Unfortunately for Phoebe, that was not the end of her story.

When Cole became the Source of all Evil and Phoebe married him without knowing his dark secret, she took on the persona of a second, more tragic fairy tale character: the Little Mermaid. The Little Mermaid gave up her life as a mermaid in exchange for human form and the chance to live happily ever after with her prince. In the original fairy tale, the mermaid fails in her quest and dies, leaving her soul separated from that of her kin for all eternity. When Phoebe discovered that Cole was the Source and that she was pregnant with his child, she chose to become his dark Queen. She left behind her family and her responsibilities to live in his world and be his wife. Ultimately, she couldn't let go of her old life or find happiness with Cole in her new one. She ended up losing Cole and the baby and nearly losing her own life—a fate only slightly kinder than that of her fairy tale twin. As if to underscore the part Phoebe had been playing, the next season's opener featured Phoebe trading places with an actual mermaid. Devastated by her losses, she tried to remain a mermaid to escape her pain, and only the love of her sisters brought her back. Love nearly destroyed her but, in a very *Charmed* twist, it was the power of her sisters' love that was able to save her.

Like Phoebe, Piper has played her share of fairy tale and fantasy characters, but the role of Sleeping Beauty, because of its association with innocence, is the one that most suits her. Particularly at the beginning of the show's run, Piper was cast as the most innocent sister, the one who demonstrated the most heart and compassion; her earthy spirit was a breath of fresh air between jaded, cynical Prue and vivacious, ready-for-anything Phoebe. And as the sister most identified with innocence and its nurturance, Piper was also the first of her sisters (and the only one so far) to become a mother—having experienced more of life and lost some of her own innocence, she is in a position to better protect the innocence of her children.

Sleeping Beauty is a princess whose life is threatened by an evil witch. To protect her, her parents hide her away as a child and let her grow up, unaware of her own identity and destiny. Similarly, Piper and her sisters had their powers stripped when they were children in order to protect them from warlocks and others who would try to harm them. More so than the others, though, Piper's sweet temperament and romantic spirit make her more appropriate to the image of the princess hidden away in the forest.

After Sleeping Beauty discovers her true identity, she succumbs to a witch's evil curse, falling into a deathlike sleep when she pricks her finger on a spinning wheel and is woken by her prince's kiss. Our first real hint that handyman Leo would be more than a love affair that didn't quite work out, and instead was Piper's true love, was when he used his Whitelighter powers to heal Piper, critically injured and hovering near death, effectively "waking" her from her sleep.

Paige plays a dual role in *Charmed*: during the course of the series she has appeared both as Snow White and a wicked enchantress. Historically, both Snow White and the wicked enchantress in her guise as queen appear in the same fairy tale as heroine and villainess, a contrast that serves to demonstrate Paige's dual nature and the eternal theme of good versus evil.

Paige and Snow White are both pure-hearted orphans with pale skin and ruby lips. Like Snow White, who, after escaping her stepmother with a kind huntsman's help, takes refuge with seven dwarves whom she cares for as a mother would, Paige is the ultimate caregiver. She worked early on as a social worker and, after leaving that job, did everything she could to care for her sisters and her nephews. She works, seemingly tirelessly, for the good of those around her, and the determination she has shown in becoming a better witch surpasses that of both her sisters. This goodness and light in Paige can be partly attributed to her being half-Whitelighter. It is in her nature to help others; it is, in fact, her destiny, as she has recently been trusted with witch and future Whitelighter charges of her own.

But just as Paige holds the potential for great goodness, she also has elements of darkness within her. She is rebellious and, of all the sisters, perhaps the one most vulnerable to darkness and the misuse of her powers. This part of her nature, the flawed witch, is personified by the enchantress character, who uses her power to gain what she wants. The wicked queen in the Snow White story wants to be the fairest in the land, and when Snow White threatens her status, she tries to have her killed. In the fourth season, Paige discovered that, in one of her past lives, she was an evil enchantress. This discovery came at a time in which she was struggling to be as good a witch as Prue was. Her frustration over not being as powerful or as knowledgeable as Prue caused problems that affected her life and her relationships; her desire to be the best at any cost was its own kind of evil and nearly cost her the good side of her personality. When Paige confronted her past self, she might as well have been Snow White confronting her evil stepmother.

Paige's ongoing struggle to balance the different aspects of her personality and her responsibilities as both witch and Whitelighter with her desires as a human woman serves as the perfect backdrop for the battle of moderation and excess, interest and obsession, right and wrong and, ultimately, good and evil that the sisters have fought in many different forms throughout the series.

Of all the sisters, Prue is the one who best demonstrates the fairy tale archetype of the hero in disguise. Prue's disguises ranged from the simple, as when she pretended to be a hitwoman, to the complex, as when she changed herself completely into a man and into a dog. In the grand tradition of fairy tale disguises, many of her adopted personas were not so much external to her as they were an expression of some part of her she had repressed—and of all of the Charmed Ones, Prue was the one with the strongest tendency to suppress her true self, a fact which was touched on when her wilder side forced itself out and nearly ruined Piper's wedding to Leo. The episode where Prue accidentally split herself into three worked similarly, showing us different parts of Prue's psyche that usually remained hidden and revealing the complexity of her character.

It's also no coincidence that the seasons before Prue's death were also the seasons in which disguising their identity as the Charmed Ones was most important, hindering the actions the sisters were able to take in fighting evil far more often than it has in recent years. Prue's death was a tragedy, but in a way it freed her sisters from having to suppress their true identity as witches. The external pressures still existed, but without Prue's influence, they were free of the internal pressure, and the show changed because of it.

The four sisters demonstrate strong fairy tale themes in their lives and personalities. Phoebe is obsessed with love. Piper is moved by innocence. Paige is torn by the conflict between good and evil. Prue was constantly disguising herself, struggling with her own identity. These four themes—love, innocence, conflict and disguise—provide the structure for the entire television show.

By touching on these classic themes, *Charmed* ensures that it makes a connection with its viewers and reaches deep into their subconscious minds. This makes the show feel welcome and familiar while at the same time standing out from other current television shows, which use older stories, not to touch on age-old themes and concerns, but to bring the same stale programming to every show on every channel. All stories are based on something: another story, a truth, a theme or a trend. *Charmed*'s strength lies in the fact that the stories it draws on are ageless and classic, not subject to the whims and trends of the networks. *Charmed* is a modern fairy tale, taking the old stories and giving them new and more complex life, and like all great fairy tales, it will endure.

Debbie Viguié is the author of several books including *Scarlet Moon*, the Wicked series and *Charmed: Pied Piper*. Her book *Midnight Pearls*, a retelling of the little mermaid fairy tale, is on the ALA 2005 Popular Paperbacks for Young Adults list. Debbie lives with her husband, Scott, and when she is not busy writing indulges her love of travel and theme parks.

A STAKE IN THE FUTURE

RUTH GLICK WRITING AS
REBECCA YORK

The history of witches like the Halliwells can be traced back to the Middle Ages and, Rebecca York argues, we've come a long way since then. With the popularity of *Charmed* as evidence, she sees an even brighter future.

CONSIDER THE HARSH REALITIES of modern life. We've got:

- The Department of Homeland Security
- The Patriot Act
- Airport screeners who make us walk barefoot toward the friendly sky

Will they keep me safe from the dark forces threatening to destroy our civilization?

I hope their efforts help. But I'm also putting a cauldron-full of faith in Paramount Studios. Their long-running television series *Charmed* is—well—an excellent good luck charm. With the three Halliwell witches on our side, how can we possibly lose the good fight?

Charmed is big-bucks entertainment. But it's also more—a cultural icon with a welcome message about modern society.

At this writing, the series is in its seventh season on the WB Network. Reruns are twice every Monday through Friday on TNT. That's astonishing in an era where a new show can appear on the horizon and vanish with the speed of light. And especially astonishing for a series about witches.

You can tell a lot about the health of a civilization by the way it treats its women and the roles they play in society. Based on the success of *Charmed*, we appear to be in fantastic shape.

I have a friend who likes to answer the question, "How are you feeling?" with the retort, "Compared to what?"

Let's compare the three witches in *Charmed* to witches in the Middle Ages.

If you were a woman living in some burg in Westphalia in 1520, and your neighbor's cow died or he couldn't get it up when he tried to boink his wife—or he came on to you, and you told him to keep his wandering hands to himself—he might denounce you as a witch.

Which meant you were consorting with the devil.

In those days, consorting was a polite word for doing the nasty. And I do mean nasty.

Wrap your head around this: In the repressed atmosphere of the times, sex was dirty and shameful: something a husband was only supposed to do with his wife for purposes of procreation—under the covers with most of their clothes on.

Witch hunts were the perfect way for frustrated guys to get their jollies.

In theory, witches could be of either sex. Usually, though, they were female. And once a woman was accused, she was on a one-way train to hell.

She was taken to the local witch processing center where she was stripped. Then all the hair was shaved from her body so the learned judges could look for witch marks—particularly in the area of her private parts.

Once a witch mark was found—and this could vary from a mole to a vaginal tear resulting from childbirth—the next step was extracting a confession. The woman was shown the array of torture instruments the court might use on her. She could choose to confess before she was stuffed into an iron maiden (a hinged, body-shaped metal case with large spikes on the inside) or had her fingernails pulled out by the roots. But, even then, escaping alive was basically impossible. Most witches were burned at the stake after writing out a confession that usually included a description of the devil's penis and an account of the orgies she had attended with him.

Many of these hapless women were raped in prison. If the executioner was merciful, he strangled the victims so they wouldn't have to endure the pain of being burned alive.

Contrast that ghastly picture of a medieval witch hunt with life in the beautifully furnished Victorian San Francisco mansion where the Charmed Ones live.

On the surface, it's the American dream, except that in almost every episode demons invade the premises, leaving a heap of shattered mirrors, smashed furniture and shredded upholstery. From time to time, you see the Halliwell sisters sweeping up the mess. But by the next time we tune in, everything is back in perfect working order.

Not so bad, considering what a "burn the witches" mob could have done 500 years ago. Still, the Halliwell sisters aren't sharing their secret with greater San Francisco. We, the viewers, and a few chosen confidants are the only ones in on their paranormal powers.

Despite our enlightened era, some people would condemn them as evil. Others want to steal their powers. And then there's the weirdness factor—a definite minus when you're trying to blend in with the neighbors like normal folks.

Consider "normal" a relative term. The interplay of the mundane, the humorous and the supernatural is one of the fascinating aspects of the series. These women spend a great deal of their time fighting the fiend of the week, yet they crack wise at the drop of a bustier. For example, in "Blinded by the Whitelighter," in the third season, a guardian angel named Natalie berated the Charmed Ones for not acting with suitable decorum.

Natalie said, "No more braless, strapless, fearless attire."

Prue mumbled, "Okay, but then I have nothing to wear."

The juxtaposition of comedy and the sisters' deadly serious mission was showcased perfectly in "Bride and Gloom" when Phoebe was captured by a warlock bent on turning the three sisters evil, while Piper and Leo met with wedding planners making chipper suggestions that would up the cost of their ceremony and reception.

Playing the paranormal against the normal works brilliantly for the show. Despite being witches, each Halliwell sister wants a stable home life with a loving husband and a family. But there are stumbling blocks. They must find a man who can accept the whole package (woman and witch). And while on their quest, they might get tricked into marriage with a demon.

Every long-running TV series must deliver what viewers crave while at the same time growing and developing. For *Charmed*, this means the writers must continually up the ante—pitting the Charmed Ones against ever-increasing supernatural threats.

Setting aside the supernatural, the rules of good drama mean that the plot must keep the sisters from living happily ever after. The moment all three Charmed Ones settle down with the right man, the series is over. So Phoebe and Paige are doomed to a string of misguided and broken relationships, and even Piper, who married her Whitelighter, must endure endless domestic and supernatural squabbles with her husband.

The interplay of magic and the mundane in *Charmed* is masterful, and the sensuality of the sisters is one of the key ingredients. Unlike medieval "witches," who hid their sexuality lest they be accused of dancing with the devil, the Halliwells dress to attract men. And they have no hang-ups about sex. Although intercourse itself is not shown on camera, there's a lot of lusty kissing and foreplay. And the camera does venture inside the bedroom door for shots of scantily clad witches and their bed partners—before and after bopping each other's brains out.

On *Charmed*, great sex is only one of life's pleasures. These women cherish moments as ordinary as dancing in Piper's club or cooking a family dinner in the mansion kitchen. Yet they drop the personal aspects of their lives in a heartbeat when they're called upon to save an innocent.

And therein lies the most important aspect of *Charmed*. Making the witches of Prescott Street the saviors of humanity speaks volumes about the maturity of our civilization. Because monumental change in human thinking had to take place before a program like *Charmed* was even possible—let alone a seven-season hit with a slew of reruns.

Burning witches at the stake, or hanging them (which was the preferred method of execution in Salem, Massachusetts, in the 1700s), is an unfortunate legacy of our past here in the west. But if you want to imagine what life was like for women in Medieval Europe, you have only to recall the recent Taliban regime in Afghanistan, where women were totally subjugated to men—who could beat them senseless for showing a flash of ankle beneath a burka or shoot them in the head in the middle of a sports stadium for teaching girls to read.

Luckily, our culture has gone from a time in history where women could be burned at the stake in the public square to an era where three gorgeous witches can grill steak on the barbecue just like any normal American can.

But it didn't happen overnight.

Anyone born in the latter years of the twentieth century probably has trouble imagining a time when men virtually ruled women. When, for example, a woman's inheritance was under the control of her husband. And when her marriage vows contained the promise to "love, honor and obey."

If you'd rather not read any ancient (early twentieth century) history, skip right to the section below on the modern kick-ass heroine. But I do think a little historical context puts *Charmed* in perspective. The literature of an era is an excellent window into that society.

You may have seen the movie made from Edith Wharton's *The House of Mirth* and thought it was a quaint period piece. But the book, first published in 1905, is a chilling glimpse into Wharton's contemporary society. It's the story of Lily Bart, a woman with an upper-class background and little money, who refuses to marry a jerk and ends up starving to death—since there are no decent-paying jobs for a female of her social station.

Even grimmer are the novels of Wharton's contemporary, Theodore Dreiser. *Sister Carrie* tells of a working-class woman who sinks to the lowest rungs of society because of her sexual choices. And you may have seen *A Place in the Sun*, based on his upbeat (not) 1925 novel, *An American Tragedy*. In the movie, George Eastman gets young Alice Tripp pregnant. To take care of the problem, he rows her out to the middle of a lake and bashes her over the head with an oar. How's that for the consequences of her letting him take her to bed? Of course, Clift also gets his just desserts—after prosecuting attorney Raymond Burr reenacts the fatal blow in the courtroom.

At the beginning of the twentieth century, women were trapped by age-old sexist conventions. Still, the times were ripe for change—as evidenced by the women's suffrage movement and Margaret Sanger's crusade for birth control.

In the workplace, women took a giant leap forward with the outbreak of World War II. With the men off at war, women stepped smartly into high-paying jobs outside the home—on assembly lines, making tanks and battleships. In the evenings, these same young women partied with the soldiers and sailors.

At war's end, the ladies were expected to scuttle back home—where they'd been since the dawn of time. But Rosie the Riveter had opened a Pandora's Box of new options for herself and her little sisters.

Men and women's roles had been set in stone for centuries. In mid-twentieth-century America, these slabs of granite were blown to smithereens.

The birth control pill ushered in the sexual revolution, and the women's lib movement of the sixties and seventies turned many women into out-and-out radicals. Feminists wrote diatribes against men and marriage. Women attacked the glass ceiling in the business world. And the media rubbed their collective hands in glee at the boundless new possibilities for profit.

Suddenly, a book about men as insensitive, self-centered jerks, like Terry McMillan's *Waiting to Exhale*, became a national bestseller. And the action-adventure hero had a new rival, the "kick-ass heroine," whose early examples include Emma Peel in *The Avengers* and Wonder Woman.

The kick-ass trend continues with such shows as *Xena*, *La Femme Nikita* and *Alias*. Or consider Captain Janeway on *Star Trek: Voyager*. For Janeway, job one was beating the guys at their own game. Only in the holodeck could the captain let down her hair and cope with her own womanly emotions.

Heroines with the balls to fight the tough guys on their own terms became a major trend at the turn of this century.

Even Harlequin Books, whose name is a synonym for "romance," has embraced this new phenomenon. Their entry in the female James Bond sweepstakes is a line of mass market paperbacks called Bombshell, under their Silhouette imprint. In their guidelines for writers, they're asking for "a strong, sexy, savvy heroine, who finds herself in a dangerous, high-stakes situation." The focus is on how she saves the day—with the romance in the story downgraded to a subplot, if it exists at all.

The early twenty-first-century kick-ass heroine is a woman who has consciously or unconsciously sacrificed her femininity to make herself into a warrior. She's essentially a man with different protrusions—breasts instead of a penis.

Like the kick-ass heroine, the witches of Prescott Street vanquish the bad guys before breakfast—sometimes with magic and sometimes with their martial arts skills. But there's an important difference. Unlike female James Bonds, they still embrace their womanhood and all it embodies. They need not be superheroes. Or special agents. Or the tough-as-nails commander of a Federation spaceship. They don't have to be loners or outcasts. They can live in an old Victorian house in San Francisco and invite the neighbors in for tea. They can own a nightclub and write a newspaper advice column and take their children to school.

In fact, their femininity is just as important as their ability to kick butt. For example, consider their on-again, off-again relationship with the demon Belthazor, who takes the human form of a sexy guy named Cole Turner.

Just for fun, compare Cole to Leo, Piper's sometime-husband. Do you ever see Leo with his shirt off? Not hardly. But the producers take every opportunity possible to showcase the broad expanse of Cole's magnificent chest. Like when he elected to strip to the waist to give Phoebe sword fighting lessons in "Enter the Demon" in season four. Or when he was half-naked and being seduced by a female demon who incinerated men from the inside out in season five's "Siren Song."[1]

Cole/Belthazor was billed as all-powerful, even gaining the coveted underworld title of "the Source of all Evil." Time and again he had the opportunity to kill the Charmed Ones—and kept making excuses for not doing it.

Why couldn't he destroy them? Because he fell in love with Phoebe Halliwell.

Ultimately, her witchcraft spelled his defeat. But along the way, she used her feminine powers on him—the secret weapons that women have always possessed in any civilization. The ability to influence their husbands and raise their children with some knowledge of "feminine" values.

I gave some examples of early twentieth-century novels where the wrong sexual choices spelled the downfall of the female characters. *Charmed* takes a different approach. Look at the very first episode, "Something Wicca this Way Comes." Police were closing in on a serial killer who turned out to be a warlock bent on wiping out the witch population of San Francisco. On a more personal level, he was Jeremy, Piper's boyfriend.

If Theodore Dreiser had written the script, the warlock would have left Piper in a pool of her own blood on the floor as retribution for letting herself be taken in by this evil guy.

Instead, she set the pattern for future *Charmed* episodes by narrowly escaping. And when Piper banished Jeremy from her heart, the Charmed Ones used the Power of Three for the first time to vanquish him from the Earthly plane.

Much of the focus of *Charmed* is on making sexual choices. And all too many turn out to be the wrong ones—at least in the short run. As Piper quipped to Paige after the Source had possessed Paige's boyfriend and tried to turn her from good to evil (in "Charmed Again II," the second show of the fourth season), "Yeah, well, you're not truly one of us until you've dated a demon, so welcome to the club."

In "A Knight to Remember," Paige was revealed to be the reincarnation of a wicked witch from the Middle Ages. In her long-ago life, she worked a spell on a handsome knight and made him fall in love with her. Magic brought him to present-day San Francisco, where all he wanted

---

[1] I could spend a lot of time talking about Cole's chest. It's not shaved, like Fabio's and a lot of other cover models', thank you very much. It's got a nice covering of dark hair that looks like it would feel wonderful to the touch.

was to drag Paige off to bed and get her with child. The three sisters and Leo traveled back in time to take the witch's powers away. Even as the reincarnation of an evil seductress, Paige escaped permanent harm and went back to life as usual on Prescott Street.

Of course, the mother of all bad dates on *Charmed* was Phoebe's love-hate relationship with Cole/Belthazor. If the intention of the show had been to punish wrong choices, Phoebe would have ended up in hell. Instead she got out from under Cole's—uh—thumb and went on to embrace life again. Rather than being punished, she was rewarded with a new boyfriend, the powerful and wealthy Jason Dean, who bought the newspaper where she worked.

In *Charmed,* feminine values are not just okay; they are a positive aspect of the series. The Halliwell sisters may be witches, but they demonstrate to viewers week after week that being normal women, being feminine, being active participants in life around them are assets, not stumbling blocks. As women, they are never afraid to show their softer side. They are never afraid to admit that their primary interest is in love and family. They all want to marry and live happily ever after. They all embrace their sisterhood. And they call on the spirits of their female relatives in times of trouble, summoning the ghosts of Grams or their mom so that they can consult their wisdom.

In a particularly touching scene in "Charmed Again II," they summoned their mother's ghost so she could embrace Paige, the child she had to give up.

After Piper became a mother, she guarded her children with the fierce protectiveness of a mother lioness. And her sisters joined in as guardians of these special children. For example, in "Baby's First Demon," in season five, Phoebe had to deal with a new boss who had just bought the paper where she works. But she was willing to risk her job to help defend little Wyatt against a hawker demon who had been hired to kidnap him and sell him at the demon marketplace. Paige risked her life at the marketplace trying to stop the parasite demons who wanted to use Wyatt's magic powers.

And while family comes first, they understand their broader mission—to save the world from evil. Even when they hate the warrior role they've been thrust into, none of them turns away from her duty to humanity.

As the sisters fight demons and other fiends week after week, they mirror a world where women are empowered as never before.

In real life, women have taken a larger role in running or influencing our society. Madeleine Albright, Condoleezza Rice, Martha Stewart,

Sandra Day O'Connor, Ruth Bader Ginsburg, Arianna Huffington, Barbara Boxer, Hillary Clinton, Barbara Mikulski, Dianne Feinstein, Oprah Winfrey, Dr. Ruth and Barbara Walters are all instantly recognizable for their important roles in our society.

And the logic circles back on itself. A series like *Charmed* is possible because our attitudes toward women have changed so radically since those long-ago witch burnings. Yet the show does not simply follow trends. It helps to set them—by creating an atmosphere where women of power are accepted by both male and female viewers.

When I go out to dinner and casually ask my twenty-something waitress, "Do you watch *Charmed*?" and she answers, "It's my favorite show," I feel a tingle along my nerve endings.

The success of *Charmed* would have been flat-out impossible before the late twentieth century. Even in mid-century, women with otherworldly powers were relegated to the role of ditz brains—like the central characters in *I Dream of Jeannie* or *Bewitched*.

Did the producers of *Charmed* know what they had wrought? Or did they just throw the witches of Prescott Street into the big media ocean to see if they would float?

Whatever the answer, viewers are treated to a television series that builds on the gains women have made in our society and at the same time breaks new ground.

By being powerful witches and at the same time women who are not afraid to embrace their femininity and their ordinary lives, they set an example for their viewers, one that empowers women and widens their horizons. And the more women we have making important decisions in government, in education, in business and in the media, the better off we are. Or put another way—the more we embrace traditionally feminine values, the less likely we are to resort to violent solutions to political, diplomatic and economic problems. And the less likely we are to let outside or inside forces threaten our very existence as a society.

For these reasons, I see *Charmed* as nothing short of revolutionary, a bright star blazing a path across the night sky, changing our perception of women and thus preparing the way for the next generation.

That so many viewers tune in to the witches of Prescott Street proves that our society has come a long way since the Middle Ages—even since the early twentieth century. And we're still on the right track. So rejoice in the success of the Charmed Ones. And stay tuned for further good news from the real world.

Award-winning, *New York Times* best-selling author Ruth Glick writes under the name Rebecca York for Berkley and Harlequin. The author of more than a hundred books, she loves writing paranormal romantic suspense. A rabid *Charmed* fan, she can't wait to read the other essays in *Totally Charmed*.

ENCHANTÉ...NOT

PEG ALOI

It's no secret that *Charmed* is on no Wiccan Top Ten lists. Peg Aloi takes the show to task not only for violating Wiccan practice but for making it harder to be Wiccan in real life. Her suggestions for improvement include more realism, such as fewer lightning bolts and instructions on how to get wax out of a ritual robe, or in Phoebe's case, a black lace bustier.

WELL SHIVER MY LIVER and toil my trouble, witches have become media darlings. Life's a witch and then you fly. Just like *The X-Files* made the world of conspiracy theory, paranormal phenomena and alien abduction sexy and glamorous, propelling a geeky subculture of obsessed Robert Anton Wilson fans forward into social recognizability (if not acceptance), the film *The Craft* engendered a whole subculture of teenaged wannabe witches, gothlets and occult dabblers into the spotlight. A witchcraft zeitgeist.

1996: The year *The Craft* opened was the year witchcraft became a social trend gobbled up by (and eventually marketed to) the youth demographic. The hot young actresses of the film (including Neve Campbell and Fairuza Balk) in black tights and noisy rosaries and glitter eyeshadow made Wicca sexy—but the film's creators made sure not to call it anything that specific. Three goth chicks who are ostracized at their Catholic high school have been waiting for their "fourth" to complete their circle, and when a new girl arrives from the West their four directions are covered. Further, the new girl already has some magical know-how and fresh razor scars on her wrist: she is beautiful, cool, scared and scary, poised to complete their dysfunctional quaternity. But things go bad quickly, when the four start to "make things happen" and only the new girl understands this is not necessarily such a good thing.

The Craft was a masterpiece of both subtlety and excess. The excess was surface: fake deities, over-the-top special effects, artful production design, gotta-have-that costumes. The subtlety, however, was not. Starting with that title: *The Craft*. Not *witchcraft*. No, no. *The* craft. The craft of the wise? Macramé? Crafty and cunning, those producers. They made sure to utilize the visual and elemental trappings any real witch would recognize. They made sure that questions of ethics and integrity were raised, along with a highbrow moral caveat that "dabbling" in magic can lead to, well, loss of popularity, if not all-out insanity.

There was Sarah, the "natural witch" with the puritanical name, whose compassionate nature allowed her to best the three "dabblers" who wanted to harness power for selfish reasons. Bonnie, the shy one with severe burn scars on her back, would, as her name suggests, give anything to be pretty. Rochelle is sweet and gorgeous but endlessly teased by a racist teammate on the diving squad. Nancy is somewhat misanthropic but quick to befriend a like-minded soul and urge complete trust among the circle of friends. Predictably enough, once the girls discover that magic works, their biggest challenges become their worst vices: Sarah becomes manipulative with a boy who treated her badly, Bonnie becomes vain and shallow, Rochelle becomes capricious and unsympathetic, and Nancy becomes a megalomaniacal sociopath. This cautionary tale was campy, sexy and surprisingly true-to-life (well, except for all the ILM-style mumbo-jumbo effects in the last twenty minutes). It was hot, red hot—like those heated iron pincers used by medieval witch finders to goad recalcitrant witches into confessing their crimes. It had glossy production design, smart dialogue and socially provocative undertones—and so it is not at all surprising there'd be interest in creating a television show based on a similar concept. At the time, supernatural and fantasy shows were already on fire on several of the major networks: *Buffy the Vampire Slayer*, *The X-Files*, *Hercules* and their respective spin-offs *Angel*, *Millennium* and *Xena: Warrior Princess*. They all did well for the demographically sensitive WB, FOX and UPN. So, lessee, how about a show about...young...sexy...witches? Booyeah!

Here was an idea for a show with the potential to entertain and edify. It could tap into a burgeoning cultural trend that was already of interest to millions of people, and what's more, make it accessible to teenagers, as *The Craft* had done. Such a show would surely glamorize and romanticize the world of contemporary witchcraft, but might also clarify its complexity, make it palatable and feel-good fuzzy for nervous parents and suspicious school administrators. Witchcraft for the new millennium, damn it.

So what happened?

How is it possible that the small-screen conceptualization inspired by this intelligently conceived, ambitious, well-researched, classy, deliciously naughty film could be so ill-conceived, bland, sappy, predictable and devoid of sophistication? And where witchcraft authenticity is concerned—forget it.

It's not that *Charmed* looks bad on its surface. In its early seasons it had much to recommend it in terms of sheer style. Its innovative use of popular music, for example, wherein obscure and often unsigned bands were given a chance to have their songs featured during (and credited at the end of) each episode, was a cool, feel-good move. Unfortunately the show's theme music remained a cover of The Smiths' "How Soon is Now?" which was also in *The Craft*'s soundtrack, when it might have been "A Charming Spell" by the Boston-based ethereal trip-hop band Splashdown. (Disclosure: members of this band are friends of mine.) They did eventually have a song or two featured on the show but the royalty checks and fame would have been far greater if the producers had taken a bigger creative risk with the show's opening. The opening credits segment, which uses the Smiths' song (covered, as in the film soundtrack, by the band Love Spit Love), clearly acknowledges *Charmed*'s debt to *The Craft*. But there, all groovy similarities end.

The show's basic premise isn't incompatible with the film's narrative structure. Prue, Phoebe and Piper are three sisters who are "hereditary" or "natural" witches living in an opulent (and ancestral!) San Francisco home. In the first episode they learned of their inherent powers and that they are meant to use them to fight evil and do good in the world. A huge, heavy grimoire of spells lives in the house, which the sisters refer to in times of need and impulsive wrong-headedness. Unfortunately, the book—solid, vibe-y, a tangible repository of learning and mystery—is the only witchcraft-related thing grounding the show in any sort of reality. The sisters' wardrobes, jobs, relationships and daily pressures are so implausibly glamorous as to make their lives appear hopelessly shallow. As a consequence, to avoid having the show look more or less like *90210*, the show relies on heavy-handed, silly special effects and implausible plotlines involving "magic" to make sure audiences know it's a fantasy, not just a glitzy teen soap opera.

If the actresses were playing characters maturing into their thirties instead of their twenties, they'd be Botoxed and aerobicized to skeletal prettiness, like the glamourpusses of *Desperate Housewives*. To be twenty-something in California is to be nubile and dewy-faced. No golden girls, these daughters of darkness: their pinkness and pallor is not only an homage to the gothic princesses of *The Craft* (even the African-American sister, Rochelle, was caramel, not cocoa), but conjures a New Englandy provenance of harsh winters, apple orchards and Puritan ancestors. And in this we have another crucial area where *Charmed* errs. The show posits a heredity-based witchcraft that only encourages naive viewers and witch wannabes to fabricate their own dubious claims to non-existent lineage. The three Charmed Ones are "natural witches" (a term also used in *The Craft* to denote innate psychic ability—the term soon became popular among teen-aged seekers, too, and was found throughout web discussion groups and teen witchcraft pages at the time) who are connected to witchcraft through their matriarchal line. Their family history has occasionally been portrayed with direct ties to the Matter of Salem.

Okay, while I'm on the subject, why is it always about Salem? The film version of the excellent novel *Practical Magic* also decided the two sisters had to have female ancestors hanged during the witch trials. Look, girls, we can't ALL be descended from them! It's every bit as implausible and tiring to suppose all modern-day witches are as-good-as-blood relations of the Puritans (sorry, *witches*) hanged at Salem as it is for us to assume we must all have been persecuted witches in a former life. I don't know if the show's producers were aware of it, but when it first aired there actually was quite a bit of this sort of posturing going on in the pagan community. You know: my grandmother initiated me, I'm descended from Rebecca Nurse, I was a witch who was burned to death in a past life, etc.

You see, when *Charmed* premiered, Wicca was becoming very popular very quickly. If you were practicing by 1984, you were still cool. But by 1988, plenty of people had at least heard of Starwood and Starhawk, and meeting a "real" witch was not as freaky an encounter as it would have been considered a few years earlier. Eighties witches were not the patchouli-dipped, lovebead-wearing, back-to-the-earth dreamers of the seventies. We had our own shops, our own music, our own fashions and plenty of books. But even in the midst of discovery, we could sense our nascent tradition was becoming old hat. No sooner did we learn that there were coven secrets than we saw those secrets published. This thanks to the granddaddy of modern witchcraft: Gerald Gardner.

An English civil servant with an encyclopedic knowledge of the occult, Gardner hung out with a group called the Order of Woodcraft Chivalry as a boy, then met some random ceremonial magicians and decided that he wanted to practice witchcraft in the Old Way. Trouble is, no one really knew exactly what that way was. So, Gardner cobbled together a number of texts (from sources like Aleister Crowley, the Kabbala and the Golden Dawn), wrote them up in a book and claimed to have "discovered" an ancient tradition. He initiated dozens of witches into his New Forest coven and, when the Witchcraft Act was repealed in 1951, immediately started publishing books and speaking publicly about what witches do. His claim that witches had been "underground" since the Middle Ages, and that what he and his followers practiced was inherited from our pagan European forbears, was more or less accepted, if not embraced, and witches' covens in the "Gardnerian" mold started springing up throughout England and eventually in the United States. It was all very hush-hush throughout the 1960s and '70s, with an occasional whiff of weirdness with the release of films like *Rosemary's Baby* or *The Exorcist*, which offered titillating glimpses of the black arts and portrayed witches as Satanists. Despite damning rumors about witchcraft, most serious seekers were not daunted and covens continued to form, although many witches remained "in the (broom) closet." Then more witches went public and started writing books which claimed to "share secrets," and it wasn't long before anyone could declare themselves a witch and be privy to the language, rituals and practices of the craft. You could walk into any bookstore and buy any one of dozens of books on the subject in the early 1980s. Nowadays, those books number in the hundreds, and most witches do not see this as a Good Thing. At the time, the increasing tendency to put a public face on witchcraft did not sit well with some of the old-timers, who had come up through the ranks looking for little hand-lettered ads mentioning meetings on the bulletin boards of occult bookshops, who mail ordered newsletters and crudely produced magazines that arrived in plain brown wrappers, who hid their robes and ritual implements away in cupboards so as not to become suspect among their neighbors or non-pagan loved ones. I recall meeting some of these folks when I first got involved in witchcraft. They were often grouchy and resentful, seemingly because this thing they had been doing in secret for so long was suddenly trendy. But some of the older folks seemed genuinely thrilled about having new blood (or is that new meat?) around for the party. That, alas, is another essay, and one I am not necessarily eager to write.

Since some of the established covens were not terribly welcoming to strangers, many younger or newer seekers attempted to move quickly beyond the standard Gardnerian Wicca-based groups to include ethnic and cultural practices; hence, Celtic-derived paths became extremely trendy for a while (*Riverdance* helped). If you weren't straight vanilla Gardnerian, why then you just might have something unique going for you. But, alas, the old chestnut "I was initiated by my grandmother" only worked for the first ten people you heard it from. The lure of authenticity and heritage is all the greater when you're told your religion/path/lifestyle/belief system/craft is actually not millions or thousands or even hundreds of years old, but dates in fact only as far back as the Second World War. To be sure, many of the trappings and activities are old, way old. Tarot, astrology, herblore, ceremonial magic...yes, all this is ancient stuff. But Gardner and his protégés put it together into a nifty anachronistic package that certainly seemed to originate in antiquity. Of course when he/they said that's exactly where it came from, no one wanted to know differently. And along with the appropriation of the (supposed) beliefs and practices of the witches of Medieval Europe or Colonial America, contemporary witches also willingly adopted a persecution complex. Even if what we believed was no longer going to get us labeled criminals or heretics (weirdos, yes; criminals or heretics, no), we understood that reclaiming the word "witch" was going to make people raise their eyebrows, if not their cudgels.

So, you started to hear whispers and then shouts and then songs of The Burning Times. Nine million witches burned, said one book, and the rest followed suit. Witchcraft, it is said, went "underground." Information was passed down orally from one generation to the next and reached us in better times. We were sisters and brothers in flesh and spirit with countless martyrs. Wow. Trouble is, it never happened. Historians waffle, but most place the actual number of victims of the witch craze somewhere between 100,000 and a million. Still, being historically aligned with the victims of torture allows for some pretty righteous self-esteem issues. Welcome to the pagan community! May I take your backbone? And you won't be needing your common sense either! Just as we started to realize aligning ourselves with history's biggest patsies was maybe not the best idea, the media representations started to pop up like mayapples in spring. Gosh, Ethel, look—witches really don't worship the devil, they really *do* do magic, and gosh, do they really spend that much time doing love spells and chanting? And look at those silly robes! And why is that cat talking?!? And we were victims all over again—but of misrepresentation this time, not of religious persecution. Suddenly, we pined for the days of being labeled Satan worshippers because at least then, people took us seriously. Perhaps it is this desire to be taken seriously that has led so many modern witches to cleave to the myth of The Burning Times, even as it has been debunked thoroughly by scholars.

If you've read your history, you know that public floggings, hangings and burnings of accused witches were akin to public entertainment, just as public torture and execution have been entertaining the masses since the gladiator days. But it is the method used that raises some forms of spectacle above others (think of Urbain Grandier's death in *The Devils* versus John Proctor's in *The Crucible*—of course, we should perhaps be thankful that Nicholas Hytner, and not Ken Russell, directed *The Crucible*). Burning is somehow, well, *sexier* than hanging. Is it that human flesh smells sweet when it's burning, like roasting pork? Is it that it's a vicarious so-glad-that's-not-me reminder of hellfire? Either way, public conflagrations sure did draw big crowds of onlookers in Medieval Europe at the height of the witch craze. Despite the fact that condemned witches in the North American colonies were never burned, dramatic literature plays fast and loose with facts and evidence and likes to consign its naughty nymphets to the flames, not the gallows. Several episodes of *Charmed* have exploited the sex appeal of the public immolation, and, the show being what it is, the magically crafted illusion (wrought by the Charmed Ones or others) of people being burned alive is as likely to be featured as the "real thing."

This is one of the more irritating aspects of the show for me: that the use of "magic" is so often merely about the use of illusion, and the transformations that occur are almost always merely temporary and easily reversed. The lessons learned after these illusory forces are tangled with are rarely connected to the nature of illusion (or delusion, or glamour, or any other concept related to it); it's usually more along the lines of "Whew! Good thing we got through that scrape! Gosh, next time we'll have to check the book and make sure we don't say those words in that order ever again!"

But I'd be willing to forgive *Charmed* its many sins: its deviation from the smart, character-driven monolithic structure of *The Craft*; its reliance upon cheap, glitzy effects to portray "magic"; its shallow, ingenuous portrayal of the Charmed Ones as professionally accomplished businesswomen who, oh yeah, just happen to be battling evil all day long before they freshen up and start their evening stint managing a successful restaurant/nightclub. Yes, I'd excuse these infractions but for one thing: the show insists on using the word "Wicca." The use of lexicon in *Charmed* is every bit as slipshod as its portrayal of history. But there is simply no reason for it if the show's writers and producers do their research and give a crap about accuracy and authenticity. I mean, is "Wicca" a noun, a verb or an adjective? Do we blame *Buffy the Vampire Slayer* for first using it as a word interchangeable with "witch" instead of its more correct usage, a synonym for "witchcraft" (albeit only in a very specific modern sense)? Or is it that the word "witch" is still too scary to some people? Or maybe practitioners wish to have a more arcane way to refer to themselves, since calling yourself a witch is still very much verboten in much of suburban America... good for being invited to a few cocktail parties, maybe, but not to the neighbor's kid's graduation barbecue.

That's okay, we have our own parties and drinking games (drink every time one of the main characters changes costumes on *Charmed*, for example). Becoming media darlings has at least made mention of us as fashionable. But is *Charmed* making it okay for us to do what we do, in terms of being respectable members of society? Or is it making TV audiences think twice when they encounter a "real" witch in "real life"? Do mundane folk think that we witches are crazy/disillusioned/naive/just plain weird for calling ourselves witches? Or, and this is the scary part, do some viewers actually believe we can do stuff like freeze time, burst spontaneously into flames, force people to fall in love with each other at the snap of our fingers and shapeshift into other people or animals? If you listen to some of the right-wing Christian rhetoric out there, it is surprising to acknowledge just how much power some people attribute to the modern witch. The power to corrupt all of the children of America, for example. Or, if we're not doing it directly, evil books like *Harry Potter and the Half-Blood Prince* are doing it for us.

I propose one, just one, episode of *Charmed* that deals with an average day of a real live practicing witch. If audiences bought it, they'd maybe buy an entire series about real witches. Not the megalomaniacal showgirls on programs like *Mad Mad House*, but witches who have boring jobs, families, mortgages, PMS and hopes and dreams. Prue would not have had some handsome, glamorous detective as a lover, but an average-looking boyfriend who was, say, an insurance salesman or a portfolio analyst. She would have stopped all the incessant wigging out and kicked back with a pint of Ben and Jerry's once in a while. She would have worn a grimy t-shirt on laundry day like the rest of us slobs. Phoebe would come back from yoga class dripping with sweat and devoid of lipstick. She would worry that her domestic know-how was not quite what it should be and check out some books from the library on, say, vegetarian cooking or furniture refinishing. Piper would get a pimple once in a while and have some sort of addictive vice like jalapeno potato chips, or scratch tickets. Paige would, oh, I don't know, have a thing for bad eighties hair bands and frosted lipstick. Oh, and their boyfriends' infractions would not involve demonic revenge scenarios or being spirited away into some misty limbo-land where they'd be incommunicado for months. This tendency of the Charmed Ones' men to just not be around in a dependable fashion would be due to very plausible reasons. Like, they'd be inaccessible because their cell phone batteries died, or because they had a not-quite-ex-wife they were still sloppily separating from, or because they just felt like watching the game with their buds over pineapple-ham pizza and Zima. No more declarations of undying love and then zapping themselves into the ether—these guys simply need to be less mysterious. Hey, better yet, make their men pagan, too! They could be Trekkies, or wood carvers, or weekend warrior types spending a few days a month in the woods with other men, banging on drums and howling at the moon.

This new *Charmed* would find its young heroines struggling with decisions such as the ones real-life witches make. How to get wax out of a silk ritual robe. What to bring to the potluck feast. Where to find broomstick-shaped cookie cutters. What to do when the High Priestess of your coven gets dumped by the studly new Harvest Lord and is left with her heart in pieces. How to tell your parents you don't want a Catholic wedding or funeral. How to comfort a friend whose Baptist family has disowned her for coming out as a witch.

No more lightning bolts shooting from anyone's hands. No more big books of spells hurling through the air. No more manipulation of the time-space continuum. No more ill-considered spells that change people's fundamental personalities. And, please Goddess, no more flawless designer hairdos. Witchcraft is earthy, sweaty, messy, frustrating and exhausting—much like life itself. And like "real life," it too can be a source of immeasurable beauty, ecstasy, insight, joy and excitement. Why can't we ever get that on TV?

> Peg Aloi has been a practicing witch for a decade and a half. She often rants about film and TV for The Witches' Voice Web site. She is also a film critic for *The Boston Phoenix* and a professor of film studies. Her favorite on-screen depiction of The Old Religion is the 1973 film *The Wicker Man*.

THEIR MORAL AND MAGICAL WORLD

GOOD AND EVIL AND BLOWING STUFF UP

The Halliwells' world is pretty simple most of the time: The Good are innocent, the Evil are vile and magic cures all. Except when the sisters go Evil, or when Good screws up, or when the magic goes away....

THREE IS A MAGIC NUMBER

JOHN G. HEMRY

The Power of Three doesn't just apply to the three Halliwell sisters, John G. Hemry says. It goes back through time and across cultures, and it makes magic everywhere it shows up.

THE POWER OF THREE. Three witches, in the television series *Charmed*, to be exact. The phrase "Power of Three" sounds both mystical and impressive. The idea behind it has made for a lot of good stories.

But why three? Why not the power of two? Was three just an arbitrary decision made by the creators of *Charmed* because they had enough money to hire three actresses? Or by Aaron Spelling because he wanted to invoke the ratings magic of *Charlie's Angels* in his new series about witches? (Though that argument just bumps the question back one series—why three angels?)

As it turns out, there are some very good reasons why three is important and why three makes very good sense as a number of witches. Some of those reasons are rooted in ancient (and current) beliefs. Some are just part of the process of telling interesting stories. Taken together, they give *Charmed* a lot of its charm.

People actually do think three is a particularly important number. The idea that the number three is special shows up repeatedly in history and across cultures. Ancient belief systems from places as diverse as Wales, Greece and Indonesia placed extra emphasis on the importance of the number three.

Start listing examples and you end up crisscrossing through human mythology, religion, literature and culture. Three weird sisters in Macbeth. Three Fates. Three Muses (originally, until expanded to "three times three," or nine). Three caballeros. Three strikes and you're out. Three Musketeers. Three blind mice. Three wise men. Three Stooges.

Folklore holds that good things come in threes, but also that famous people die in threes. Lighting three cigarettes from one match ("three on a match") is supposed to cause bad luck as well as creating risk of burnt fingers.

It's been believed in many cultures that the soul resides in the body for three days after death. (As Miracle Max from *The Princess Bride* would say, for the first three days they're only *mostly* dead. On the fourth day, they're completely dead.)

Speaking of which, the Bible says Jesus rose from the dead on the third day.

Names (especially true names) were regarded as very important in many ancient beliefs. Speaking a true name three times would variously invoke or give power over the one named, so repeating a name three times was a chancy thing to do. The belief that saying a name once or twice was safe but that saying it a third time would have a magical effect gave rise to an expression that's still common—third time's the charm. (People today are most likely to remember this from the movie *Beetlejuice*, in which saying his name three times either summons or vanquishes that sleazy spirit and his love for old Harry Belafonte tunes.)

Trinities show up in many belief systems, and even those with many gods usually declare three of the gods to be the leaders (as in the three brothers Zeus, Poseidon and Hades). Today, the Christian Trinity (Father, Son and Holy Spirit) and that of Hinduism (Brahma, Vishnu and Shiva) are widely revered.

Three pops up a lot in the Christian Bible, as a matter of fact, both as the number itself and in concepts grouped in threes. The famous passage from I Corinthians reduces those things that abide to "faith, hope and love," which is as nice a threesome as anyone could hope for.

Three, it turns out, can be a special number even to those who are trying to understand the universe as philosophers or scientists. Aristotle, an ancient Greek philosopher whose thinking heavily influenced the development of Western science (and who tutored the young Alexander the Great), declared that there were three kinds of motion, three kinds of friendship, three reasons for being attracted to something and three forms of government. But wait, there's more! In his treatise *On the Heavens*, Aristotle flatly states that "the world and all that is in it is determined by the number three." (If you happened to have been Aristotle's pupil and couldn't remember the answer to a question he tossed your way, "three" probably would've served as a good guess.)

Modern witchcraft also finds special meaning in the number three. One prominent example is the Law of Return, also known as the Law of Three or the Threefold Law. The law is basically a motivational tool and states that anything a witch does, good or bad, comes back multiplied three times over. Do good and get three times greater good in return; do bad and get hammered three times as hard back. If you do the math, it seems pretty clear that crime (and evil-doing in general) wouldn't be a paying proposition for a witch.

Charmed usually seems to reflect this particular rule in spirit if not to the letter. The early episodes dealt with the witches not only learning to use their powers but also learning not to *misuse* their powers for personal gain or other selfish purposes. A typical example of following the rule can be found in the season two episode "Morality Bites," where the three used magic to punish a thoughtless neighbor. This small malicious act had serious consequences (including the future execution of Phoebe for murder), so when given the chance to relive events the witches chose not to use their powers against the neighbor. Sometimes, however, there's more than just the Threefold Law at work. In season five's "A Witch in Time," Phoebe kept saving Miles from being killed only to learn that his death was required by the Angel of Death. If Phoebe kept saving Miles, she herself would have to die, which isn't exactly a reward for what should have been a good deed. In the end, Phoebe had to let Miles die.

There are other ways in which Wicca and witchcraft place a special significance in the number three, such as the Triple Goddess (also known as the Threefold Goddess), who has three aspects but is one being.

While the divine being with three aspects, which together make up one, has been and is a common theme in belief systems, it's also a big part of *Charmed*. Together the three witches command a great power (the Power of Three), even though they're not divine in the literal sense of being heavenly goddesses. (Though ten out of ten warlocks doubtless wouldn't agree, most men would probably describe the Charmed Ones as being divine in the figurative sense: they're all women with smarts, courage and pretty darn good looks.)

A couple of other overt mystical references to the number three in *Charmed* are the Triquetra on the cover of the Book of Shadows and the description of magic as having three essential elements (timing, feeling and the phases of the moon).

In short, *Schoolhouse Rock* had it right. Three *is* a magic number.

Exactly why the number three has been held up as special by humans for as far back as we can tell isn't known. It's not impossible that there's some natural quality which influences humans to subconsciously see three as special, in the same way the Golden Mean (the ratio of 1 to 1.618...) is found throughout nature in things like the curve of a nautilus shell and repeated by humans in things like the proportions of playing cards because it just feels good when we look at things proportioned that way. (As a matter of fact, humans are proportioned that way, too.)

There's certainly any number of things that from the human perspective very naturally divide into threes: past, present, future; left, right, center; above, below, even; tall, medium, short; birth, life, death; hot, cold, tepid; blue, yellow, red (the three primary colors). Goldilocks, dealing with three bears, keeps finding things divided into three states (too big, too small, just right) in a fairy tale which seems designed specifically to emphasize the way in which many aspects of the universe seem to fall easily into threes.

Then there are the ways people choose to define things that gives a special significance to three. Such as the fact that two people, married or not, make a couple. It takes a third (a child) to make them a family.

When it comes to literature, people thinking of multi-volume book series usually think of trilogies, and trilogies remain the default form of book series (the first book series I wrote was a trilogy). Non-writers may assume that's because trilogies are easy to write compared to other lengths. They're not. Writers will tell you that, on the contrary, it's actually harder to do a trilogy well. The basic problem is that middle book, which neither starts the story nor ends the story but just carries it along. Anyone who's read the first book wants to get to the end of the story, so making the middle book as powerful and interesting as the beginning books is not a simple task. Even in the great Lord of the Rings trilogy the second novel (*The Two Towers*) is usually regarded as the least of the three books.

Making that middle book a great read can be done, of course, and the most well-written trilogies are those in which the author has been able to generate enough new characters, story lines and plot developments to keep the middle book from suffering by comparison (as in *The Subtle Knife*, the second book in the His Dark Materials trilogy by Philip Pullman[1]). But it ain't easy.

---

[1] Insert shameless plug for BenBella's book on His Dark Materials, *Navigating the Golden Compass*.

So there really isn't any reason why trilogies should be the common rule for multi-book series. In fact, they ought to be the exception. In addition to the extra difficulty inherent in that middle book, publishers are notoriously reluctant (unless you happen to be a best-selling author) to shell out for multi-book contracts if they can get by with only committing to buy one or two books until they see if the public really wants to buy what an author is writing. Somehow, though, the three-book series continues to reign as the norm while two-book series often feel too short and four-book series can feel somehow awkwardly long.

It's reasonable to suggest that we're hardwired inside to see things in threes, or else that the universe is put together in a way that favors dividing things into threes. If you believe the universe was put together the way it is for a reason, that could be taken as evidence that the number three matters in some fundamental way—though whether it matters because of some arbitrary principle of physics, or because of the wish of a divine creator is another question. Whatever the reason, people do seem predisposed to see three as a special number.

From a human cultural perspective, then, using three witches as the lead characters in *Charmed* makes a lot of sense. But *Charmed* isn't a documentary television series. It's entertainment. *Charmed* tells stories in every episode, with all the events in each episode contributing to a slowly developing overall story. If *Charmed* didn't do a good job of telling those stories every week, if it didn't build a compelling and interesting larger narrative to frame all those episodes, then it would fail no matter how culturally relevant and mystical its underpinnings were.

Anyone reading this probably thinks *Charmed* does a good job of telling stories. This is where the number three has another special significance. When it comes to telling stories, three is a big help. No, not the dreaded trilogies. Characters.

Because when it comes to characters, just as in culture, three once again is a magic number.

You get a clue to this in the career of the Three Stooges. A total of six men played Stooges, but when the slap hit the stick there were always just three in front of the camera. While Moe and Larry stayed constant, Shep was replaced by Curly who was replaced by Joe who was replaced by Curly Joe. Meanwhile, the Marx Brothers are remembered as another threesome (Groucho, Harpo and Chico) even though a fourth brother (Zeppo) was part of the group during many of their movies.

Why? Because it worked. Three nuts interacting made for sustained, long-term comedy success. There have been successful comedy teams made of two people, but try to think of one as well-known and enduring as the Stooges. And even two-person comedy teams recognized the need for a third person in their movies, where there's invariably another major character added for the two comedians to bounce off of (think of Dorothy Lamour in the Bing Crosby and Bob Hope Road movies). The three *Ghostbusters* added a fourth late in the movie, but that fourth character remained a minor player compared to the original three (played by actors named Murray, Aykroyd and Ramis—which, as the animated *Ghostbusters* series pointed out in one episode, sounds a lot like a law firm).

It works in drama, too. Think of the romantic triangle. Two happy people who are happy with each other make for happy endings but also short, dull television series. Throw in another man or woman, and sparks start flying.

Or consider the phenomenally successful *Harry Potter* series. Yes, it's about Harry, but Harry doesn't wander through Hogwarts alone. In one way or another, his friends Hermione and Ron are almost always there, too. The trio support each other, help each other, argue with each other, hang out together and so on. It's hard to imagine Harry without his posse, and Hermione and Ron play important roles in the outcome of each book.

Three works for stories because three people is a small enough group that you can really get to know everyone, but also large enough not to become stale and predictable. If you only have two primary characters, their relationship ends up pretty much set in stone after a little while. Every situation produces the same reactions because they're the same two people pinging off each other.

Three characters expand the possibilities a great deal. Arnold and Brittany gang up on Carmen this week, then next week it's Brittany and Carmen bonding while Arnold insists he needs time to himself, then the week after that Arnold and Carmen team up to help Brittany with a problem. The relationships are both solid (within the trio) and constantly shifting.

So, if three is better than two, why not use four characters? Or five? You can, but it gets a lot more complicated if you're really working on relationships, because four or more characters have, potentially, a lot more and different ways of interacting. You start to need line diagrams to keep track of who's doing what with who and why. That's soap opera territory, and for the dedicated fan it's fun, but when characters are in constantly altering relationships with several other people it limits how much time you can spend exploring those characters. If you're also trying to tell compelling stories about events those characters are caught in, then the burden of trying to follow a lot of characters can easily detract from the story. Instead of following the action involving three characters, you have to hare off in different directions to find out what the others are doing.

One of the best examples of the allure of threesomes in storytelling is found in *The Lord of the Rings*. At this point, someone's objecting that there were nine in the Fellowship, and many more characters wandering in and out constantly. Yes, but (even without going into the "three times three" business, which makes nine important to people who think three is important), Tolkien kept breaking his larger groups down into threes, the most prominent of which was Frodo, Sam and Gollum. Meanwhile, Aragorn, Gimli and Legolas keep ending up together, while Merry and Pippin form a group with Treebeard for a while, then in Minas Tirith it's up to Gandalf, Pippin and Denethor to form another character triangle. Merry, left behind in Rohan, partners with the characters of Eowyn and Theoden. Even though the main conflict, between Sauron and the West, is a two-sided affair, Tolkien keeps rendering it into three-character events. Rohan versus Mordor and Saruman. The armies of Mordor versus Gondor and Rohan at Minas Tirith. Sam versus two groups of orcs (who obligingly wipe each other out) at Cirith Ungol.

Why did Tolkien keep doing that? Because it makes a great story. Writing of a war between only two players is like writing about a hammer beating on an anvil. The first stroke can be dramatic but by the third or fourth the glow is gone. Throw in a third party and the fun begins. Deceit, betrayal, faith, honor and politics are all in play.

Another famous character threesome, one revered among science fiction fans, is the original *Star Trek* trio of Kirk, Spock and McCoy. No matter what alien species or worlds were encountered, the interactions between those three usually formed the heart of each episode. And like the concept of divine beings with three aspects, the three starfarers were seen as each epitomizing a different quality (Kirk action, Spock brains and McCoy emotions). Together, they made great stories. Subsequent *Star Trek* series have lacked such a leading trio, and none of those series hold up well by comparison to the original.

Which brings us back to *Charmed*, which in its own way very much follows the model the original *Star Trek* had such success with (not to mention *Charlie's Angels*). The three witches are each distinct personalities. They're all strong in their own ways. Each has unique powers. Each has her own individual hopes, fears and dreams. They don't always get along. They're real.

The core of *Charmed* is the relationship formed by the three witches.

Every story is anchored somehow in that triangle, in the interactions of the three as they face challenges both mundane and magical. One may marry a Whitelighter or a half-demon, boyfriends come and go, children arrive, an endless array of warlocks, demons and other malign spirits attack them, but every story is grounded in how the three witches relate to each other. That's the great strength of the series. That's what makes *Charmed* both fun and compelling to watch.

Indeed, this strength was great enough to overcome a huge inconsistency as a result of Shannen Doherty leaving the series. From the first episode, *Charmed*'s storylines had been built on the overarching concept that the three Halliwell sisters (Prue, Piper and Phoebe, also known as the Charmed Ones), working as one to harness the Power of Three, were fated to become the most powerful witches of all time. Having one of those sisters die (because the actress playing Prue was leaving) created a bit of a hole in that concept. A really big hole. The writers of *Charmed* solved the problem in what was likely the best way they could, by retaining the basic concept but discovering a fourth sister (Paige). That meant there were still three Halliwell sisters left to become the most powerful witches of all time, and still three sisters to form the core of the stories. (And why shouldn't destiny have ensured the existence of a spare Halliwell sister to guarantee the prophecy even if something happened to one of the original three? Stranger things have happened.)

I assume everyone is grateful that *Charmed* didn't attempt to follow the model of an earlier show about witches, *Bewitched*, and simply replace the actress playing Prue with another person. It didn't work with Darrin and it wouldn't have worked with Prue. Prue, the character, had simply been too well-written and acted. She was as real a person to those who watch *Charmed* as if she actually lived down the street, a testament to how well the three-witches formula in *Charmed* works. Good series concepts help writers create characters who become so genuine that they don't seem to be fictional characters anymore, but rather actual people.

This isn't to say that choosing to use three witches automatically guaranteed that *Charmed* would work well as a series. The decision to use the Power of Three helped the series writers, but it alone didn't write episodes full of great word-play and clever ideas. The writers did that, taking advantage of the opportunities offered by the set-up. The witches could've been written as silly stereotypes instead of as characters who act and talk the way we'd think modern women would if they suddenly found themselves confronting the weird and wonderful things their powers cause them to encounter. The magic of good acting and good writing doesn't, so far as I know, depend on the number three.

So whatever the reason or reasons for deciding to base *Charmed* on three sisters who discover they're witches (and it could've been as simple as Aaron Spelling thinking it'd be funny to do a series with three witches to contrast his earlier series with three "angels"), the decision has worked very well. It provides a strong cultural basis for the assumptions underlying the series. It may even benefit from a human predisposition to think three is a really special number. And it gives the writers what I'd say is an ideal number of primary characters to work with.

You don't have to take my word for it. Just ask Aristotle.

> John G. Hemry may have been fated to write about a television series dealing with the supernatural because of a very strange coincidence involving high school names. Buffy the Vampire Slayer originally went to Hemry High School. Meanwhile, the Halliwell sisters of *Charmed* went to Baker High School. Baker is John's wife's maiden name. He's not sure what this double coincidence means and isn't sure he wants to know. John is the author of several novels, including the first and so far only legal thriller military science fiction series (a.k.a. *JAG* in space) beginning with *A Just Determination* and continuing through *Burden of Proof*, *Rule of Evidence* and the forthcoming *Against All Enemies*. He's also the author of the Stark's War trilogy (his first series; he knows better than to get caught in the trilogy trap now) and numerous short fiction stories, as well as non-fiction articles on topics like interstellar navigation. A retired U.S. Navy officer, he lives in Maryland with his divine wife "S" and three children.

CHARMED INTO GOODNESS

ANNE PERRY

In a world where Good and Evil are so clearly marked—the Good wear white robes, the Evil wear black leather—being moral should be simple. But as Anne Perry points out, with great power comes great responsibility...and great temptation.

A FRIEND OF MINE asked me why I, as an adult, would waste my time with what are essentially fairy stories. My mind teemed with answers and I tried to put them into order to explain why the best fairy stories are more than fun, terrific special effects, horror, romance and superb imagination. Stories of magic, supernatural forces of good and evil and the ways in which we deal with them, have been part of our legend and folklore for centuries. In fact, they stretch back for as long as mankind has sat around the fire at night and frightened, entertained and delighted each other, making each other laugh and cry, sharing our terrors, our dreams and trying to understand who we are. We have sought to find the meaning of life and to come to terms with the forces that we cannot govern.

To give these forces names and appearances helps us to face them. We create heroes who can vanquish the demons we fear, magical creatures of good as well as of evil, so there is a balance in the universe, and hope. We are not alone any more, and that is perhaps the greatest help. Then there is not only hope, there is also courage. In time there grows a measure of wisdom.

Charmed is among the best of "fairy stories." It is set in present-day San Francisco, but it could be anywhere: three sisters in their twenties discover their powers as witches, powers which they have inherited from their mother and grandmother, both now dead.

To begin with these powers were slight, compared with what they later became. Prue, the eldest, could move things with a wave of her hand. Piper, the middle sister, can freeze people and events long enough to effect changes before restarting time. Phoebe, the youngest, has no "active" power, but has flashes of precognition of events, very bad ones. After Prue's death, half-sister Paige added the ability to orb objects by calling them by name. These gifts give them all the opportunity to prevent evil from happening, and together they use the "Power of Three" to vanquish demons.

But then, maybe we all need help in vanquishing our demons?

Of course with talents come responsibilities. Over and over the stories in *Charmed* tell us that the gift of power must be honored. You cannot change what you were born to be. Abdication may bring a respite, but ultimately it is destructive. You have given up a part of yourself; you will never be whole after that.

How many people have great skill or talent, but somehow never live up to the expectations we have of them? Is it bad luck? Is it that the big break never came? Or is it that along the way a demon—fear, loneliness, the risk of failure or being laughed at, the inability to move beyond the barrier of despair—was not faced, recognized and vanquished, at whatever the cost might be?

If you want the prize, you pay the price. We all have moments when it seems we have made a bad bargain. We had not realized how much it was going to cost, how much the payment would hurt, and we cry out, "Stop the world! I want to get off! This wasn't what I meant—I've changed my mind!" But there is nowhere to "get off" to. We are here for the ride—win, lose or draw. Some things are meant to be—have to be. But the fact that it is your destiny does not make it any less frightening, or less painful! Over and over again this advice is given to a novice forced to accept new powers.

Have we not all made bargains with fate and then found the price higher than we were prepared for?

The powers of the sisters were small to begin with, but with use, like all talents, they increased, and learning how to use power wisely is one of the most difficult challenges one can face. The history of the world, from individuals to nations, is marred with examples of how power can corrupt; even with those we had thought the wisest and noblest. It does not take long for us to imagine ourselves invincible, or believe that because we *can* do something it is all right that we do it.

As the sisters' powers increased—the power to be in two places at once, to throw fire, to cast even stronger spells, to read the thoughts of others—it became harder to use them judiciously. The temptations for abuse magnified, as did the dangers and the costs. We watched each sister struggle to control her new abilities like a driver trying to manage a car whose engine capacity has suddenly tripled—it is very hard to keep it on the road. How many wrecks come from a mixture of arrogance and inexperience?

There has been more than one *Charmed* episode where a character has stolen a power that was not meant for him only to find that he cannot control it. In the end it often destroyed him. There have also been very graphic examples of the burdens of power and responsibilities. It is far from an easy thing or an unmixed blessing. We are shown the loneliness, and occasionally the regret and self-doubt, that come with greater understanding and responsibility. If you are capable of love, and the Charmed Ones very definitely are, then you are also capable of pain, of jealousy, of fear for the safety of others, conflicting loyalties, the temptation to take your own happiness at too great a cost to others: all the excitement, the confusion and the pain of being human.

With powers like those the sisters possess, there are rules. You can—and must—strive to save the innocent, but you cannot punish the guilty. Consider the possibilities if you could! Guilty of what? An act, a word, a thought, the omission of an act? Indifference? A misunderstanding, a willful abdication, or just sheer unwillingness, to think or care or to accept responsibility? Who is the judge? And if a judgment is wrong, or partial, who undoes the mistakes?

How many times are our own vengeances wrong? In outrage we punish, and it is the wrong person, or we know only half the story. There is much in that principle of the use of power alone.

Over and over again the sisters are warned by circumstance not to take their powers for granted. "If you abuse them," they are told, "they can be taken from you!" And they were, for a space. Arrogance brings its own downfall. Their calling is not a choice—it is a fact. It also makes them a target for evil, and sometimes being a victim is part of their job. It puts their gifts into perspective. Magic is far from an easy answer.

But then is it not salutary to have the gifts of power put into perspective? Would we not all like to do that for a few politicians, from local government level up to dictators and despots? However, the ones who matter most, and for whom we are accountable, are ourselves.

The sisters' powers are based in their emotions. We see it in the stories again and again. Prue's anger triggered her powers, and it was anger she used to show Phoebe how to wield them when a spell gone awry switched their gifts. And, as Piper learned early on when she took on Leo's to save his life, the source of even Whitelighter powers lies in emotion—specifically, love. Is this a general truth? Perhaps powers of body can develop physically, and of the mind intellectually, but is it not emotion which drives them all? Good emotions such as love, compassion, the desire to heal and to right injustice—they impel us to acts that indifference would never achieve. Even less specifically moral desires, like the hunger for knowledge or to see the world as we would like it to be, can drive us beyond our normal strengths. And the reverse of such passions are equally powerful: hatred, rage, terror and appetite also push us far beyond our ordinary limits. Though these are not our thoughts, or our feelings, they are still ones it is healthy to be reminded of. To be told in words means little. See it in images, played out in a story about people you identify with, see the demon roaring into violent and destructive life, and it stays in the mind.

All the sisters' powers are severed by hate or fury, especially if it is directed against forces of good and most particularly when directed at each other. Lose your temper, harbor anger and nourish it, and it allows the demonic to enter into you. Usually the surrender to evil is slow and invisible to the observer. Nobody said demons are stupid, and evil is very good at covering its tracks. It is possible to be clever, but unwise. Be careful to whom you give power, what you buy and at what price!

It requires wisdom and humility to know whom to trust, and sometimes mistakes can cost dearly. It takes great courage simply to be alive, to face the unknown with the possibility of danger around the next corner. We don't face dramatic demons who suck the life out of us by siphoning our thoughts with fingers like talons, or who drive us to unnatural, uncontrollable rage; our demons are not hollow-eyed and all-devouring, consumed in fire or cold as death. We only face failure, loneliness, disease, weakness, pain, loss of those we love, hunger of the mind or body, confusion, perhaps despair—the dark and bitter sides of human life. But the same courage is needed for us to fight them and bear both victory and defeat with dignity. Stories help; they tell us that we are not alone.

Even witches do not always succeed. There are episodes of *Charmed* in which the sisters have to accept failure and learn to overcome their guilt because they did not save the innocent. Sometimes it is our reaction to failure that defines us more than our successes. It helps to see our heroes' human fallibility as well. Most of us can win with grace; losing with grace is very much harder. It is an unpleasantly familiar "demon" to face.

One episode, season six's "Soul Survivor," raised the age-old question of Faustian bargains. If pacts with the powers of good exist, then surely similar pacts within the powers of evil must also? But evil lies and betrays, so when it does, do we have to keep our side of the bargain? Can evil which has tricked us still collect its payment? Is the question a legal one, a moral one or both? Marlowe's Faust suggests it is legal, Goethe's that it is moral. *Charmed* says it is legal, with a moral redemption possible through the intervention of an advocate with not only the skill but the willingness to fight, risk and sacrifice. There is also the implication that one who can advocate has the obligation to do so. Can anyone afford to waste a chance to do good? Some things are not offered more than once.

In this instance Paige did succeed in saving the man, not perhaps entirely an "innocent." He did knowingly make a bargain with a demon, even if part of his intention was good. But is that not the nature of rationalization? The end justifies the means? But Paige was reminded by her sisters that she could not save everyone. None of us is promised success all the time. We cannot blame ourselves for the actions and decisions of other people in which we had no part. They had a choice, which was their own. We should not overrate our own power or importance, or imagine that we are responsible and could or should control the decisions of others. But it is not easy to let go.

There are many demons in *Charmed*, all imaginative portrayals of an evil, a weakness or a temptation. The special effects are superb, enough to give nightmares to those with a sensitive disposition. More relevantly, they give face and form to aspects of our nature that we all recognize. Each demon preys upon a certain vulnerability, but all have qualities in common.

Evil has a genius regarding seduction; over and over again it is shown to know our vulnerabilities and our dreams. We are all cut from the same cloth, whether we aspire toward God or descend until we become devils. Evil is the passion and the intellect of the good which has been twisted by sin. Its power to mislead and enchant rests on its resemblance to what can as easily be right. There is nothing corrupt in the love of beauty, knowledge, laughter, excitement and, above all, in the hunger to live and be loved. It is only what we will do to gain these things and keep them that can be wrong. Demons know this and use it!

As Prue told Phoebe in season two's "Pardon My Past," when Phoebe flashed back to a past existence in which she was utterly selfish and used the power of her beauty to gain money, manipulate people and live a self-indulgent and manipulative lifestyle, it's as much a part of human nature to be bad as it is to be good. The key is how we tell the difference, and that we choose the good.

Several times the show touched on the concept of possible different futures. Which one comes to pass will depend upon their choices, some of which need all the courage the sisters can muster, and may require considerable sacrifice. There is no such thing as a path that is without cost or pain.

You cannot win by retreating from the fight. Love can hurt, but hate is a choice of weakness, not of strength—of fear, not of courage. That can be a hard lesson to learn. Like all of us, each of the sisters experience days when all she wants is a normal life, with time for herself, a job she enjoys and can be good at and the freedom to do the normal, everyday happy things that other people do, especially find someone to love. They have all the usual frailties as those without magic have. They can suffer headaches, be so tired they hardly know what they are saying or doing, be embarrassed, self-conscious, nervous on a date, bad-tempered, frightened, clumsy—anything the rest of us feel, even just ordinarily lonely and unhappy. Magic, like any other power, is a gift to be used, not an answer to the needs of mortality. It does not make you wise or good. It makes you admired sometimes, but not necessarily loved. It sets you apart, and that can be one of the most difficult things to bear.

If the gift must be honored, then it must also be protected, and that means kept secret. The few who have it are often unable to deal with its burdens. They choose ordinariness instead. Watching the stories we side with the sisters, but in life would we really have that courage? To ask that is difficult. To answer it with honesty is even more so.

To engage the enemy you must first know who he is, and what it is he wants: your destruction, certainly! But in what sense? What weakness of yours will he test? What strength might he pervert? Some in particular can read your greatest terror and make you live in it. How much easier would it be to go by a different route and avoid confrontation?

Evil believes that personal ties and loyalties are a weakness that it can exploit. Good knows that they can be vulnerabilities or weaknesses if they are corrupted, but also the greatest of strengths if they are refined by honor and the willingness to sacrifice should sacrifice be necessary. Many of the episodes have focused on that theme.

One of the strongest involved the return of the four horsemen of the apocalypse, demons with the power, at certain special times in history, when the world is ripe, to bring about the world's final destruction: season two's "Apocalypse Not." At the beginning the sisters were asked one of those questions that people think of at parties: If you were in a burning theater and could save either one sibling or five strangers, which would you choose? All answered one sibling.

While fighting the horsemen, they managed to send one of them to a nether region—but accidentally sent Prue as well. Joined together, the four horsemen could destroy anything. With breaking hearts, Piper and Phoebe made the difficult decision to sacrifice Prue rather than let her and the horseman both return—because they knew that was what she would have chosen.

That nobility was enough to turn the tide. The master of all evil destroyed the horsemen because evil betrays its own servants when they fail. It has no honor, and to trust it is a fool's decision. Those who will betray a foe will betray a friend also. The cause is immaterial; it is the nature of evil to deceive and to use and to destroy. That core is part of the violence of existence: it is necessary for evil to exist in order for good to exist also. That essence cannot be vanquished.

At the end of the story the sisters were asked again, would they save one sibling or five strangers? And without hesitation they said, "Five strangers." Honor won over personal love, and it was enough to save everyone, at least until next time.

In "How to Make a Quilt Out of Americans," a favorite aunt, now old and ill, sought them out to steal their powers by trickery in order to bribe a demon who could restore her youth, beauty and, above all, health. The price, as always, was her soul.

She explained to the sisters that for some the "golden years" could be mostly regret for that which was lost or wasted. She only wanted another chance.

In this visual, appearance-obsessed age, how many of us would trade honor for the youth and beauty we believe will make us loved? We all want acceptance—but at what price? We are so afraid of death, fearing the unknown that lies beyond it.

A normal fear, and a very human one. This aunt learned hideously the price of giving into it and of doing business with demons.

A similarly themed episode, "My Three Witches" from season six, showed the energy contained in unfulfilled desire and how it can be used against us. And yet balancing that risk is the knowledge that without desire there can be no passion, no life and, in the end, no joy either. What use is the sweetest fruit on earth if there is no hunger? It leads to deeper thoughts of the nature of joy. Is heaven not so much a different place as a greater ability to see, hear and taste the glory that there is everywhere? To borrow from William Blake: "to yearn for eternity and find it in an hour, to hunger for infinity and see it in the sky, heaven in a wild flower, to cease to be alone in the touch of one hand."

Perhaps hell is to have no hunger, to be incapable of that soaring happiness of touching the stars.

Another episode, "Love's A Witch," featured Phoebe given wildly enhanced powers of empathy, reading other people's thoughts in alarming detail and showing her more of the future than ever before. It was a painful demonstration of how intensely we all need privacy for our own dreams and mistakes, time to deal with them where others do not see our battles. We also need the protection of not knowing those of others. Sometimes we cannot even function properly if we know what other people think of us, good or bad. We cannot cope with knowing everything. Living with the unknown requires a great deal of knowledge and faith in order for us to go forward, head high, but an overload of knowledge is paralyzing. Some things need to be thought alone. Some events need to be met only when they happen. We are given such limits to our vision for good reason.

Threading through all the individual episodes are the unfolding stories of the main characters. Prue fell in love with a mortal man, and it cost him his life. She later died as well and was replaced by a half-sister, Paige, who has so far not found a lasting love.

Phoebe fell in love with and married a man half-mortal and half-demon. For many episodes he struggled to become fully his better self, and in the end he lost. Was it ever possible that he could have won? I don't know. For me the jury is still out on that. Perhaps any redemption is possible, but so is any loss. Is there a depth from which one cannot rise? That's not any human's right to judge.

Certainly there is no height from which we cannot fall. And that brings us to the most thought-provoking stories of all. Piper fell in love with Leo, a Whitelighter—in effect, the sisters' guardian angel. They had a baby, Wyatt.

For a while life was happy, then virtue brought its increased power, responsibilities and a price. Leo was promoted from Whitelighter to Elder, one of the supreme order in the progress of natural beings. Leo, like anyone else, could not deny the calling. No matter what the cost, Piper also could not stand in the way of his progress. At one point she accused him of refusing to tell her the truth because he knew it would hurt her. Her anger, confusion and terrible loneliness is easy to understand. She cried out that sacrifice was not fair. "Sacrifice never is," he replied.

And for her there was more to fear because their child, Wyatt, had powers, even as a baby, that outstripped both of his parents' as well as a destiny to become one of the most powerful of all beings. Now Piper faced bringing him up almost alone while protecting him from the demons eager to destroy him in his infancy, when he was most vulnerable.

With Leo gone, another Whitelighter, Chris, was appointed as their guardian angel. He had come from the future especially to save Wyatt from the demons who threatened him. But what the sisters did not know, and Chris did, was that it was not death that was the danger to Wyatt, but seduction to the side of evil. One possibility for the future was that his immense power would corrupt him, as all power tends to and absolute power almost always does.

The potential for the greatest good is also the potential for the greatest evil.

To ease some of Piper's pain at being left, Leo magically dulled much of her memory of their time together, a sort of emotional anesthesia. The ability to have one's painful memories removed is an intense temptation. But the story that followed raised a vast new field of thought. How much of our own character and xx springs from what we remember? Without memory, character and instinct remain, but what of whole areas of morality that come from experiences of guilt and remorse, the need to forgive and be forgiven? From knowledge of suffering, and therefore pity? Compassion is *feeling with*; without one's own lifetime to draw on, without the knowledge of cause and effect that living brings, what wisdom is there? What growth built upon understanding?

What is perhaps even more frightening, and with consequences every bit as great, is that if you escape pain by detaching the mind from the knowledge that caused it, you are also escaping reality. It is a matter of proportion and degree, but carried to its extreme, is that not what madness is? We build a framework of reason from good and evil, joy and pain, light and darkness. When we refuse one, we deny the other. Only by accepting them both, and with the capacity to choose and to learn, to feel and remember, can we grasp the beauty of truth and moral reality.

It is the courage to feel that is the core of life.

Recognize your demons, give them names and face them!

In the Greek myths the gods are personifications of qualities of good and evil, or great natural forces which are neutral, such as fire or water, and can be either according to their use. When they symbolize great passions, unfaced and ungoverned, then they are the elements of classic tragedy. That is why they have lasted for millennia, and why we use them now in our own stories to explain the enormity, the magnificence and the fears and griefs of our own lives.

Fairy stories paint pictures of the strongest of our common experiences, heighten them and make the familiar new and amazing. We see with a greater clarity and understand more deeply. In our wildest moments, the ones that most stretch the imagination, we are least alone in our journey. We are hearing the voice of every man who has sat around the fire at night with the same terrors and same dreams since the days of the caveman, and who always will, even if we tread the stars.

Anne Perry is the best-selling author of several historical detective series, including the Thomas Pitt series and the William and Hester Monk series. She has also written two fantasies, *Tathea* and *Come Armageddon*. Visit Anne on the Web at www.anneperry.net.

WHY ARE THE ELDERS SUCH JERKS?

OR, THE BAD PORTRAYAL OF GOOD IN CHARMED

RICHARD GARFINKLE

The neat division of the Halliwells' world into Good and Evil has a few narrative flaws, Richard Garfinkle says. The Evils are all petty jerks. Unfortunately, so are the Goods.

WHY DID THE ELDERS try to prevent Piper and Leo's marriage? Why, all through the series, do they come across as insufferable twits? What accounts for the abuse Leo's character has taken in the last two seasons? Why can't he or any other Whitelighter handle a simple crisis of faith? In short, why are the "good guys" so annoying when they are good and so prone to falling toward the bad when adversity strikes?

While stated in terms of *Charmed*, I do not think these questions can be fully answered within the context of the series. However, the show does give excellent illustrations and illuminations of what seems to me a large-scale problem in modern writing. The examples above are symptoms of a difficulty present in nearly all modern literature and certainly all pop culture. That difficulty is this: Modern writers appear to have an extraordinarily hard time depicting transcendental good. This trouble is partially rooted in the nature of writing, but even more so in modern views of people and what makes them good and interesting.

"Good" and "evil" are terms thrown around with reckless abandon in shows such as *Charmed*, but what they mean—indeed, what it is to be good or evil—are fuzzy concepts for both the creators and the audiences of such shows. Sometimes it seems that good and evil are nothing but t-shirts that mark out which side is which. There is a video game psychology in this: As long as the target is wearing the correct t-shirt you can blow them up with impunity.

Generally a moral code is outlined that declares whom you get to blast and whom you must leave alone. But this morality is usually racist, speciesist or dimensionalist (the humans-good/other-dimensional-creatures-bad prejudice). *Charmed* shares with *Buffy the Vampire Slayer* the concept that killing demons is good and killing humans is bad. This is regardless of the actions the demon or human takes. In *Charmed* there was the classic case of Prue's contempt for Cole when he killed a human who was trying to kill him (this showed Cole descending back into "evil"). It is true that the human could not have hurt Cole, but if he had vanquished a *demon* too weak to harm him, Prue would not have blinked a mascara-ed eyelash.

It might be argued that this black hat/white hat simplicity is necessary for the purposes of an hour-long drama, since good and evil are complex concepts. I don't agree. It seems to me that there are simple definitions of good and evil that fit most people's ideas of these concepts and which hold up even in the rarified reaches of Heaven and the pits of Hell:

GOOD: Seeking to reduce unnecessary suffering.
EVIL: Seeking to create, or not caring about the creation of, unnecessary suffering.

In other words, a good person or entity would work to cut down the amount of suffering in the world. An evil person or entity would either seek to increase suffering or simply not care about the suffering of others.

These two definitions also illuminate the inherent opposition between good and evil beings. A good being would oppose the actions of someone who created suffering, regardless of whether the action was deliberate or through indifference. An evil being who sought to increase suffering would oppose a good being's attempts to alleviate it. An evil being who was indifferent to the suffering of others might—*might*—oppose one who works against such suffering, assuming there was some other reason to do so.

Indifferent villains may sound wimpier than actively evil ones, but some of the best nasty characters (as well as the worst nasty real people) come to their evil through indifference. A well-known example is Ebenezer Scrooge, who created suffering by not caring about the fate of the poor.

This opposition between good and evil also exists within each human being. Nearly all of us have desires to ease the suffering of others. But we also have desires to create suffering in those we hate and are often indifferent to the pain of others, particularly if they are far away from us or not the "right" sort of people. This internal battleground is the source of the mythological conflicts between good and evil, the struggle for the human soul.

Stories that take this internal struggle and paint it across the real world are as old as storytelling itself. The major point of such stories is the overcoming of evil or the effects of failing to overcome it. The former tales are hero/saint stories; the latter are morality plays.

In the process of overcoming evil, a hero or saint transforms himself— or herself— individually and the world universally. One of the basic principles of such spiritual tales is that a person who defeats the evil within becomes capable of helping others overcome that evil. This kind of story is almost never shown on TV. The last example I can think of was on the show *Northern Exposure* in the shamanic education of Ed.

Shows like *Charmed* are necessarily set on the battlefield of such conflicts. The characters are the warriors of good and evil. Traditionally, such characters would be allegories for virtues in the forms of gods, demons, etc. The demons and other nasties (warlocks and Darklighters, in *Charmed*'s case) would represent particular dangers to the human soul. The gods (or, here, their witch and Whitelighter analogs) would stand for particular human and divine capacities that could overcome the dangers. The means of defeating them (that is, the plots of the stories) would illuminate processes by which people could free themselves from those ills in the real world. In other words, such tales are instruction manuals that exist to aid people in living good lives.

In *Charmed*, however, allegory has been supplanted by butt-kicking and spell-chucking. The dangers are dramatic, the heroes are...well, we'll get to the heroes later, and the means of defeat are clever and visually exciting but rarely enlightening.

This kind of cool but meaningless conflict takes us away from these instructive stories and puts us into the realm of the modern superhero story. The ongoing conflict between good and evil is watered down into an episodic battling between nice and nasty. The characters on *Charmed* are much like the postmodern superheroes who populate today's comics. The characters on *Charmed* are cool to look at; they kick butts and take names, are vaguely concerned with good and are on the whole nicer than their opponents for a given value of "nicer," but most of the fundamental distinctions between good and evil have fallen by the wayside. Instead, good and evil are separated by distinct special effects (Whitelighter orbing versus demonic fading), costumes (demons have funny-looking heads) and occasional bouts of motivation (we save innocents, they harm them).

The transformative character of the allegories is completely lost. People in *Charmed* do not become better for overcoming evil. The Charmed Ones did not attain any greater goodness for their defeat of the Source (which in an allegory would generate sainthood). Nor have they gained any control over themselves for all the evils they have vanquished. They have grown some as human beings over the course of the series, but there is no correlation between that growth and their triumphs and tragedies.

A lengthy but worthwhile example of this failure to transform can be seen in Phoebe, who presented an opportunity for a story great in goodness. Phoebe, who began as the most airheaded of the Charmed Ones and who went through the messiest interactions with evil (i.e., Cole), could have been a source of fascinating tales illuminating many elements of human life.

Phoebe's basic power was to see the future, allowing her to act to prevent the dangers she foresaw. Given this great gift, she griped that she couldn't blow stuff up. But suppose instead of complaining she had embraced her power, let it into her soul and, delving deep into forethought, developed an understanding of the consequences of actions both human and spiritual. She could have learned from her gift, could have come to understand how people affect other people and how good and evil work in the world. She could have become a larger force for good if she had realized she had the greatest of the Charmed Ones' gifts. She could have guided her sisters, the Whitelighters, other witches, even the Elders themselves in their conflict with evil.

Okay, you might say, so Phoebe becomes a great oracle. What then? Doesn't that end her plot line since she now has no flaws or conflicts?

No. Now Phoebe, who sees so much, would have to deal with her physical limitations. She would see more suffering than she could act to prevent. How would she chart the course of doing good while always knowing more suffering than she could affect? That is a long-term, complex character arc that can last for seasons without once falling into maudlin wallowing.

Furthermore, when this Phoebe discovered (as she would have) that she was married to the Source but that Cole still existed inside it, her true task would unfold. She would have a titanic struggle ahead of her, to help her husband overcome what had been placed in him and to make him master and subjugator of the Evil Source. This Phoebe would have had a fascinating magical and moral challenge. A battle would have ensued between her and the Source for Cole's soul that could have had a place in an entire season's worth of episodes.

Instead, we were presented with Phoebe having a crummy marriage, being manipulated by the Source, losing the child she never really had, losing Cole, etc. All perfectly normal soap opera stuff, nothing charmed about it. And her foresight, her great gift, has done nothing but push her into being a watered-down oracle: an advice columnist.

The Charmed Ones' battle against evil is not really a conflict with evil, because no evil is truly overcome. Rather than there being any deeper meaning to their conflict, the characters are relegated to the roles of foot soldiers in a magical war. Instead of Phoebe's struggle being to win Cole's soul back from evil, it was to survive the emotional tragedy of losing her husband to evil. Phoebe's growth and changes have come about because of her attempts to retain her humanity despite her place on the front lines.

This struggle to stay human in the face of battle is an important story, well worth the telling. But it is better told about real soldiers fighting other real soldiers in the moral ambiguity of the human battlefield than about black and white conflicts between demons and angels.

But the main reason *Charmed* fails as an allegory, despite its good-versus-evil premise, lies in its depiction of good—particularly good that goes beyond human niceness.

Evil, consisting as it does of jerks, is largely the same whether on a human or transcendental scale. A jerk is a jerk regardless of whether he wants to stomp on anthills or cover the world in darkness. The creation of suffering is always a petty goal. It may succeed on a horrific scale and create vast pain for millions of people, but the originator of that goal remains petty in mind. Despite his hype, the Devil (or whatever name you choose to give to a large spirit of evil) is a whiny jerk who said, "Whaa, I want to sit on the shiny throne. It's not fair! You can't kick me out! All right, I'll kick over your sand castle, see if I don't!" All the black clothes, fiery special effects and menacing plans cannot undo the fundamental pettiness of evil.

Evil is the same regardless of scale, but good is not. The scope and depth of suffering that one can overcome depends greatly on the depth and complexity of one's goodness. Any doctor can tell you that while it is very easy to cause damage, it can be very difficult to undo it. A brutish punch in the face may require a highly trained surgical team to repair. The necessary skill of the surgeon does not glorify that of the puncher. Likewise, the deep goodness needed to rescue a person who is wracked with wrath and fear over tortures they have suffered does not magnify the torturer into some vast figure of demonic grandeur. A bully is still a bully.

Since one of the major elements of storytelling is the transformation of characters, it is on the side of good that the struggle works or does not, since only in good will there be real and subtle change. (Conversion from evil to good—or vice versa—can be a real change, but often it is portrayed as simply swapping t-shirts; the characters act the same way but for the other side.) And in *Charmed*, as in so many modern tellings, good and the change in good are weakly represented.

In *Charmed* the side of good is composed mostly of witches and Whitelighters. The Whitelighters include everyday guides for mortal witches and future Whitelighters (what Leo was when he started out) and Elders, who direct the actions of the side of good. There is an implication that there is something greater that can be called God for whom the Whitelighters work.

This structure of mortals with angelic guidance is classical, as is the distinction between lesser and greater angels. What is modern and weak about the *Charmed* version is that the Whitelighters, especially the Elders, act like obnoxious prats.

This is not unique to *Charmed*. On *Angel*, for example, the Powers that Be, whenever they manifested or spoke through some oracle or set a test, were always shown as snooty, self-righteous twits.

Herein we find the crux of the modern image of good: self-righteousness, the arrogant sense that one has a complete monopoly on right and wrong.

Where does this idea of good come from?

I believe it comes from the self-righteous humans who declare themselves the messengers and speakers for God, the self-anointed prophets, the ones who show up on TV all the time. These persons tend toward extreme overconfidence in their own goodness and in the truth of their own words. But if you know any really good people (as opposed to self-declared good people), you may have noticed that they tend not toward confidence but toward caution. While they may speak with clear conviction, they will be careful in what they say and do and will rarely render harsh judgment on anyone except themselves. Of all the virtues the self-righteous claim to themselves, none has an ounce of humility.

One might object that angelic figures like the Elders cannot, as agents of the divine, have humility. But if we consider them as agents of a power that seeks to end suffering, then clearly they must be humble. The first principle of ending suffering is to do no harm. One must be careful in one's actions, cautious in order to make sure one does not harm another unnecessarily.

Human beings have a hard time being humble because they tend to live alone in their own heads. Unless they stretch out their attention they need never feel the suffering of another person. This means that the most self-absorbed person can feel like the center of the universe, because he or she never needs to realize that there are others in the world.

But the Elders, who exist in a divine presence, should feel their own smallness, sensing as they would the vast majesty and depth of all around them and the great honor and difficulty of the task laid before them. Traditionally, even the greatest of angels understand how small they are compared to the omnipotence that guides them, and how humbly they must undertake the holy tasks which are set for them.

Let us examine the actions of the Elders in the case of Leo and Piper's romance. The Elders did everything they could to try and stop it because they had a rule: "No nookie between witches and Whitelighters." They declared the Rule more important than Love. This is a military attitude—No fraternization between officers and grunts!—rather than a holy one, in which love is more important than nearly anything.

Even if, in humility, the Elders could enforce their rule in general, the Charmed Ones were prophesied as being unlike regular witches. Classical angels would have been cautious and humble and wondered if the love between a Whitelighter and one of the Charmed Ones might have a higher purpose than they could understand. And they certainly would not have made deals with evil in order to crush this love.

But, being self-righteous, the Elders did whatever harm they thought necessary in order to enforce the rule. This too comes from our everyday experience of the self-declared good people. They will stomp as hard as they want on people's lives and make whatever alliances are needed in order to ensure their rules are followed. Rarely do the self-righteous take any notice of the pain they create, or the degradation of their principles that often comes from their enforcement of them. This is a crucial difference between real and apparent good. Real good, whenever it must create suffering (and sometimes it must) feels pain at doing so and seeks to minimize the suffering. Any good parent who has had to punish a child feels the punishment and wishes they did not have to inflict it.

The depiction of transcendental good, which derives from the worst examples of the self-righteous, is not uncommon these days. It is frustrating, from the writing perspective, that this is the dominant view of goodness. It is particularly annoying because all modern writers have had in the last century examples of really good people to draw upon in creating holy characters.

In part the problem may be that the best public people of the last century—I would note for example Mahatma Gandhi, Dr. Martin Luther King Jr., Pope John XXIII and Mother Teresa—do not make good warrior figures, so they do not fit well into the aforementioned butt-kicking-spell-chucking kinds of shows. But Gandhi and Martin Luther King Jr. fought against empires using love; John XXIII fought against damaging teachings; Mother Teresa fought against the direct manifestations of human suffering. In allegorical terms, each of them was stronger and more terrible to behold than the greatest dragon-slaying knight or the most babe-like, spell-wielding witch.

Another difficulty in stories like *Charmed* lies in the lack of implications for the characters' accomplishments. In a world like the one depicted in the show, much evil comes from demonic influence. Therefore, if a demon is vanquished, there should be a lessening of the evil that demon represents. Each vanquishing should make the world a better place. When the Source was destroyed the world should have become transcendentally more hospitable and people should have become better, at least until a new Source was crowned.

This did not happen for two writing reasons: First, it is difficult for many people these days to conceive of what a truly better world would be like. Second, the world of *Charmed* is supposed to be sort of like ours. In our world evil comes from people, and the only demons are the ones in those people's minds (the bad thoughts and ideas they accept). Therefore, while it is dramatically necessary for demons to be defeated on *Charmed*, it could be argued that it is impossible to put the consequences into effect.

Even if one accepts that argument, the battles should at least have implications for the Charmed Ones themselves, making them better people and increasing their ability to confront evil both inside and outside of themselves. In short, each demon overcome should bring the Charmed Ones closer to goodness and make better their lives and the lives of those they later help. It has not done so, and here lies the real writing difficulty as well as the point of this essay (finally).

Today's writers are taught to see their characters in the framework of psychology. Psychology as a branch of medicine is capable of seeing what is wrong with an individual person, but not what is right with them. Hence there is a blindness to goodness, one inherent in the creation and evolution of characters.

More simply, writers are taught to see their characters as masses of problems, as bundles of flaws. This is because messed-up people are, supposedly, more "realistic" than people who are not juggling neurosis grenades. Some writers argue that no one wants to read about or see healthy, well-adjusted people going about their lives handling things capably. But if you look at the world we live in or any of its fictionalized parallel worlds (such as the world of *Charmed*), you will see that there are enough inherent difficulties and challenges for even the most capable person, and that a trial of the good within someone is at least as interesting as the repeated hammering of that person's flaws. The above discussion of Phoebe serves as an example of this as well.

There is another writing problem invisibly coupled with the conception of characters as flaw-packets. Modern writing is based on the unstated assertion that the best solutions available for people's difficulties are those that already exist in our world.

To take an example: When Leo and Piper were having marriage difficulties they went to a mortal marriage counselor. Angst and minor humor ensued as they translated their magical problems into commonplace marriage gripes punctuated with scenes from earlier episodes.

Surely somewhere in Heaven there was a Whitelighter so deeply imbued with transcendental love that he or she could have offered better assistance than some mortal with a medical degree. Had there been such an Elder, the confrontation between them would have made for a very different episode. Rather than a semi-humorous retelling of past events, Leo and Piper could have confronted the mind-shattering reality of true love, unencumbered by the petty problems of their lives. They would have seen each other as they are and known how much they meant to each other. This is actually much scarier, and makes for better viewing, than just sniping at each other for forty minutes before the inevitable reconciliation.

Charmed is not alone in resorting to everyday psychology in the face of characters who should have deeper insights into the mind than students of Freud and Jung. I would cite as annoying examples the telepaths on *Star Trek* and *Babylon 5* who, despite an ability to roam around in and mess with other people's minds, have no advice or assistance beyond that available in self-help books today.

Let's take another charming example of an inconsequential matter: Death. In particular, life after death. The Charmed Ones not only know there is life after death, they also know that the dead (particularly dead witches) can come back and bug the living. Prue died, but apart from actress problems there is no reason she could not come and offer advice from time to time. Leo is dead, but that doesn't stop him from having post-mortem children. The Charmed Ones' mother and grandmother are dead, but they can come and go on occasion, nudge the Three as they need to be nudged and see their living descendants presumably unto the nth generation. (Imagine Grams butting into the lives of generation after generation of Halliwells. *Shudder.*) Death in *Charmed* is not the ineffable tragedy it is in the real world. But all the characters act as if it were, because it is an implicit rule of modern writing that one cannot do better than what is available in real life. In real life death is "that undiscovered country from whose bourn no traveler returns." On *Charmed* they not only return, they bring souvenirs.

If nothing better than what exists commonly in the real world is permitted, then one cannot actually depict any real good beyond the superhero-ish rescuing of people in distress and the smacking down of nasty things. Holding to this rule means no great good can ever be shown. Great evil, no problem. All that is necessary for great evil is for someone to be mean to lots of people, or intensely mean to one person. The more people or the more intensely mean, the more evil.

There is one more writing principle which gets in the way of the depiction of goodness. All writers today are taught that stories need "conflict." This dictum is pounded so deeply that few question what it means. Rarely does anyone ask what conflict is and why stories need it. Unchecked conflict writing means that stories written according to modern precepts will always have a heavy dose of characters going at each other, one way or another.

The dogma of conflict is such that the most desirable story is the one in which there is as much conflict as possible—not just fights between good guys and bad guys, but struggles between friends (and sisters), disputes between inferiors and superiors (such as Leo and the Elders), bouts of internal torment (as with Leo and Cole) and so on ad nauseam. The need for varieties of conflict means that no character can rise above the everyday pettiness that creates most character conflict, nor can anybody master him—or herself—well enough to transcend self-flagellating angst. The idea that conflict is necessary to stories means that no character can be good enough to minimize the conflicts in his or her life.

If I may continue my heretical views, I venture the opinion that conflict is not a needed element of stories. What is necessary is an unresolved element that comes to resolution, in whatever form the writer chooses. Conflict is only one kind of unresolved condition, the easiest kind to show and the one best adapted to the use of gaudy special effects. But that by no means makes it the only or the best kind.

The case for the weakness of conflict can best be made in the matter of love stories, of which *Charmed* has had quite a few. Traditional romance is filled with conflict: struggles over desire, over which member of a triangle gets cast out into the cold, over subordination of one person to another and so on. Television has presented many such conflicted romances, some of them quite well. But it has routinely run into trouble when romance ends successfully and life together begins. As many an analyst of television has pointed out, romances that were fun to watch fall flat when the couple gets together. Writers presented with these situations usually resort to the introduction of artificial troubles, of which temptation and adultery head the list, followed by having children and griping about the life changes needed to rear them. In short, they create artificial conflict to keep the tension of romance going long after it should have been replaced by the unresolved matters of life.

The mistake here is in thinking that a story about two people growing together is inherently boring. But in reality the fitting together of two lives is such a great undertaking that nothing compares with it in terms of commitment and character change and flow. There are stories to be told of all elements of life and many of those stories really only start when two people get together. There have been occasional movies and TV shows about this sort of thing, but they are rare because they are not very visual and require skilled acting. *Charmed* would actually be one of the few shows where such things could be shown, with as many special effects as desired. Allegorically, there is as much drama going on in the everyday reconciling of two people's different customs as there is in the most violent demon-whacking.

Spiritually, most cultures have a handful of gods, angels or saints devoted to warfare, but often thousands devoted to everyday living. The struggle against evil and the doing of good is found more vividly in the hearth than on the battlefield. In order to save an innocent, the Charmed Ones might need to mend a family, or fight some demon that exploits hunger and poverty, or overcome an evil teaching that pervades a particular family or business. Even on just a personal level, they might begin by seeking to unify their destinies and their personal lives—instead of whining about them—or preparing the world for the coming of the next generation of Halliwells.

I do not wish to sound too missionary on the matter of writing methods, but I do think it necessary to compile the factors that have weakened the depiction of good, and from that demonstrate why it is possible to do better. Here are the weakening elements: a superhero view of the conflict between good and evil; an image of good that comes from self-righteousness; characterization that relies on personal weaknesses rather than strengths; a refusal to have the world or the characters change in accord with their actions; and a reliance on conflict as the most vital element of storytelling.

Put together, these chains hobble the good characters and give them no hope of reaching any greater good. Even stasis in goodness is too much to hope for. In order to sustain the conflict, anyone who is greatly good and not a jerk (such as Leo) must undergo crises of faith and fall from grace in order to fit into the kinds of stories that fit those constraints. Paradoxically, the characters in *Charmed*, white robed or black, are all stuck in a hell of *faux*-goodness.

None of these constraints are truly necessary. Any and all of them can be thrown away, to the betterment of storytelling and character development, and to save the good name of goodness, which has been badly sullied over the years.

Great good requires depth. To save a soul involves deeply dredging out the darkness within someone and showing them how to replace it with light. That takes more than a well-placed boot to the backside or a quatrain delivered in the last five minutes.

Some might argue that you can't do that in a one-hour (okay, forty-minute) TV show. That is true, but in the long span of a season there is plenty of time to both kick backside and explore the deeper recesses of the human heart. What could be more proper in a show rooted in Heaven, Hell and Magic?

> Richard Garfinkle is the author of two science fiction novels: *Celestial Matters* (which won the 1996 Compton Crook Award for best first novel in science fiction) and *All of an Instant*. At present he is engaged in the more dubious practice of writing non-fiction science popularization. He lives in Chicago with his wife and children.

EVIL: CAN'T LIVE WITH IT, CAN'T QUITE VANQUISH IT

KATE DONOVAN

The Halliwells have been fighting Evil daily for seven seasons now. Are they ever going to get a break? Not according to Kate Donovan, who argues that the story is about the battle, not about the outcome.

EVERYONE KNOWS ABOUT the Charmed Ones. They're Good witches who battle Evil. Make no mistake about it, these females are the real thing—true warriors.

And like any true warriors, they want to *win*—to completely vanquish Evil for all time, not just for the thrill and satisfaction it would bring them, but so that they can start living somewhat normal lives, knowing that they have fulfilled their Destiny.

Unfortunately, there's a catch.

The very essence of Goodness is having the strength and willingness to resist Evil.[1] If there were no bad options out there to tempt us, wouldn't the concept of Good become meaningless? In other words, without Evil, wouldn't Goodness cease to exist as well? What would be the point in the Charmed Ones fighting and struggling and sacrificing the way they do on behalf of Good if victory would mean the end of the very thing for which they fight?

The genius of *Charmed* is the way it presents and explores this para-

---

[1] And as we'll see later, it's actually more than resisting Evil. It's resisting it for the right reasons.

dox, teaching us that the battle itself is the goal. The sisters fight Evil so that Evil won't get the upper hand. They keep the playing field level so that humans have a meaningful choice between Good and Evil. If the battle is kept even—if demons aren't allowed to subvert Free Will with their sin balls and spells and illusions and fire balls—the Charmed Ones have faith that humans will choose Good more often than they will choose Evil, and therefore Good will triumph when the battle finally comes to an end.

Good Versus Evil

It has a Biblical ring to it, doesn't it? Think of the Garden of Eden. God gave humankind three things: paradise, one simple rule and free will.

Free will—a.k.a. the power to *break* the "one simple rule" and *lose* paradise. And we all know what happened next. On the other hand, if no "bad" choice had been available, could Adam or Eve have been seen as "good" or worthy of paradise, rather than simply phenomenally lucky? Without Free Will, would they have been human beings at all? Happy? Yes. Human? Not in the sense we think of it. In our world, each person is, in reality, a micro-battleground for Good and Evil. Apparently, so were Adam and Eve.

The list of people—real and fictional—who have made poor choices since the Garden of Eden is impressive. For example, think of King David, another Biblical figure who succumbed momentarily to worldly temptations; Brutus, an honorable man except for that time he stabbed his close friend and ruler; then there's Guinevere, who.... Well, you get the idea.

Interestingly enough, those folks are not famous as evildoers, but rather as humans with truly admirable qualities who just happened to falter in a fairly spectacular way.

So what about the Halliwell sisters? Where do *they* fit into this lineup?

The Charmed Ones

Destiny chose them to fight Evil, and it gave them amazing magical powers with which to do so. The sisters must be practically perfect to have earned that sort of honor, right?

Hardly. In many ways, the Halliwells are regular, albeit extremely good-looking, females. In one of the many strokes of genius that typify the series, the show's creator resisted the temptation to give the girls such do-gooder occupations as ER nurse, ex-nun and cop. With the exception of Paige, who came to her powers later and was drawn meanwhile to social work, none had careers that screamed selfless hero/martyr. And even though Phoebe eventually became an advice columnist, which is arguably a service to her fellow humans, she did that *after* she became a witch and not wholly for altruistic reasons.

But these sisters did have a few things in their favor. A rich legacy, even though they didn't know it. A line of good-hearted, powerful ancestors. A bond, however strained at times, as sisters. And as their story unfolds, we learn that they have evolved and are continuing to evolve. Phoebe may have been Evil in a past life, but perhaps that isn't the badge of weakness it appears to be. Maybe having been Evil once, she can better appreciate the Goodness that now thrives in her heart.

All in all, these females meet the definition of Good in the sense that they do a great job of resisting Evil. On the other hand, they're human. Or, as they jokingly reassured newcomer Paige, you aren't *really* a Charmed One until you've dated a demon and, I would add, probably not a full-fledged One until you've *become* a demon! The very fact that they are a target of Evil, and come up against it every day in their battles, makes them bound to slip occasionally, especially where dark magic is involved. So Piper was turned into a Wendigo; Paige into a vampire; Phoebe was possessed by the Woogy; Piper became a Fury[2]....

Okay, so these things are bound to happen. But once again, *Charmed* doesn't take the easy way out. Most shows would have the heroine get in touch with her inner Good in order to overcome her possession by Evil. But in *Charmed*, when a sister goes Evil, it's to the bone! The unafflicted sisters, or Leo, or *someone* had better save the day, because the Evil sister is having *way* too much fun to worry about doing the right thing. Proof? In an episode where all three sisters turned Evil, Piper actually reduced her beloved Leo to a pile of debris because he was getting on her nerves. Fortunately, when the spell was reversed, Leo came back, but that's the sort of high-stakes fun *Charmed* can't resist doling out.

It's easy to behave well when there's no Evil around to tempt you. The challenge is to be Good in the face of almost overwhelming temptation. And the Halliwell sisters find ways to handle that challenge better than most.

---

[2] This particular episode illustrates the true genius of *Charmed*—its deft mixture of serious situations and humorous ones. Metaphysical subjects? Absolutely. Drama and tragedy? You bet. But interspersed with the heart-wrenching scenes of Piper, transformed into a Fury because of her grief over losing her older sister, we have scenes of Paige experiencing the hilarious backfire of personal gain from a spell she cast. Okay, maybe chest-fire is the more appropriate term. She inappropriately used magic to make a man irresistible to women to teach him not to be sleazy, and she ended up with an excess of "charms."

Charmed 101

One of the best episodes for purposes of this essay—not to mention, one of the best episodes period—featured an Infector with a box containing seven sin balls, which had the ability to find a germ of sin in a person and magnify it until that sin consumed its host. The Infector's goal was to use the balls to infect seven humans. But not just any humans. He needed to corrupt seven "paragons of virtue"—humans who would ordinarily excel at keeping their bad tendencies under control, assuming Free Will was at play. But the sin balls completely subverted Free Will.

We were told that no amount of magic, however strong, could counteract a sin ball. Only a selfless act by the infected person could do that. We were also told that for one of these Seven Deadly Sins—the sin of Pride—there was no such thing as a selfless act. Even when a prideful person does something for someone else, it's from a sense of invincibility, not sacrifice. They do it for the rush of pride they experience for having acted so nobly.

Another Catch-22. And unfortunately, this meant that Pride was the one sin that couldn't be beaten.

And who got infected with Pride? The sister who was arguably the ultimate paragon—Prue.[3]

For Phoebe, the Infector selected the Lust ball, thereby exploiting her natural playfulness and big heart with hilarious—but potentially deadly—consequences. For Piper, who has a tendency to overdo, he chose Gluttony. And in one of the inspired moments that make this show great, laid-back Leo was hit with Sloth.[4] Yes, even Leo has a tiny germ of sin!

The point is, the Charmed Ones aren't perfect. They have flaws, and their flaws make them vulnerable to the very Evil they're trying to fight. But that's a Good thing, as it turns out, because every bout with Evil makes them stronger, wiser and more evolved in their ability to fulfill their Destiny.

---

[3] Unbelievably great lines of dialogue ensued. If you haven't seen this episode, camp out in front of your TV until it airs. I don't want to disclose/ruin anything more about it.

[4] Leo delivered an all-time classic line when the sisters asked him if he had checked with the Elders about the box of sin balls, and he replied that he orbed halfway there but then got tired and came back!

Cole

There's no better example of the battle between Good and Evil in the *Charmed* universe than Cole Turner. He *literally* embodied the fight! Cole, the well-intentioned man with human weaknesses, and Belthazor, an upper level demon with centuries' worth of practice being Evil: they coexisted in a physical form that could morph between two appearances, the handsome guy and the scary one. We watched in amazement as the battle raged, knowing that at the height of his battle, Cole was facing the most frustrating choice of all: whether or not to use Belthazor's Evil powers for Good, knowing that if he did so—if he dared tap into that Evil once too often—he might never come back from it.

He faced temptation in forms we can't possibly comprehend. And we're not just talking about the choice between Good and Evil. There was that third choice, the one that was both his strength and his downfall—his love for Phoebe. He would do anything for her. It was his reason for being Good, and we can see the danger there. He would be Good for her, but to protect her, he would also be Evil. He was a man completely lacking a moral compass and, eventually, that caught up with him. But even when he became the Source of all Evil, it wasn't because he wanted power for himself. It was to save Phoebe.

Ironically, Cole—the half-demon—illustrates what is best about being human: the ability to be unselfish—to put another person above oneself—even if that impulse is misdirected.

Love

So where *does* Love fit into this Good and Evil equation? Clearly Love is never really Evil but, as in the case of Cole, it can make a person vulnerable, and Evil will exploit that weakness for its own purposes. The Halliwells have a lot of experience with that particular concept.

But Love has also been the source of a long line of Halliwell strength—the unselfish ability to put another person's needs, and sometimes their very existence, above one's own. Knowing that others—including their mother, their beloved Grams and Melinda Warren—have gone before them gives them confidence and a sense of responsibility. And it also gives them the knowledge that even after they're gone, their magic—their fight on the side of Good—will be a legacy to future generations of Halliwells.

Personal Gain and Personal Loss

We know instinctively that a Good witch should never use her powers for her own personal gain, and the sisters have learned it through experiences both dramatic and humorous. For the Charmed Ones, however, it's not enough to use their Magic for Good and to resist the temptation of personal gain. Destiny takes it one step further and asks them to experience tremendous personal loss as well.

They lost their eldest sister in the fight against Evil. That fight took their mother from them at an early age too. Prue lost Andy. Phoebe lost Cole—more than once, in fact. Because of their commitment to the battle, they have had difficulty maintaining friendships with outsiders, having romances, building careers. And even though Piper now has children, the stakes are so very high in regard to protecting and guiding them that, should things go awry, her son could grow up to be the most powerful force for Evil the world has ever seen. Beyond these sacrifices loom the future tragedies they know in their hearts will assail them. Yet they continue. They have evolved along with their powers, understanding that the prohibition against personal gain is only the tip of the iceberg for a Charmed One.

The poignancy of their losses, and the nobility of their continued sacrifices, proves beyond a doubt that Destiny made the right choice with them. They are human, yes, and they will always falter on occasion, but they are also Good—not just because they choose Good, but because they choose it for noble, unselfish reasons.

The Elders

What can we say about this bunch? They're above the fray—dedicated yet removed. They were once human, once capable of such uniquely human experiences as falling in love, but they no longer have such "petty" feelings. They are detached from emotion and, as a result, their definition of Good doesn't really work for the sisters, or for us.

They didn't want Piper and Leo to marry because it could cause complications for the Battle. They have allowed the sisters to experience painful trials to become stronger, more committed. Judging by Leo's example, Whitelighters still feel compassion for their charges' trials, but we get the impression the Elders have almost lost that ability.

When Leo himself became an Elder, he became detached too. The very qualities that earned him Whitelighter status—the amazing generosity of spirit and the desire to ease suffering he demonstrated as a human—began to fade on an individual level. And by individual, I mean his wife and his children! It was only when he came face to face with the anguish he caused Chris that he was jolted back to being a caring person. And ironically, that jolt made him too human to be a successful Elder anymore.[5]

We admire the sisters because they have to control their emotions and make heart-wrenching choices. Do we admire the Elders? I don't think so. Once again, it's easy to be Good when there's no temptation and, for the Elders, temptation has been greatly minimized.

The Elders are the ultimate proof that the battle between Good and Evil is an Earth-bound one. Humans *have* to fight it. The Elders and the Demons, while seemingly major players, are really on the fringe, because the battle does not rage *inside* them as it does for the Charmed Ones. The show is at its most brilliant when the sisters are fighting the external battle and the internal one simultaneously. Those shows leave us drained. They also inspire us.

The Rules

Want more proof that Good and Evil need each other, whether they like admitting it or not? How about the "deals" and the "rules" and the so-called "neutral" entities that keep popping up? For example, there's the clean-up crew that comes in when Magic has been exposed. These fellows don't make value judgments—they just clean up the mess. Then there's the Angel of Death—seems like a nice enough guy, but he's got a schedule to keep and that's that.

There's even a rule, respected by demons as well as the forces of Good, that a witch who is first coming into his or her powers can choose whether or not to be Good. Evil can tempt the witch, but cannot directly subvert Free Will, which meant, when Paige's time came, a demon could present her with a truly reprehensible human specimen to kill, but couldn't make her kill him. And being a witch destined to do Good, she didn't.

The best illustration of this principle of mutual rules and agreements was the episode about the Hollow, an entity so dangerous that Good and Evil work cooperatively to keep it confined for fear it will consume *all* power. It nearly decimated Magic once, whereupon Good and Evil

---

[5] Gideon of course went a little too far in the *other* direction. Talk about your unsuccessful Elders!

pooled their power and confined it, with one representative from each camp keeping guard, apparently whiling away the time by playing a never-ending board game.

Why did the Source decide to unleash the Hollow anyway? Because he could not defeat the Charmed Ones without it. He had reached the point where complete destruction of *everything* was preferable to allowing them to exist. This Source was no longer precisely Evil. He was insane.

Free Will Versus Destiny

We've shown that there can't be Good without Evil or, more accurately, without a meaningful choice between them. The Charmed Ones fight to protect that choice, using their Magic to restore but not tamper with it.

Do the sisters have Free Will? And how does Destiny fit into the equation?

In *Charmed*, Destiny is a person's promise. Their potential. Their highest purpose, cosmically speaking. They may be destined to do great things, perhaps eventually to become a Whitelighter, but anyone can turn his or her back on Destiny. And Evil can throw a monkey-wrench into even the best Destiny, such as when a demon or a Darklighter tries to destroy or turn a human before that human is able to accomplish all the Good he or she is destined to do.

Obviously, the Charmed Ones have an amazing Destiny—to make a lasting contribution to the world by saving innocents, the downside being that every warlock and demon is gunning for them. But the sisters also have an escape clause, courtesy of Free Will.

For one thing, the Book of Shadows provides them with a Relinquishment spell, and while they resist using it, the concept is clear and recurring. Even though they destroyed that page in the book, the spell lingers in their memories, always haunting them, always available to be exploited, as the Source tried to do.

When the sisters managed to defeat the Source ahead of schedule, the Angel of Destiny himself visited them to offer an amazing opportunity: in reward for their unselfish heroism, they could now choose to give up their powers and lead normal lives.[6]

---

[6] Otherwise, the battle would go on. Even though the Charmed Ones vanquished the Source of all Evil, Evil still existed. It just wasn't consolidated in one convenient being who could dole it out to ambitious demons in exchange for their allegiance. With the Source vanquished, the demons began battling one another to take over the underworld. Thus they were distracted from coming after the Charmed Ones, but not for long.

It seemed like an impossible choice: their magical powers in exchange for the security of love, motherhood, friendship and the other human wonders so often denied to them. When they were young and new to the craft, the idea of giving up their growing powers—their heritage—seemed insane to them. But several years and many losses later, Piper and Phoebe had grown weary of the battle, and the yearning for a normal life had grown stronger.

Again, the show didn't take the easy way out by having the sisters decide they owed it to the world to give up their own needs for those of the greater Good. It was more complicated—more human—than that. The sisters were given a reminder of how it felt to *have* power at their disposal, power they could use for good, and to protect themselves and their loved ones, and they couldn't imagine life without it. Sure, they were being unselfish to a point, but keeping their powers also meant keeping that rush, that excitement, that confidence, and they didn't want to give it up.

For the Charmed Ones, Destiny is a particularly interesting concept because their destinies are so intricately intertwined. Yes, they can relinquish their powers, but it is an all-or-nothing proposition. Yes, they have amazing individual powers with which to battle Evil, but in the battles that really matter, it takes the Power of Three. That shared Destiny is the source of their strength, not just because their Magic is strongest when they work together but because it always reminds them that they are not alone in the fight.

Chris

If the Cole storylines were the most enthralling on *Charmed*, the Chris arc was the most profound in terms of the battle between Good and Evil as it intersects Free Will. Chris had seen a world in which Evil had taken over, and he was sent back to our time[7] to prevent that from happening.

There were two ways for Chris to fix the future: either stop the event that would turn his beloved baby brother from Good to Evil, or kill Wyatt before he grew too powerful to ever be stopped. It was only because Chris had seen Evil at its worst—its most pervasive—that he could accept this mission. He was desperate to save the world without harming his brother, but if all else failed, he *would* have killed Wyatt.

---

[7] Off topic, but worth noting: *Charmed* does time travel better than *any* other television series, including past and present (and future?) sci-fi giants.

At first we were appalled by Chris' methodical approach to his task. Then we began to glimpse the pain it was causing him and we slowly began to trust him—to worry as much or more about him as we did about Wyatt, because Chris was just a child too in a sense, and saddled with the fate of the world and the prospect of killing a loved one.

Once again, *Charmed* at its best.

Demons

The Charmed Ones fight for Good. Do demons fight "for" Evil? Actually, a demon fights for himself or herself. Period. The show makes that clear again and again. Even the demons who do the Source's bidding do it in hopes of moving up the demonic ladder, not out of any sense of allegiance. A demon who works for the Source has two options: gaining more or stronger powers if he succeeds in an endeavor; fiery, agonizing destruction if he fails. On the other hand, a demon who doesn't work for the Source can't get ahead at all. Not much of a choice. (But then again, they're not really into choice, right?)

Evil

Okay, so what about Evil? Can it exist without its counterpart? Is it *really* trying to wipe Good off the face of the Earth?

Maybe some of the lower-level demons are that shortsighted, but the brainy ones know the truth. Evil likes to tempt. To corrupt. If everyone were Evil, then who would be left to corrupt? Isn't that how demons move up the ladder? They need victims!

In theory, at least, Evil has as much a stake in preserving Free Will as Good does, but in practice, the preferred technique for a demon is to subvert Free Will with a spell, an illusion or, as noted above, a good old-fashioned sin ball. Why? If Free Will is the essence of Evil, why do demons keep subverting it?

The only explanation, other than their apparent inability to defer gratification, is that they seem to know that Good would triumph eventually if humans were given a real choice.

There's also the fact that those who fight for Good have the purpose of protecting and advancing Goodness, while a demon has the purpose of protecting and advancing himself or herself. It's all about the demon's own self-interest. We often hear the expression "the greater good," but never "the greater evil," and there's a reason for that.

And ultimately, that gives Good an edge in the battle, doesn't it? True unity behind a common purpose—a greater Good—and the willingness of the individual combatants to sacrifice themselves for that goal is a powerful concept. And it's never more evident than with the Charmed Ones, who know that their power is a legacy from Melinda Warren and countless other ancestors, and know also that their children will inherit it. Demons don't waste time thinking about such things.

Another point in our favor? Humans have a lot of practice struggling against their own base tendencies. Demons, in contrast, don't have any Good in them at all. Because of this, they can't understand Goodness and can constantly underestimate it. And when they do have the bad luck to get infected with a little Good? Consider Cole as the Source: that little glimmer of human love that the Source couldn't extinguish led to his downfall. He couldn't understand it, so he couldn't beat it.

Of course, Evil has its edge too. The warriors of Evil have no problem taking Free Will away from a victim, and oftentimes they choose as their victims the very warriors who have chosen to defend Good.

Demons resort to magic as a sign of desperation. The Charmed Ones use magic too, but only because the demons and assorted evildoers do, and only to restore balance and fairness to the battle. The sisters know in their hearts that when Good finally triumphs, it won't be because of magic. It will be the power of love, the strength of unselfishness and faith in something greater than oneself that will carry the day.

Good versus Evil. It's a story as old as humankind and destined to last just as long—which is very good news for *Charmed* fans.[8]

Post Script

I wrote this essay before the Avatars bullied their way back into the show, and now that their arc has come and gone, I thought I'd add a note about them. In many ways, the Avatar storyline reaffirms the basic principles of the show in regard to the concept of Good versus Evil, but was it necessary? First of all, Cole clued us in years ago as to their true nature, in an episode where they tried to recruit him, insisting that they were a power beyond Good and Evil, and he responded that he knew Evil when he saw it.

The Avatars claimed to be getting rid of Evil. Yet to do so, they employed Evil's hallmark tactic, i.e., robbing humans of meaningful choice.

---

[8] There are so many more examples of Good versus Evil, *Charmed*-style, and no more room in which to discuss them. There's Darryl, the best nominee for future Whitelighter; Grams, who is an essay all by herself; the Manor, built on a spiritual nexus that can be either Good or Evil. The list goes on and on, as does the battle. Pick almost any episode, and you'll see it unfolding.

Once again, it's *Charmed* 101. We can't blame Leo for forgetting it for a while, since he's been through a lot lately. And apparently, the sisters needed a reminder as well. But like Cole, *Charmed* fans weren't fooled for a minute.

> When Kate Donovan isn't watching escapist TV, she's writing books or practicing law in Northern California, where she lives with her very understanding husband and two children. Her first published novels were time travels and paranormal romances, one of which, *A Dream Apart*—her first and still her favorite—was the story of a young woman who discovers that she's really a witch and has to learn to embrace her powers and a very unusual Destiny. Is it any wonder Kate became a *Charmed* fan? Her latest is *Exit Strategy*, a female action/adventure story from Silhouette's Bombshell line. Kate can be reached at katedonovan@hotmail.com.

THEIR
A DIFFERENT KIND OF REAL
MATERIAL WORLD

The Halliwells must pass for normal in San Francisco or face the consequences (the only time their secret got out, they lost Prue). Yet they dress in bad drag and don't seem to be living in any recognizable place. This is real?

WHAT IS SHE WEARING?
A COSTUMING CONSPIRACY

TANYA HUFF

The Halliwell women are all beautiful but their taste in clothes is, well, Ho Lite. With the exception of Piper, who often dresses like a depressed nun, the sisters could be picked up for public indecency any day of the week. And then, to make it worse, sometimes Phoebe *runs*....

IF THIS PIECE were an electronic presentation rather than print—if you were watching this rather than reading it—I'd open with a montage of shots in which the Charmed Ones themselves ask each other variations of the title question, ending with Phoebe's season three observation in "The Primrose Path": "Look at me. I am a fashion blunder. A '*Mademoiselle* Don't.'"

For the curious among you, she's referring to a beige scarf top decorated in an almost frightening number of clip-on feathers. That's right: clip-on feathers, the kind you can buy by the bag at most decently sized craft stores. It's...well, unattractive is putting it mildly.

Given the way the costuming on *Charmed* headed during season three, Phoebe could easily have been making a prophetic statement. Perhaps she'd had a vision of wardrobe choices to come. Probably not the red and grey fleur-de-lis arm warmer ensemble of season six's "Crimes and Witch-Demeanors," or she'd have sounded more horrified than frustrated. Maybe her powers were kind and only allowed her a glimpse of that pink newsboy's cap.

Yes, the Charmed Ones have clothed themselves in some interesting outfits over the years. Who can forget Paige's green sleeveless mini dress from "Witch Wars"—not a time travel episode, however much this outfit may lead you to believe otherwise. Or the unfortunate incident in "The Bare Witch Project" when Phoebe's head was attacked by a green burlap, blue denim, purple-ribboned thing masquerading as a hat. Or Prue's stretch pants in "Bride and Gloom" that were the exact same shade as her skin tone and therefore essentially not present for much of the scene. Or Piper's... actually, Piper comes off pretty well most of the time, being the responsible sister and all. Occasionally she's crossed the line between practical and frumpy in what may be a valiant, if doomed, attempt at fashion balance.

We've had a variety of spaghetti-strapped, one-shoulder, no-shoulder tops—including a couple so low cut it must have taken very powerful magics indeed to maintain a PG rating. And while there's clearly been a frequent application of spirit gum, there's been a distressing absence of supportive undergarments. We've had cropped pants, flared pants, artfully distressed pants—where distressed is the operative word—and pants cut so low that the tattoo at the base of Phoebe's spine gets full exposure. We've had miniskirts, translucent skirts, skirts over pants and dresses on all the sisters that were supposed to be alluring but, quite frankly, weren't. The unflattering sleeveless pale crepe number Paige wore in "Charmed Noir" is a classic example—the color was bad (the tone was bad, at any rate, since her part of the episode was shot in black and white) and the fit was worse.

But it wasn't always like this.

In season one in particular all three of the Charmed Ones dressed in ways that could only be considered normal. "Attractive young women on television" normal, perhaps, but normal nevertheless—if a tad heavy on the wearing of witchy jewelry. Prue had an interesting insect-dangling-off-of-a-necklace thing going for a while mid-season three.

What changed?

Two things.

The first change was obviously Prue's death. Prue, the strongest-willed of the Halliwell sisters, had always been more than capable of keeping Phoebe in line. With her influence removed, Phoebe's fashion choices became steadily more bizarre. Given those choices, poor Paige (as the new, youngest sister, never subjected to Prue's eye rolls of disapproval) has to go to amazing lengths to be the blithe, young, free spirit she's meant to be. Unfortunately, those lengths have included a pale blue fake fur jacket ("Hyde School Reunion") and a pink plaid and lavender fantasy schoolgirl outfit ("Ordinary Witches"). Neither Phoebe nor Paige seems to have any concept of work-appropriate clothing. And age-appropriate? Phoebe's age was given as twenty-seven in "Size Matters" in season four. Three years later, she's thirty and still baring skin like a teenager.

Piper, who runs a club and could get away with a lot more glam, shows the only restraint remaining in the family.

The second change takes us outside the world of *Charmed* and into the world the rest of us have to live in, where "the rest of us" includes the people who produce the show. *Charmed*'s first episode aired on October 7, 1998. While various Christian coalitions for family decency no doubt existed back in the waning days of the last millennium, they didn't have the power they acquired two short years later, during the middle of season three, when a new government came to power in the United States. *Charmed* is a show about witchcraft. Good witches battling evil and saving innocents, granted, but the new administration brought with it the prevailing opinion that there's no such thing as a good witch.

Charmed, while never a phenomenal breakaway success, had a solid core audience that followed it from time slot to time slot—solid and loyal and large enough to make advertisers happy. Happy advertisers make for happy studio heads. They wouldn't have wanted to cancel the show, but they certainly would have wanted to keep from attracting the attention of the religious right and the perception of its growing power.

What could they do?

They could rework the show so that no one could possibly take it seriously.

But *Charmed* was already a contemporary fantasy with little or no connection to the real world, up to and including a distinct disregard of San Francisco's weather and its effect on what the sisters might be wearing. Season seven's "A Call to Arms," canonically happening in January in Northern California, featured gauzy summer clothing at an outdoor wedding. It also featured a sari and heaven only knows what to call that outfit Leo was wearing—but their foray into ethnic clothing is an entirely different story. Given that it is a fantasy, how could the producers of *Charmed* make the show even less real and therefore less likely to attract the attention of rising right-wing hysteria?

I have a theory. It came to me while shopping for a present for my eldest niece. As I walked down the bright pink aisles at the toy store, I recognized the clothes: the Capri pants, the gauzy flowered blouses, the out-of-scale accessories.

The Charmed Ones are now dressing like the world's most famous eleven-inch doll.

Some of this doll's clothes have to be very, very tight in order to stay on. Some have to be loose enough to get over inflexible legs and arms, so they fit badly in other areas. Just generally, the way that they fit has little actual relevance to the bodies of most women. Your average little girl is perfectly happy to slide a pink mini dress on a redheaded doll. And at forty-plus, Barbie is still wearing clothes designed for teenagers.

The Halliwell sisters have been turned into Barbies with enough cunning little outfits that they never have to wear the same thing twice. Let's not even talk about the shoes. Some of the ridiculous footwear on this show is remarkably familiar to anyone who has ever rolled over and been rudely awakened by the presence of a purple plastic pump in the sheets.

Is there anything less threatening to Middle America than a doll that's been around for over forty years? Mothers played with these dolls as children, dressing and undressing them, and now, as feminist author Tracy Quan has observed, their children are playing with the dolls "in homes all over North America. Barbie has become one of the family, and nothing can stem this tide. Even the most committed feminists have been known to buy Barbie dolls for their daughters, as have fundamentalist Christians."[1]

Barbie can be a witch because it doesn't mean anything. She's Barbie. Barbie can be anyone—from astronaut to veterinarian to equestrian to member of the USMC. It's been that way right from the beginning and we're all used to it by now.

What's that? What about Barbie's blatant sexuality? The completely out-of-proportion figure? Well, you said it yourself: it's completely out of proportion. So far out, in fact, that it can be dismissed as unreal, plastic, de-sexed. Neuter the witches, neuter the sexuality that has always clung to witchcraft.

So, my theory in a nutshell: after observing the changes in the costuming over the seven years of the show, I conclude that the producers have disguised the Halliwell sisters as Barbie in order to slip a show about witchcraft past the rising power of the religious right.

Is this a bad thing?

I don't think so. Okay, let me qualify that: some of the outfits, yes, they were bad things—I'm thinking particularly of that pale blue fake fur jacket here—but overall, no.

---

[1] Quan, Tracy. "The Littlest Harlot: Barbie's Career as a Role Model." In *Whores and Other Feminists*, Jill Nagle, ed. London: Routledge Incorporated, 1997.

Just as Barbie is ultimately a toy to be played with, slipping the Charmed Ones into Barbie outfits has given the writers more room to play. Freed by their adoption of a classic symbol of childhood, the writers have walked off with a barely disguised Hogwarts as well. Phoebe became a mermaid—a terrific-looking costume by the way. Paige slipped into a gritty detective novel. Piper became Death's assistant—and picked up pretty much her only "What are you wearing?" of the series for the shapeless black coat that seemed to come with the job (although Death himself looked considerably more nattily attired). The girls ended up on reality TV, demon style. Even Leo got captured and caged by Amazons.

A moment's digression about the men of *Charmed*; the bad guys are significantly better dressers. Cole was always well dressed—when the writers allowed him to be dressed at all. Julian McMahon spent a fair bit of time out of his shirts (season three's "The Primrose Path" and "Power Outage" being prime examples). Poor Leo not only had to spend most of his time in baggy t-shirts, flannel, saggy butt jeans and white socks in brown shoes, but when he became an Elder the poor man had to shrug into a gold velour robe. He didn't catch a break with the wardrobe department until his alignment got dicey in season seven and he became an Avatar. And Chris...actually, Chris' clothing mostly suited his age, and that's really the best that can be said about it. Young men aren't generally the picture of sartorial elegance, nor do they want to be.

It's not easy being an accessory, and that's really all the men on this show ever were. Good luck finding Ken even half a dozen outfits in the double aisle of Barbie pink; Ken has always had significantly fewer fashion choices. And the less said about what isn't beneath Ken's saggy butt trousers, the better—like Barbie, Ken has only the appearance of sexuality, having also been safely neutered.

This is not to say that *Charmed* is totally free of sexuality. It's there. But it's bad.

The bad guys wear a lot of tight black leather, shiny boots and metal studs. The bad girls also get the leather, boots and studs, but also show considerably more cleavage. When any of the Charmed Ones go temporarily bad, the black leather and cleavage is a dead giveaway. This costuming shorthand allows us easy identification of evil without having to think about it much, which is always a big crowd pleaser with the religious right. Barbie in black leather? I don't think it's ever happened.

Here's the really clever part: the Halliwells haven't only become Barbie; given their preoccupation with clothes, they're also the girls playing with the doll. You can't get much less threatening than that. Clothing at the Halliwell house is chosen for any and every occasion with all the attention to detail of a seven-year-old sorting through scraps of fabric looking for the perfect tiny outfit. Seven-year-olds generally don't care about age-appropriate, or work-appropriate, or that redheads cannot and should not wear certain shades. Little girls are "in the moment," and if that moment includes a sleeveless, rhinestone trimmed cocktail dress to be worn on a date that doesn't include either cocktails or, in point of fact, actually going out ("Witchness Protection," season seven), then at least they're playing quietly and the grown-ups needn't worry about them for a few moments.

How preoccupied with dressing up are the Charmed Ones? When Paige died in "Styx Feet Under," the season seven episode where Piper went to work unwillingly for Death, she stalled her final passage by confessing to Piper that she stole one of her favorite jackets and a pair of earrings. On *Charmed*, Death itself has been delayed by fashion choices.

Lest Death have the final word, let's finish up by replaying the opening montage and revisiting the question: "What is she wearing?"

If I'm right, there's only one answer.

Camouflage.

Tanya Huff lives and writes in rural Ontario, Canada, with her partner Fiona Patton, seven cats and an unintentional Chihuahua. Her twentieth book, *Smoke and Shadows*, came out in paperback in the spring of 2005. Its sequel, *Smoke and Mirrors*, came out in hardcover in July 2005.

SITTING ON THE DOCK OF THE BAY, CASTING SPELLS

WHERE THE HECK DO THE CHARMED ONES ACTUALLY LIVE?

NICK MAMATAS

Halliwell Manor has been like home to viewers for seven seasons, but where is it, really? Not San Francisco, Nick Mamatas says. Maybe not Earth.

A LIFELONG NEW YORKER, I finally decided in 2004 that I needed a change of scenery and began making plans to move to the Bay Area. I was living with my sister at the time and she decided that I should watch the entire syndicated run of *Charmed*—her favorite television show—so that I could learn about San Francisco, which is apparently full of fairly incompetent demons.

Well, having lived in the Bay Area for just over half a year now, I have to say that I am very disappointed.

It's not all that difficult to meet witches in SF and the surrounding areas. I live about four blocks away from a "metaphysical supplies" shop that's larger than any apartment I've ever lived in. A good fifty percent of the people I've been introduced to since moving here have revealed themselves as pagans or witches of some sort, and surprisingly frequently as part of the construction "And she was like, 'I want an exclusive relationship,' and I was all like, 'You knew I was a bi poly pagan when we met on the bipolypagangeek board'...." Not that the town is half pagan or anything; this is just the milieu a young and nerdy writer of dark fantasy finds himself in these days.

There are plenty of places in the Bay Area for witches to congregate. One friend of mine offered to take me around to various hangouts and stores frequented by her part of the greater witchcraft pagan scene. B (we'll call her that to protect her privacy) wanted to show me the Sword and Rose, a witchcraft supply store she stumbled upon just as she was finishing up college and "looking for something" to believe in. The store is at 85 Carl Street, but good luck finding it as it's hidden between two buildings and through a garden pathway. The owner, a fellow named Randy who is said to be a "master of conjuration" (not sleight-of-hand stuff; he claims the ability to bring various supernatural entities to some sort of physical appearance), put his shop in such an out-of-the-way space, according to B, "So that only those who are meant to find his store discover it." And indeed, The Sword and Rose is hard to find from the street and is also seemingly the only place of business in town not to have its own Web site. (It does have a phone number, though.) Enough people find the store to keep it open, that's for sure. Earth religions, and even claims of magical powers, are as common as nipple piercings in this town, and the crowd tends toward the alternative and the countercultural.

But the Halliwell sisters? Mundanes. Squares. I'd call them nerds but nerds are cool now, apparently. And wherever they live, it sure isn't SF. It is more like the San Francisco Bay Area as imagined by someone vaguely familiar with some elements of the city (or as they have it out here, "The City," though "The City" will always be Manhattan to me), but who had never actually been there. I mean, there's a bridge and a park. In most episodes of the series, however, the action might as well be taking place in Columbus, Ohio, during a pleasant spring day.

There are some elements of SF-themed action in the show. An early episode shows Prue going to the beach to unwind and get over some emotional issue. She, seemingly *contra* one of *Charmed*'s major charms, is fully clothed the entire time. The lack of skin makes sense, though: the Bay Area is a lovely sunny place where the populace simply pretends to experience nice weather. Mark Twain was being funny when he said, "The coldest winter I ever spent was a summer in San Francisco," but he sure wasn't joking.

The Halliwells live in a very nice Victorian (and indeed, they must be powerful witches to be able to afford its upkeep and property taxes given their day jobs), but even the exterior shots of the house betray a certain plainness that many of the great Victorian and Edwardian (post-1906 earthquake homes) in SF don't have. Bright, sometimes garish paint jobs that bring out all the decorative details of a classic home are the local fashion. Halliwell Manor is a bit too much *Home And Garden*, not nearly enough Mission District.

Another San Francisco element appeared in the first season episode "Power of Two" in which Phoebe went sightseeing at Alcatraz and encountered the ghost of a serial killer looking for revenge against those that executed him. Nitpickers have pointed out that nobody was ever executed at Alcatraz, but the more egregious sin was that Phoebe went there at all. Locals don't go to Alcatraz unless they're children on a school trip. I know because I've asked around and gotten confused looks.

"So, how do you get to Alcatraz? I'd like to see it," I asked a whole bunch of SF residents when I first showed up here.

"I don't even know; I've never been there. A boat?" was the usual answer. "Try an elementary school field trip," was the second most popular.

Now I know how the tourists who used to stop me on the street to ask me how to get to the Statue of Liberty felt.

Piper's nightclub, P3, is also the most mediocre of music venues, far below the standard SF hangout. Given that Piper's about as hip as the official seamstress for the Mormon Tabernacle Choir, we can't be too surprised at the shape P3 is in—but how on Earth does the club even stay open?

P3's décor is late backlot lounge set-dressing. The "P3" name brings to mind nothing so much as some sort of urolagnia fetish club. As a music venue, it's a damn nightmare: Dishwalla, The Goo Goo Dolls, Cranberries, Orgy and other alternative pop bands that a) would in real-life fill up much larger venues, b) would likely not play a newish club and c) suck somehow manage to keep enough drinks flowing to keep the girls in business. I will give the devil his due, though, as SF-area alternative industrial band Snake River Conspiracy appeared in season three's "All Halliwell's Eve"; local music is big in the Bay and the band has enough of a following to make a P3 club appearance viable but not overcrowded. (SRC also does a great cover of The Smiths' "How Soon Is Now?" which is, as performed by Love Spit Love, the *Charmed* theme—the show gets extra credit for not having had the band play that song during the episode.)

There are other issues too: where are the damn hills? How come even the non-witches can find parking so easily? Nobody ever nibbles on a See's Candy, or complains about the fog and the rain, or spends any leisure time on their computers. When Prue turns into a man in "She's a Man, Baby, a Man!" it's as though none of the sisters had ever encountered a transgendered person before.

The ultimate problem is the Charmed Ones themselves—they just don't come off as Bay Area witches. In "Witch Trial" Phoebe and Piper attended a celebration of the Equinox in a park. "Wild" Phoebe was willing to join the other women in stripping for the ritual, saying "When in Rome," but Piper balked: "No-no-no! We're not in Rome, Phoebe. We're in California. And it's illegal here." Ah, but in SF, public nudity is not illegal unless the nude person is engaging in lewd behavior. Pagan rituals, the annual Dyke Parade, the Folsom Street Fetish Fair, UC Berkeley's Naked Guy and, heck, even the fellow who does naked yoga in front of the tourists at Fisherman's Wharf are just the most famous examples of public and legal nudity that have made the national news. One need not be a resident to know that SF is one of those cities where we let everything shake, dangle and sag. And a native nightclub-owning witch had never contemplated or even heard of a skyclad ritual before? It might play in Peoria, but not in the Bay.

The arrival of Rose McGowan and her portrayal of Paige did lend the show a bit of hipster cred, and her character was used to play off some of the stereotypes of the Bay Area. "Witchstock" featured Paige trying on red go-go boots left behind by Penny Halliwell (Grams) and finding herself projected back to the Summer of Love. Well, sort of—the Summer of Love and hippie culture as presented and described in the episode was a mish-mash of half-remembered clichés. Grams was a hippie and also wore go-go boots? Timothy Leary's Human Being-In was mentioned as happening during the summer, but it actually occurred six months prior. Allen (Gramps, though in other episodes Gramps is called Jack and died in '64) was a beatnik instead of a hippie, though he did have a VW Microbus. Police batons were turned into daisies, which was a cute touch, but Penny's pacifism (even backed by magic) was generally derided for macho action heroics. And, of course, drugs were still a no-no. Young Penny said to Paige, "There's no acid allowed in the Manor, Paige. We're all on a contact high." Well, that's boring. It must run in the family.

I don't want to make it sound like I'm too down on the show, or too overly impressed with San Francisco. *Charmed* is a very cute show; I'm a great admirer of the early, darker episodes and enjoy watching a program that successfully combines the fantastic with a plausible and emotionally appealing depiction of a modern family of thirty-something women. *Charmed* doesn't delve into the banal dysfunctions that drive so many television dramas and shows that family is important and love is possible. And as far as The City goes, I'm a bit too old and cranky to be endlessly fascinated by leather vests, "cool" workplaces that lay everyone off as readily as any Old Economy factory ever did and the psychodramatics of polyamorous relationships. The real-life witches I've met often claim expansive psychic abilities, but most of them can't even predict with regularity that the rent is due on the first of the month.

As writers and readers of the fantastic have long known, setting itself often becomes a character. Lovecraft's Arkham is more recognizable and memorable than any of his human protagonists. Stephen King's Maine, the New Orleans of Poppy Z. Brite and Dennis Etchison's Southern California all speak to the reader by presenting the quotidian realities of the area and then subtly (and later, not so subtly) warping them to make the environments both frightening and liberating. Frightening, because anything can happen. Liberating, because, again, anything can happen.

But in the San Francisco of *Charmed* what is remarkable is that almost nothing happens. Much of the supernatural action takes place in the Manor or in other dimensions. The City proper is almost never shown, and the daily lives of the Halliwell sisters almost never involve the city—there are no late BART trains, no Giants or Raiders games, no Halloween down on The Castro, nothing. SF does serve a purpose in *Charmed*—its big city and freak-friendly aura allows the writers to avoid the otherwise inevitable "nosey neighbor" character—but other than that there is no reason at all for the show to take place where it does.

Instead of using San Francisco to provide both color and scares for the audience, the show uses the Charmed Ones to drain SF of all that makes it special. Its radical past is pooh-poohed and trivialized; its vibrant present is reflected only in the evil outsiders that the Halliwells face down every week. *Charmed* represents the gentrification of the soul of the Big City; The City is rendered safe for virtual tourists/viewers who are too frightened (or complacent in their own homes) to even get on the plane and come visit. It's too bad, as there is an enormous amount of material one could work with: Emperor Norton, the "painted ladies" houses, the many ethnic cultures and their myths and supernatural systems, the winding, sometimes sinister streets and alleys, the changing nature of the family and, of course, the embrace of the weird that makes SF such a great place to live. These sorts of plot hooks and overarching themes can turn a good show into a great one.

Unfortunately, the San Francisco of *Charmed* is no deeper than a postcard.

Nick Mamatas is the author of the Lovecraftian Beat road novel *Move Under Ground* and the Marxist Civil War ghost story *Northern Gothic*, both of which were nominated for the Bram Stoker Award in horror fiction.

He has published over two hundred articles and three dozen short stories in venues ranging from the men's magazine *Razor*, the *Village Voice* and various Disinformation Books anthologies to *Strange Horizons*, *Polyphony* and *ChiZine*. He is a regular columnist for both Forteanbureau.com and *Flytrap*. After spending a year in the Bay Area, he recently pulled up stakes again and moved back to the East Coast, where he splits his time between NYC and Vermont.

TALENT AND THE SOCIALISM OF FEAR

JODY LYNN NYE

You'd really think the sisters would dress more quietly, go to more local gathering places, join a few organizations...anything to fit in with the rest of the populace because, as Jody Lynn Nye points out, if anybody ever gets suspicious and their secret gets out, demons will be the least of the Halliwells' problems.

"From each according to his ability, to each according to his need."

– KARL MARX, *THE COMMUNIST MANIFESTO*

IN BETWEEN DEALING with their very complicated love lives, their interpersonal relationships with one another and with non-family members, and now the responsibility of children, the three Halliwell sisters are busy saving the world on a nearly daily basis. Problems of a serious magical nature frequently stumble into their laps, forcing the three to drop their own lives in order to resolve the threat. When a crisis is resolved, however, the ladies resume the semblance of a normal life, working jobs, taking care of their house, themselves and one another, and dealing with neighbors. But wouldn't karma demand that these extraordinary women extend themselves even further, using their special abilities more broadly to save still more worthy people from the evils that threaten them? After all, the Power of Three is unique; most of the malign forces of the *Charmed* universe burst into the Halliwell home on a regular basis, seeking to destroy the sisters or subvert that power for themselves.

In a perfect world, one might reasonably ask such a question. And, in a perfect world, witches such as the Halliwells might give of their power when it was not being otherwise demanded. They are obviously meant to do as much good as they can. Why else would fate have caused such a confabulation as the Power of Three to come into existence in the first place? Why else would the Elders have assigned semi-angelic Whitelighters to guard their backs? The problem is that the sisters live in *this* world.

Karl Marx's words, quoted above, voice an ideal, one in which no one would demand more than she or he required and those who were capable of filling those requirements would give willingly of their time, talents and resources. However, human beings have a tendency to increase their demands to suit their wants rather than their needs. It's all very well to argue equal access to all resources, but who is to arbitrate when such resources are to be allotted, and to whom? Without other complications the Halliwells might be able to slowly educate their friends and neighbors to ask for help only when in dire need, as George Bailey did in the classic film *It's a Wonderful Life*, if only it weren't for that other factor accompanying the knowledge that your three lovely neighbors are witches—real ones, with actual powers equally capable of banishing demons, summoning the spirits of the dead or saving your baby from being hit by a car. That factor is fear.

Fear is animal in nature. While modern humans pride themselves on their rationality and almost certainly believe that they live in an enlightened world, most respond from the most primitive part of their brains when it comes to dealing with the unknown. For all the technology we possess, for all the scientific arguments that we supposedly espouse, human beings still fear what they do not know. It's a complicated fear, one that a simple assurance of safety is not enough to allay.

Should the Halliwell sisters go public with their talents, even in a limited fashion, they would stir up that dread of the unexplainable. Most likely strangers would not take their claims of magical ability seriously until receiving proof positive, at which point they would be almost certain to have one of two reactions. The first, and rarer of the two, would be the "Hey, *cool!*" response, evoked from people whose curiosity is stronger than their native caution. The second, and far more likely, would be terror and withdrawal pending a more emphatic, even violent, response of self-defense. In season three's "All Hell Breaks Loose," the sisters were exposed in the media and an angry mob appeared on their doorstep, terrified to discover witches living secretly in their midst. The threat to the three Halliwells could be removed only if no memory of their exposure continued to exist. Though the effort to reverse the chain of events resulted in Prue's death, allowing the situation to stand would almost certainly have claimed the lives of all three sisters.

The sisters have also had a few near misses, such as in "Forget Me...Not" and "Crimes and Witch-Demeanors," in which their magic was almost revealed to the world. But these episodes also introduced a squad of neutral entities known as the Cleaners, whose job it is to expunge the evidence of witchcraft accidentally performed in public, à la *Men In Black*, showing that even the normally out-of-touch Powers That Be—both good and evil—understand the disruption such knowledge could cause.

The sisters must also consider the effect of their talents upon intimate relationships. They are only human, after all, and want to have normal love lives like any other women. Unfortunately, they risk provoking the same fear and revulsion from any would-be inamorato that they do from the public. It has happened at least twice. Even though Andy and Prue had known one another since high school, and even though he had been the sisters' strong ally through several uncanny situations, in "The Truth Is Out There...and It Hurts," he admitted that he was not prepared to accept her newfound powers. Phoebe lost a boyfriend, Jason, when the truth frightened him as well (though to China rather than to death). Fortunately the men's response was not physically violent in either case, nor did the sisters' revelations result in public betrayal.

The Halliwells felt that they have had to keep their talents secret not only to prevent generating fear, but also jealousy. Those without magical ability would wish that they had it. They would feel entitled to benefit from it in some way, or else feel the need to deprive any person who does have it from deriving any perceived personal gain. That way everyone is even, even if no one is happy.

Anyone who was ever rapped over the knuckles by a teacher for going faster than the rest of the class will understand the phenomenon. (If it didn't happen to you, ask your friends. It will have happened to one of them.) The "I hope you brought enough for everyone" philosophy ignores the hard fact that life is not fair. Talent belongs to the ones to whom fate gives it. It can't be distributed and it can't be destroyed, though, at least in *Charmed*, it can occasionally be stolen—as it was by the Stillman sisters in "The Power of Three Blondes," and by the occasional demon. But those were all magical attacks, not mortal ones. Those who have talent in the mortal world cannot have it taken away; they can only be ostracized. Conventional wisdom states that those who have talent had better use it for the common good or face being considered evil and selfish.

Not every inequity works this way. The very rich, for instance, have merely achieved financial affluence; anyone can do that if he works hard enough. Choice possessions fall into the ownership of those with good timing and the means to obtain them. The "man on the street" might envy the "man who has everything" but understands the reasons for the discrepancy between his means and the latter's. Anything that can be achieved by effort is okay. Ah, but being able to bat .500 or sing in perfect pitch—now that's unfair. Talent is not earned. It's dropped upon the undeserving without regard to the feelings of those who must do without. It is Not Fair.

Magic is an extreme example. Anything that allows one person to achieve a desired end without having to work for it makes others jealous. The average person might admire or even worship a celebrity, whose natural talent has won them wealth and fame, but even so, a simmering resentment exists deep in the average fan's breast, eagerly awaiting the appearance of some weakness which proves that the star does not deserve the status he or she enjoys. (Look how rabidly the press follows celebrity felony trials, from Michael Jackson to Martha Stewart. Bringing a mighty person low satisfies the socialistic hunger for making all people equal.)

Any ability that could give the user power over another person is feared and hated, especially if there is no authority that can command obedience from the user. Not every powerful person is a bully, but the adage "Power corrupts, and absolute power corrupts absolutely" has a basis in psychological fact. Those who have power always pose a threat to those without it, unless they can be controlled. If you think you'd hate being pushed aside by some star's posse when that star wanted to shop in a store you were innocently browsing, think how you would feel if that star was capable of "zapping" you into obedience with the whisk of their hand. Only vulnerability makes the power-wielder a potential friend or ally.

This fear of the powerful creates a terrible atmosphere of distrust and underhandedness. Is it any wonder that our fictional "friendly" alien visitors always proclaim, "We come in peace" upon landing? And even then it is unlikely that we fully believe them. A cynical whisper in our heads continues to insist that any being that came to Earth aboard a spaceship that could cross light years must be here to enslave us or eat us, or both.

Historically, witches—or rather, those accused of being witches—were persecuted, burned and hanged, not necessarily because they had already hurt anyone with their witchcraft, but because they posed a *potential* threat to people who feared becoming victims. Many of the complaints were based not upon fact but upon jealousy or hatred. It would have made no difference if the accused witches had pleaded that all they wished to do was use their powers for the good of others. Mobs do not believe in altruism. We may want, romantically, to believe in it. And we understand, rationally, that witches who practice it, who seek to right the karmic balance for the sake of all existence, have far more to lose than we do and therefore are careful to safeguard their abilities. But emotionally, we're sure they're going to get us when our backs are turned, so we have to get them first. This is part of what made the retirement of the superheroes in Brad Bird's fantastic animated feature *The Incredibles* so believable: though the heroes willingly risked their lives daily, the public became jaded and contemptuous of them, ready to destroy the generous impulses and selfless deeds of the superheroes with endless litigation. It's a vivid example of how the best of intentions can produce the worst results.

The Halliwell sisters have had no choice but to keep quiet about their talents except to a select few trusted friends. Otherwise, the sisters would either be forced to share their talent endlessly to prove their good intentions or be constantly threatened with death or harm. Still, by revealing themselves to the public, the sisters have it in their power to do a tremendous service for the magicians and witches who will follow them. Taking the terror out of the traditional image of the witch—the crooked-nosed old crone—would do much to help human beings dispose of yet one more needless fear.

So, how would they reach out to potential "clients" to offer their aid when a gap appeared in their schedule? Tradition frowns on psychics and witches charging for their talents, but that seems a hard knock for those old hedge herbalists who seek out and prepare their own remedies, let alone modern homeowners with property tax and electric bills to pay. Surely modern witches would be able to collect enough to cover their overhead while still satisfying the karmic requirement not to profit. Though the sisters would need to budget their available time, surely the Power of Three merits a more stylish attempt to reach out than the 3x5 card in the supermarket. Any advertising agency worth its salt would jump at the opportunity to advertise enchanters for hire, but even local advertisements would make national or worldwide news. Introducing them with a cute campaign could begin to erode the visceral fear of the witch, but the unfortunate outcome of even the most discreet and well-targeted public advertising would be an overwhelming influx of demands for aid, most of them spurious or self-interested. And since the Halliwells would be unable to respond to 99% of the applications, any good a positive ad campaign could do would be reversed. An Internet site, one bespelled to open only to those people who are genuinely in need of magical assistance, might be a better answer. Let fate handle the details; the sisters have too much to do to host a Web site in addition to performing rescues and changing the world. This is not an ordinary small business, after all. Perhaps the Elders could form another support group like the Cleaners to handle positive PR in the mortal world.

Another solution might be to acquire a patron, a powerful person of means who could supply the Halliwells with expenses while at the same time protecting them from the fearful. That was surely one of the reasons that kings and dukes had court magicians: the arrangement was to the magicians' benefit as much as the rulers'.

Having an enchanter in one's retinue was a mark of a prosperous and powerful regent. It proved that such a monarch commanded forces not only in this plane of existence but in the astral one as well. Having a witch or wizard in a monarch's service was acceptable to the public because, presumably, the master of so many subjects would be able to keep control over their magician as well. That way, also, the magician's talent would not be squirreled away selfishly, but acceptably employed in the service of the monarch for the public good. Working for a universally recognized authority precludes the magician from having to win over every doubter one at a time.

In the absence of a supreme governmental authority, however, good and evil matter. "Are you a good witch or a bad witch?" Glinda the Good Witch asks Dorothy Gale in *The Wizard of Oz*. The farm girl Dorothy protests she is not a witch at all, but neither Glinda nor the Munchkins believe her. Who else has the power to lift a house and drop it on one of their most dreaded enemies but another witch? If she is a good witch, the Munchkins are happy to interact with her, because they have grown up used to witches and other miracle workers, such as the Wizard himself. A good witch is one who is constrained by morality to aid the greater good. A bad witch is driven only by greed and self-interest and should be feared and destroyed if possible.

The Munchkins are willing to take Dorothy's word on her moral inclinations, though, while it's difficult to imagine human beings on this contemporary Earth doing the same. We have no experience with genuine, proven magicians and have a hurdle to leap that Munchkins and other inhabitants of fantasy land do not: we must accept the existence of magic before we can even begin to judge whether or not a magician possesses ethics and self-control.

Moreover, magicians on this contemporary Earth have even further obstacles than similar beings elsewhere: paranoid governments that wish to control such talent or, if they cannot control it, destroy it so it will not hurt their nation or fall into the hands of their enemies. Effective witches would be taken into "protective custody" and tested and/or tortured to discover the depths of their talents. This would apply not just in the United States, but in any country. If by some miracle these witches and warlocks were freed to go about their business, which a practical assessment of human nature would suggest is unlikely (it's a wonder that FBI Agent Kyle Brody never thought of turning the Halliwell sisters in to the government), they would be kept under tight rein by the powers that be, much as a court magician would be, and thereby be unable to perform any works not strictly licensed by the ruling monarch, president, premier or oligarchy. The paperwork that would necessarily follow each use of magic would be interminable: imagine having each time to report the details of your actions, the outcome thereof and a list of the beneficiaries. An "outed" witch might be forbidden to act for the well-being of an enemy of the state, even if that enemy was being wronged. Being "traded" to another country in exchange for a special favor would not be out of the question. All of a sudden, what seemed to be a great gift would become an unbearable burden. A witch who was even a casual student of human nature would never allow her gifts to become known. Any witch with sense would run for the hills.

The Halliwell sisters are wise to keep their talents concealed and work for the good of humankind behind the scenes. No good deed goes unpunished, as the old saw goes. Without the protection of a higher authority or mass public acceptance of what they are, they cannot go public. Doing so would mean more time spent fighting the fears of their neighbors than fighting evil itself. They serve the universe best by keeping from engendering that fear in the first place. It is better, then, that their own common sense and fate itself remain the arbiters of where their talents are applied. Should an evolution in society come that embraces the assumption that witchcraft is as acceptable as superheroics, the Halliwell sisters might come forward to accept the thanks that are due them. In the meantime, they will have to be content with the superhero's own daily protection—keeping their identities secret—and be content with doing their job for the job's sake.

Jody Lynn Nye lists her main career activity as "spoiling cats." She lives northwest of Chicago with two of the above and her husband, author and packager Bill Fawcett. She has written over thirty books, including *The Ship Who Won* with Anne McCaffrey, a humorous anthology about mothers, *Don't Forget Your Spacesuit, Dear,* and over eighty short stories. Her latest books are *Strong-Arm Tactics* (Meisha Merlin) and *Class Dis-Mythed*, cowritten with Robert Asprin (Meisha Merlin).

THEIR MEN
LEO, COLE AND OTHER TRANSIENTS

For all their astonishing beauty, the Halliwells have a heck of a time holding on to men. Even the loyal Leo goes AWOL on a regular basis. Is it because they'll always be more loyal to their sisters than to their misters (poor Cole)? Or is it because their misters come and go, but their sisters are forever?

WHY CAN'T THIS WITCH GET HITCHED?

OR, GIRL POWER AND THE MEN WHO CAN'T HANDLE IT

MAGGIE SHAYNE

It's not easy for a tradition-bound man to commit to a woman who can turn him into a newt. Maggie Shayne argues that it's this imbalance of power that ruins the Halliwells' love lives, not the fact that they keep falling for bad risks like demons, dead men and baseball players.

RELATIONSHIPS—the fun kind—those being the ones that include sex—are my specialty. I love watching them unfold, analyzing them, picking them apart and predicting what's gong to happen next. I've lost friends that way.

So you can probably imagine what a blast I've had watching the women of *Charmed* work their way through men so fast they make the ones in *Desperate Housewives* look like blushing virgins.

I mean, come on. Does anyone have that much sex? With *that many* men? Had the Halliwell women been notching their bedposts, they'd have been reduced to sleeping on mattresses on the floor by the end of season three.

But that's beside the point of this essay, which is this: none of the Charmed Ones will ever have a stable, long-term, monogamous relationship with a man.

The basis of my theory is twofold. First, there is the haunting refrain that still echoes through the minds and hearts of everyone in the TV biz, and has since the tragic ends of such classic series as *The Scarecrow and Mrs. King* and *Moonlighting*. It goes something like this: "When the yearning yet resisting couple finally get together for keeps, the story is over."

Hell, it's a refrain we romance novelists hear in our *sleep*. It's taped to our office walls in large fonts. It might even have been encoded into the lyrics of our mothers' lullabies. We know it well. We don't forget.

But that reason is too easy, too obvious and far from the subject of my thesis here, which is the second, and most important reason Phoebe, Piper, Paige and Prue have never and will never have a stable, long-term, monogamous relationship with a man: they are powerful women. In the *Charmed* universe (which I like to call the "*Charm*iverse" or else "The Land of Very Bad Clothes"), the Halliwell sisters are probably the most powerful women ever. In fact, that's what this series is really about, deep down in its cleavage: Girl Power. Is there a more perfect metaphor for Girl Power than Witchcraft[1]?

Let's count the ways, shall we?

- In Witchcraft "God" is most often "Goddess."
- While logically, we know there are male Witches, society views Witchcraft as a female thing.
- The Girl Power embodied by Witchcraft is so incredibly threatening to men that they launched an all-out attack on it during the Witch Hysteria that gripped Europe and the US 400–600 years ago. Some refer to that time as "The Women's Holocaust." Some claim up to nine million women may have been murdered.

Most men can't handle Girl Power. Even today's men, who are far more enlightened than their torture-loving forebears, can't help but feel a bit uncomfortable with it. Oh, there are exceptions. I'm married to one of them and am a devoted friend to others—after all, men like that are a rare find and deserve notice! But they are, sadly, in the minority. For the most part, men still like to believe they are the powerful ones, the ones in charge, the ones on top. Both in real life and in fiction, they labor under this false illusion—an illusion constantly being validated for them by regular infusions of Vin Diesel, the Rock and Viagra.

---

[1] When used to refer to the fictional witches of *Charmed*, I have used the normal lowercase spelling of the word "witch." But when referring to real Witches in the real world, people who are following the spiritual path of Witchcraft, I have capitalized the W.

(Not that I have anything against Vin or Rocky. In fact, looking at them for long, uninterrupted periods, particularly shirtless and sweaty—them, not me—is one of my favorite pastimes.)

Be that as it may, men in general don't want to face the fact that they are, in truth, the weaker sex. And *Charmed*, just like any good fiction, is a reflection of the society in which it lives.

The witches of *Charmed* are super-chicks. If real women were as much in tune with their own power as the Charmed Ones, we'd be getting equal pay for equal work, the Equal Rights Amendment would have been ratified ages ago and sex crimes would be death penalty offenses.

The men of *Charmed*, like many of their real-world counterparts, can't deal with women who are more powerful than they are, so they find various ways to ensure their state of blissful ignorance, or else they try to make themselves more powerful in order to regain the supremacy they never had.

Let's take it from the top, shall we? I've always been a big Prue fan anyway, and while I adore Paige and think her presence adds a wonderful energy to the show (a sex kitten who enters her first episode licking a lollipop—how can you not like her? She's like a Britney Spears video with a slightly less tasteful wardrobe), the show hasn't been the same since Prue died. I miss her.

Back in the beginning, Prue's steady banging was a cop by the name of Andy. Andy was a great guy: strong, powerful, a man in charge. And maybe he figured that since he was a cop, he had enough power to hold his own in a relationship with a powerful woman like Prue. But then it turned out Prue was a witch, and not just any witch, but one of the Charmed Ones.

Naturally this threw Andy for a while, but he bounced back, apparently still convinced he could maintain his illusion of power. When it became clear that he couldn't, he died. *Died!* Can you imagine going that far to escape the inevitable truth that your girlfriend is more powerful than you are? I mean, come on, guys. That's taking it over the top.

Okay, so we all know he didn't *really* die to escape Prue, at least not on a conscious level. But deep down...who knows? Either way, it was unsuccessful. He should have known there was no escaping a determined witch. Prue died, too. Just how do you think you're going to get away from her now, Andy? Huh?

Schmuck.

Okay, so Andy and Prue, tragic love story, but really not the steamiest one of the series. For that we must look to the tale of the hottest character ever to grace the halls of Halliwell Manor: Cole.

Mm, mm, mm. You know, I've built an entire career on the premise that women love a hot-looking bad boy. And Cole really fit the bill—not only was he prime, top quality grade-A hunk, he was actually half-demon.

Cole and Phoebe had great chemistry. But Phoebe had something Cole didn't have (besides the wardrobe from Hell). She had Girl Power. And even a half-demon found himself paling in comparison. But Cole was not easily dissuaded. He wanted Phoebe, and he wanted to be the alpha guy. For a while he tried it on his own, just relying on his human side and his good looks, charm and apparent skill in the sack to bring himself up to Phoebe's level.

This was probably a good idea. But it didn't work.

One episode that perfectly illustrated this point was season four's "Lost and Bound." (Get your mind out of the gutter—it's not referring to anything with leather or buckles, although you can find an episode that covers S&M and bondage fantasies if you look. Try season five's "Stormy Leather.")

In "Lost and Bound" Cole was working with Social Services, living as an ordinary mortal, and had put an engagement ring on Phoebe's finger.

Immediately, Phoebe turned into June Cleaver. She started baking cookies, wearing clothes straight out of a 1969 issue of *Good Housekeeping* and vacuuming in pearls. She lost all interest in battling demons.

You know for a while there, Cole had it made.

The subplots in this episode back up my thesis as well. While all this was going on with Phoebe, Piper was having a spirited debate with Leo over their unborn baby's powers. Surely the child of a Whitelighter and a Charmed witch would be one powerful little rugrat. And Leo was pushing for a spell to "bind" the baby's powers before it was even born. My theory? He wanted to do this because, up until the actual birth, they were all convinced the baby would be a girl. He couldn't bear the idea of one more powerful female in the house. Piper was against the idea, of course.

This debate is further proof that men want to be the most powerful beings in their immediate vicinity—or, you know, once they get into the White House, the entire world.

Meanwhile, in a home nearby, a little boy with powers of his own accidentally set his bedroom on fire. Did I mention my theory that males can't handle Girl Power? Even if they happen to HAVE IT?

At any rate, eventually the sisters figured out what was going on with Phoebe, and she took off the ring and got in touch with her inner witch again. Thank Goddess!

Having learned that he made a lousy Darrin to Phoebe's Samantha, Cole began to embrace his demonic side.

Now, this isn't where the story of Cole and Phoebe ended. He really put up a valiant fight to elevate himself to a position of power so he could stay with her. He tried getting her pregnant with demon spawn, but that didn't work out. When being the groom in their Satanic wedding didn't do it for him, Cole went for even more power. In fact, he managed to claim the throne of High King Muckity-Muck of the Demons (not the official title).

And you would think *that* would do it, if nothing else would. Right? Well, at least, you might think that if you hadn't ever seen an episode of *Charmed*. If you had, then you probably knew that *these witches' reason for being is to vanquish demons.*

Hello? Cole, come on. You really should have thought this thing through.

There was a lot more stuff in between, of course, but in the end, Cole couldn't out-power Phoebe, even when he became the Dread Dictator of Darkness (again, not the official title), so Phoebe vanquished his ass and washed her hands of him.

Undaunted, Cole got himself nipped and tucked and started a lucrative little plastic surgery practice in L.A. where he wound up being nominated for a Golden Globe. Think he's feeling powerful enough yet?

Ahh, but we have not yet touched on the most fascinating relationship of all: the saga of Piper and Leo.

Leo started out as the Halliwells' handyman. But naturally, that role wasn't nearly strong enough. He couldn't even get to second base with Piper while wearing a tool belt. So eventually he revealed that he was in fact (insert harp music and tinkling chimes here) a Whitelighter. He was *their* Whitelighter.

The sisters' reaction? "What the hell is a Whitelighter?"

Determined to impress them, Leo explained that he was a sort of guardian angel. Every witch has one. (Mine must have been held up at the border or something.) As their Whitelighter, Leo had certain powers. He could heal their injuries, bring them back from the dead if he got there soon enough and the script said it was okay and, best of all, he sort of got to tell them what to do.

Ahhh, that Leo. Clever, clever, clever. He set himself up in a way that couldn't help but put him in a position of power over the witches, basically introducing himself with the phrase, "I'm the boss of you."

So Piper fell for him, knowing something he didn't: that his plan was doomed to fail. Maybe Leo was in a position to tell the girls what to do—but like all women, the Charmed Ones were never very good at doing what they were told.

So for a long time, as the relationship between Piper and Leo grew, Leo spent all his time *trying* to be the boss of them—and learning that controlling witches is very much like herding cats. It can't be done. He yelled; they yelled louder. He told them not to do something; they did it anyway. He told them *to* do something; they avoided it at all costs. He gave advice; they ignored it.

I can't even blame him for wishing to have more power than them. The poor guy wasn't exactly treated with honor or respect. After Prue died, for example, in season four's "Hell Hath No Fury," Piper's grief turned to rage. She became one of the three Furies, taking out her anguish on any demon unlucky enough to cross her path. When Leo tried to talk her down—after all, she was enjoying the kill a bit too much—she flipped him. *Flipped him!* Sent him flying ass-over-applecart, as they say in my neck of the woods. Luckily, he landed on the pillow-covered sofa. Phew! Close call. How's that for respecting your Whitelighter?

Basically, Leo, in all his angelic Whitelighter glory, became little more than another tool in the witches' arsenal. They kept him around and pulled him out when he was needed, like a faithful old athame or an heirloom wand, or their notorious Book of Shadows. (I think mine's busted, by the way. It *never* opens to the page I need all by itself. I'm thinking of sending it back for a refund.)

Leo wasn't in power at all. He might have been off twinkling on a cloud someplace, doing whatever it is he did when he wasn't on the screen, but if the witches called his name, he had to appear. And they did call him. When one of them was hurt or when they needed to pick his brain or use him for some other purpose, like killing a big spider or changing the oil filter in the car.

He was like a genie in a bottle, a virtual slave to the witches, which is way lower on the power-pole than a handyman.

Okay, so he screwed up. Leo realized it after a while. And like many men down through history, his first idea for a solution involved sex. He got Piper into the sack, of course—and frankly, just between you and me, I don't think he could have been anywhere near as good as Cole probably was. I mean, who's going to blow your socks off in bed, an angel or a demon? It's fairly obvious, right?

Anyway, he proceeded to knock Piper up and to marry her, not necessarily in that order. He's not alone. A lot of men think keeping a woman "barefoot and pregnant" is a good way to control her.

They are, of course, dead wrong. While getting a woman pregnant might seem like a good way to keep her in line to a man, for a woman it is the most powerful time of her life. She becomes a Goddess, a creator, the bearer and nurturer of life. All of a sudden, she's thrumming with more power than she ever felt before. And for most women, the pregnancy has the effect of moving the man *down* a notch on her list of priorities. It's the baby who holds the top position now.

In Piper's case, this was illustrated beautifully and perfectly when her pregnancy rendered her invulnerable. And so, left with little other choice, Leo got himself a promotion. He became (twinkle-twinkle-twink) an *Elder*!

All together now: "Ooooooooh. An Elder."

Yes, Leo became an Elder. And I hear what you're asking. "What the hell's an Elder?"

Well, it's fairly easy to explain. The Elders are a combination of major angels (or perhaps minor deities) and Supreme Court Judges. They seem to be in charge of deciding what's right and wrong, of governing affairs on Earth and of guiding Whitelighters in their duties protecting witches, while the witches do their duties vanquishing demons. Elders are definitely of higher rank than Whitelighters. Just the same way Whitelighters are of higher rank than witches.

And you would have thought Leo would have considered that being of higher rank had not necessarily made him more powerful up to now before deciding to take the job. But he probably figured, what the hell? Piper had the kid, she wasn't going anywhere. Let her and her sisters deal with that. He'd just shoot off into the stratosphere and take care of important things with a bunch of other white-robed, sober-faced types.

It's important to note, I think, that Leo became the only Liberal on the bench at that time. The other Elders were clearly Conservatives.

As an Elder, Leo was not required to spend a lot of quality time with his baby son, Wyatt. ("Why?" for short. I mean, come on, Wyatt is Leo's last name. So is the baby's legal name Wyatt Wyatt? Ugh!) Leo could swear (not to God, of course; there is apparently no supreme being, God or Goddess in the *Charmi*verse, which is odd considering there are witches, angels and demons, but there you go...but I digress) that he wanted to spend more time with Piper and the baby, and display remorse and even frustration at being constantly called away by the rest of the Elders, and no one could prove he wasn't sincere.

By the way, did you ever notice that the Elders sound like Tinkerbell? I mean, you hear this little tinkling sound, and Leo looks up at the ceiling as if he expects to see the Elders perched up there, hanging upside down like bats from the crown molding or something. And then he'll say, "They're calling."

Did anyone ever think to have the Elders just say, "Yo, Leo!"?

I suppose it would lose something of its mystical nature, huh? Yeah, that's why I don't write for TV anymore.

Okay, so Leo thought he had it made. He was not only the boss of the witches, he was, as an Elder, boss of the Whitelighters now. But once again, he'd failed to think ahead. First of all, he and his wife were no longer on good terms at all. Their marriage was basically over. And secondly, once he left his former position, there was room for competition. A new Whitelighter showed up in town—a young, hot-looking fellow named Chris, who was the tastiest thing to walk onto the *Charmed* set since Cole.

And of course, Leo reacted in typical male fashion. His henhouse had been invaded by another rooster. Too bad that he was the one who flew the coop and left the door wide open. (Why am I suddenly craving KFC?) He felt threatened by Chris, was convinced Chris was up to no good and was determined to get rid of him.

I submit to you that he would have had the same reaction to *any* hot-looking male Whitelighter who had shown up to take his place.

This one turned out to be his son—Wyatt's little brother, the one lucky enough not to have been landed with the name "Wyatt." He was visiting from the future in order to save his own life (and, okay, the rest of the world from his big brother gone bad): unless he could ensure that Piper and Leo got it on one more time, he would never be conceived and therefore would never be born, and thus would not exist to come back from the future. So if he existed in the future, he had clearly already been conceived, so why was he bothering to come back to ensure something would happen that had already happened?

(Deep breath.)

Think about that one for a while if you want. I tried, but it gave me a headache, so I'm moving on.

Here was Chris, coming all the way from twenty-odd years from now, just to help Leo get laid. You'd think Leo would have been grateful. It's not like he'd been getting much on his own. But no. Leo wanted to blast the poor kid to Kingdom-soon-to-come. Ungrateful bastard.

And poor Chris. I mean, come on. He was a male too. And he'd apparently been raised by three women who were oozing Girl Power from their very pores. You gotta know he'd been in therapy for a while.

Well, eventually Leo and the girls figured out who Chris was, and Phoebe stopped hitting on him (ewwww!). Leo and Piper knocked boots, and Chris was conceived and all was well.

I liked the grown-up Chris better than the baby one. Baby Chris just can't hold his own on the screen. He's a little stiff and a bit of a drinker—always with the bottle in his hand, you know? I, for one, hope baby Chris gets ensorcelled by a demon and turned into an adult again, so we can get back to ogling hunky, grown-up Chris. I mean, it's the least they can do for us loyal viewers. If we want to look at babies, I imagine most of us have access to the real thing. Can you say the same thing for hunks?

I didn't think so.

Okay, so Leo was back to square one. He got Piper preggers for the second time, but he no longer held out hope that it was going to give him any sort of power over her. So he was left with no choice. (This guy just doesn't give up. Then again, if you'd been frozen into a chunk of ice by your beloved and then drop-kicked into a zillion little Leo-sicles, or called a stick in the mud and then turned into a literal stick, in the mud, as he was in season three's "Bride and Gloom," you'd want to ensure your personal security too!) He moved on up the food chain and became Chief Justice...er, that is, head Elder. Note here that a bunch of other Elders had to get killed in order for that to happen, but it wasn't directly Leo's fault, so I guess it's okay.

And P.S., how do you *kill* an Elder? Aren't they immortal? They seem to exist up in the atmosphere somewhere, sitting around in the clouds with white robes and tinkly voices and the power to appear and disappear and see all and know as much as the writers need them to know at any given story arc. Shouldn't someone have *told us* that Elders could die?

And while we're at it, how about Whitelighters? They seem to live forever unless their dying serves the plot. So what are the rules here? Someone clue us in!

But back to the subject. Leo became head Elder.

Did it make him powerful enough to feel comfortable as the husband of a woman like Piper? A witch? A Charmed One? Well, what do you think?

Mostly, the Charmed Ones spend their time proving the stodgy, stubborn (dare I say, "stick-in-the-mud"?) Elders wrong. They defy their edicts, deny their rules, do just about what they please no matter what the Elders decree and, usually, they're vindicated in the end. The Elders, in all their wisdom, are usually wrong, which makes one wonder where it is they get their wisdom and knowledge in the first place.

So Leo elevated himself to the level of head Elder—someone who is wrong most of the time, can't enforce his laws or rules on anyone even if they somehow turn out to be right, and is viewed by the witches as an out-of-touch figurehead who doesn't know what it's like to be on the front lines in the war on demons.

Maybe that's the key, Leo must have thought. Maybe it was all that demon-vanquishing that made the women so powerful. Maybe being able to annihilate living beings at will and basically being in possession of a license to kill tends to make a woman go a little bit power crazy.

So what if there were no demons to vanquish? What if there were no evil to fight? What if the entire world became some sort of...Utopia?

Leo apparently passed this notion along to his friends, the muses, who whispered it into the ears of the writers, who wrote season seven of *Charmed* for our viewing pleasure.

In it, lo and behold, there was a whole other level of beings even more powerful than the Elders! They were known as the Avatars. They had so much power they could blast Elders, and humans, and demons into oblivion with lightning bolts that surged from their fingertips. And naturally, beings with that sort of destructive potential were pacifists. They didn't believe in violence. They, like beauty pageant contestants the world over, wanted only world peace: a world in which no demons interfered and people didn't even argue over fender benders because they were so brimming with goodness and love and *grckkrspa!*

Sorry about that, I threw up a little. Ahem. That's better.

Back to the story. Aside from everyone on the planet being in a diabetic coma from an overdose of sugar, the world under the rule of the Avatars would be perfect.

Now, the Elders didn't like the Avatars, didn't trust them. (I wonder why.)

Neither did Paige's latest boyfriend, Brody. He was so sure the Avatars were evil that he killed one of them. He used the tried and true method for killing supernatural beings in the *Charm*iverse—that is, he threw a harmless-looking bottle on the floor. It broke, and its ghostly tendrils (a.k.a. the "potion") snaked up into the air, into the Avatar's nostrils and the Avatar then died. It's just the natural order of things.

Unlike Brody, Leo believed the Avatars were truly good and before you could say, "Does this sound familiar?" Leo had become an Avatar himself. When the Elders found out, they zapped him with the lightning bolts from *their* fingertips. (Yes, of course they can shoot flames from their fingers—they're pacifists too!)

But lo and behold, Leo didn't die! And he returned to the witches, triumphant and sure of his power. He even *looked* sexier than he had in a long time, what with his shirt torn and his face and arms all sooty from the attack.

Where was I?

Oh, right. Leo returned from his confrontation with the Elders, wounded and dirty but unbeaten. He must have been certain that he was the most powerful person on the set. Maybe at last he could have his cake and eat it too. He could restore and even maintain a relationship with one of the most powerful women in the *Charm*iverse, and keep his own, even greater power intact.

Do you think so?

Have you been paying attention?

The Avatars wanted ultimate power over all. They thought they could rule the world by doing away with all evil and brainwashing everyone to their way of thinking—their form of government, so to speak. (Why is this reminding me of the latest White House press release?) Once that was in place, the witches were expected to give up their powers on the grounds that, without evil to fight, they no longer needed them.

But if that happened, there would be no one left with the power to challenge the Avatars' authority. This would, one would think, be fine by Leo, him being an Avatar and all. At last his power would be secure.

But the world would have been out of balance. Everyone knows you can't have day without night, darkness without light or good without evil. Even the writers of TV shows! Something disastrous would result, and the only way to restore the balance was by removing the Avatars from power.

The witches had no choice but to join forces with some of the dethroned, disenfranchised demons in order to overthrow the new order and restore the balance. Leo, having realized he had chosen the wrong side and placed himself at risk of being vanquished by the women he loved, fought the Avatars right beside them. And you know, you really have to give the guy credit this time. For once, he had ultimate power in his grasp, but he gave it up for the greater good, and more than that, for love. His decision to swan dive *City of Angels*–style off the Golden Gate Bridge and return to regular mortal-hood instead of leaving his family alone forever was an even more impressive demonstration.

Maybe he's starting to figure out that love is where the real power is. And maybe, among all the male characters in *Charmed*, he'll be the one to finally accept that. If he does, he might just last after all.

For now, he's back to coming when he's called, helping when he's asked, having his opinions ignored and often looking damn good, but otherwise staying out of the way.

And that, my sisters, is as it should be.

But I fear it won't last. Leo, I predict, is destined to keep on trying to out-power his powerful lover until he either dies in the effort or gets an offer from another network. Happiness in love never lasts for the Charmed Ones.

They've got too much Girl Power to ever be tamed by any man. Be he cop, demon, Whitelighter, Elder or Avatar.

Maybe we all do.

Maggie Shayne is the *New York Times* best-selling, award-winning author of more than forty novels, ranging from stories about Witches, vampires, psychics and ghosts, to bone chilling, edge-of-your-seat romantic suspense and beyond. She has also written for CBS daytime dramas *Guiding Light* and *As the World Turns*. One of Maggie's novels, *Eternity*, has been optioned for film. She is a working, modern day Witch who, in dull moments, wonders aloud, "Why don't the Charmed Ones just put the potion into a spray bottle instead of wasting all those cute little glass vials?" Maggie's new romantic suspense novel *Darker Than Midnight* goes on sale in November. Visit her on the Web at www.maggieshayne.com.

HOME IMPROVEMENT IN MAGIC LAND

VERA NAZARIAN

It's difficult to tell what criteria the Halliwells use to choose their men—at first glance they appear to be "tall and breathing"—but Vera Nazarian says they're smarter than that: They're all choosing men who are good with their hands.

"I always thought you threw a bunch of [wild] parties...things breaking, people screaming."
—Innocent neighbor to Piper and Phoebe ("Ordinary Witches")

"It's gotta be better than cleaning up after demons all the time."
—Piper, contemplating an Avatar utopia, to Phoebe, sweeping wooden banister remains with a broom ("Ordinary Witches")

"I am tired. Of all. This."
—Paige, as the Charmed Ones clean up yet another end-of-episode domestic mess ("Ordinary Witches")

How do magical superheroes handle life's less-than-super problems? Even a witch gets a stopped-up sink or a broken toilet and requests a service call from a handyman.

But what about when those everyday household problems happen with an annoying frequency and daily regularity, like hellish clockwork? Let's explore some of the extra-wacky fun mundane problems take on when there is magic happening all around.

Case in point: It's Monday in the Halliwell Manor. Random demon pops into the kitchen—mostly out of the thin air but sometimes crashing like a gorilla through the stained-wood front door—and unleashes fireball. Fireball misses a Charmed One who's engaged in prepping potion ingredients or peeling potatoes. It continues moving like a meteor along a curveball trajectory out through the kitchen door and hits the living room wall. On a particularly lucky day, it first smashes into an antique lamp, a vase, a sofa or side table. Wall gets scorched in a crispy, apocalyptic black-hole pattern that does not quite match the rest of the Victorian decor. Demon gets vanquished by exasperated Charmed One. But apocalyptic barbeque burn-spot remains on wall while the pretty and priceless vase lies in shards, lacquered door in splinters... You get the picture.

On Tuesday, repeat of the above, with minor demonic species variations and possibly residual goo. On Wednesday....

Makes a girl want to cry. Even when she's a Halliwell. And if she's an antiques specialist like Prue, it makes a girl want to—well, let's just not go to that dark, ugly place of the artistic soul.

What to do? Get out the broom and bucket yet again? Visit the hardware store? File an insurance claim? Call your friendly handyman Whitelighter?

Obviously magic is not all "poof and everything's okay now." And shows like *Charmed* are not afraid to portray the practical, even pragmatic, aspects of life for its magical protagonists, juxtaposing the mundane with the decidedly not. Whether it's refinancing a mortgage to get the P3 club going, home repair and improvement or even those very odd jobs to make ends meet, the Halliwell sisters have plenty to do in order to keep the Victorian manor they call home.

The TV tradition of using magic to both create and solve, and have episodes hinge upon, down-to-earth problems in the home is a long one. In the 1964–1972 Screen Gems comedy *Bewitched*, the practical and charming suburban witch Samantha Stephens wiggled her nose (accompanied by that great little "clackety-clack" sound) to repair various living room damage brought about by the antics of her chaos-loving witch relatives, primarily her delightfully wicked mother Endora, the bumbling Aunt Clara, sheepish Uncle Arthur, wicked party-girl Cousin Serena and anyone else who might drop in through the brick chimney (recurring structural damage) or land on a coffee table (can you say "carpentry job"?).

In the 1965–1970 Sidney Sheldon sitcom *I Dream of Jeannie*, the blissfully un-emancipated, never-liberated and perfectly willing to do anything magical harem ditz Jeannie scrunched up her adorable face and blinked her eyes (accompanied by the equally familiar "boing" sound) in order to please her handsome master, the oft-confused and flailing astronaut Maj. Anthony Nelson. A blink and Jeannie the genie would take care of regular housecleaning in a matter of seconds, or completely rearrange the interior of the major's bachelor pad or desk at the office—whether he wanted it or not, but always for his own good. Such constant magical domesticity more so than any other large-scale miracles drove the show. And while it annoyed Major Nelson and amused his buddy Major Healey, it seriously scrambled the brain cells of the military base medic Doctor Bellows, who just couldn't take it anymore, poor fellow. Really now, was that pencil standing in the mug or lying on the table a second ago? Did it float in midair? Or was it his reputation and credibility, flying away on swift, loony, decommissioned wings?

Jump forward several decades, as TV magic and its rules, not to mention SFX, got decidedly more sophisticated. We saw Joss Whedon's 1997 *Buffy the Vampire Slayer*, with the Slayer herself battling a bevy of demons all over her mother's house. The last straw for Buffy came in season six, when the rowdy M'Fashnick demon thoroughly busted up the Summers' living room and kitchen. In vain Buffy scrambled to protect valuables before they got in the demon's way, but he continued his trashing party down into the basement. Soon, the battle raged right next to the brand-new copper pipes. Buffy's construction-savvy friend Xander had just arranged to have this pristine plumbing installed after a recent flooding. And now one of those shiny new pipes broke again, unleashing a torrent and Buffy's fury, and inspiring her to pound and trounce the demon, finally drowning him in three feet of water, a flood of his own making ("Flooded," 6-4). The deceased Joyce Summers' life insurance money ran out at this point (though it had come in handy during previous times when the home was trashed) and only Giles' timely financial help saved the day. However, Buffy still ended up having to get a fast-food job at the terrifying Doublemeat Palace to pay for it all and to stay ahead of the piling bills. Oh, if only bills were bloodsucking vampires instead of mere financial forces of darkness....

Which brings us to Aaron Spelling's 1998 magical WB drama *Charmed*, where all of this magic domestic mayhem is taken a step further. Not only do the three Charmed Ones witness the repeated destruction of much of their heirloom house, but they are often destroyed themselves, only to be brought back as good as new by the life-affirming force of white magic and the help of a loving guardian angel Whitelighter, Elder, Avatar and, more than anything else, the ultimate Handyman, Leo Wyatt.

Now, about that Leo Wyatt fellow. He's a hunky WWII hero, the gentle and loving father of Piper's children and a guy with a heart of 24-karat gold, if not better. So, okay, he's also sort of... well, dead, and an angel. Even so, Leo's almost too good to be true for an angelical entity (compared, for example, to the bumbling Clarence from Frank Capra's 1946 classic *It's a Wonderful Life*), and sometimes so good that you want to put a collar on him. You can just bet that there are times that thought passes through Piper's mind, and she's tempted to say something to the extent of "Down, boy. Good puppy. Here's a pork-flavored eye of newt, now go sit in the corner. Behave, and I'll let you lick something else later...."

Well, this Leo puppy can certainly fix things. And more than just fix—he can make them as new. While another plumber might put on a hasty patch-up seal under the sink, Leo can *heal* those copper pipes, soothe away the sprung leak, make it better than it was before. Some other less magic-macho carpenter would go to the hardware store and buy a replacement door, but not Leo. After he's done with that damaged wood, you won't even know where the break had been. Smooth and oh-so-sweet.

And even better yet, Leo comes to help within seconds when called, orbing in to get the job done now, pronto, guaranteed. Not by appointment between eight and one, not in an hour or your money back, not just on weekdays, with the weekend and after-hours service bearing a high-cost emergency surcharge. Nope. Leo is instant handyman gratification, 24/7. And you don't even need to crack a phonebook. For that matter, you don't even need a phone.

The Victorian mansion where Leo so often practices his handymanly charms, and where so much of the demon trashing and furniture breaking happens, is a very special place. For starters, it is the ancestral home of the Charmed Ones, having been in their family for generations and most recently belonging to Penelope "Grams" Halliwell who bequeathed it to Prue, Piper and Phoebe. And the Manor's formerly rundown and now remodeled attic houses The Book of Shadows, which is in so many ways the seat of the white witch powers.

Since it's the psychic center, the home base and the safest place, then it might follow that the ability to keep it so—to make it stable, to keep it in tip-top shape, to restore damage at any moment and to guarantee that the home remains a white magic haven—would be the ultimate sexiest thing that magic can do.

Yes, sexiest. We'll get to that in a moment.

Sure, the Charmed Ones' destiny and mission is to save innocents and to vanquish Darklighters, demons, warlocks and all the other evil supernatural scum that fills the world like roaches. But when it comes down to it, without the Manor to call home, without a home for the family and the Power of Three and without stability in their lives and the pure *trust* that such a home represents, the sisters' international and far-ranging mission of Good might very well be compromised.

Everyone needs the comfort of home, and most people are more than willing to fight for the place they think of as home. The Charmed Ones have to do it so often that they take this fight a bit for granted.

Really, there are a thousand and then some ways that the Manor can sustain damage, and does.

Foremost of course are demon attacks and consequent vanquishings. They are as routine as making a pot of coffee, and they result in ugly burn marks on walls, broken furniture, piles of ashes and soot and damp goo spots on the carpet and floor, not to mention broken knick-knacks, vases and anything else in the way of the energy balls or other magic projectiles. Usually vanquishings are accompanied by fire and explosive action. And the cleanup's a bitch.

The sisters are real champs about it—well, for the most part. There are exceptions, such as Piper being under the influence of a witch doctor's house cleaning spell ("House Call") or Phoebe refusing to deal with the house altogether ("The Power Of Two"). But on the whole, the three of them take it all in stride. After one particular nasty vanquishing, Piper mentioned that she really should stop leaving nice things around the house. Hello, Piper? Took you all this time, girlfriend? Non-magical cleanup usually requires sweeping, washing, scrubbing, cleanser and paint. And of course using magic for minor domestic messes can fall under the no-no category of personal gain.

A related problem is forced entry by demonic forces of darkness, which usually choose to ignore physical barriers. In other words, when they find no entrance they make one, and they don't often bother to check first if a door is unlocked—no one ever said forces of darkness were all that smart. This often results in broken walls, windows and doors and is resolved by carpentry work and parts replacement to the merry accompaniment of the hardware store cash register's "ka-ching" and the depletion of Halliwell finances.

What about orbing? Chances are excellent that, upon materializing, someone could break furniture, or even end up *inside* objects or even walls. Granted, Leo was always pretty good about carefully selecting his landing location, but Paige has been known to sneeze herself semi-corporeal and precariously bump into things, even if that time it happened to be all Cole's fault ("Centennial Charmed").

Spells gone awry? Goodness, yes. How many times have herbal ingredients ended up splattered all over the kitchen or the attic? And that's not counting Piper's failed cooking experiments. Even a master chef makes mistakes.

In short, everyday life at the Manor is an exercise in maintenance and repair. And whether the Charmed Ones like it or not, even their more personal life choices are colored by it.

Ever notice how the good men in their lives are good with their hands? Darkly conflicted half-demonic bad boy Cole Turner never showed any interest in picking up a power tool. And neither did the glamorous dot-com millionaire, Jason Dean. But the big-hearted Leo Wyatt is a plumber and handyman, while the handsome and ordinary guy-next-door Dan Gordon was a construction worker. No wonder it was tough for Piper to choose between Dan and Leo. Decisions, decisions. But still, decisions within the same home remodeling niche.

And maybe that's why Phoebe still hasn't found the right man. He's probably out there remodeling someone's bathroom, not being a corporate lawyer shark or a newspaper magnate. Not even an attractive police inspector. Think about that, Phoebe. And that goes for you too, Paige. Next time you get the dating itch, forget the mysterious federal agent and call a general contactor for an appraisal. Doesn't matter what kind, just do it. Better yet, simply break something and then wait for your repair-god soul mate to knock on the front door....

We were talking about sexy, weren't we?

Think about it: what's the most empowering, vibrant, virile metaphor of magic? *Magic is the ability to fix things.* Redress mistakes. And the sexiest practitioner of this kind of magic is not a warlock or a demon but the ultimate *handyman*.

Yes, we're back to Leo.

The best metaphors go both ways. Not only is Leo a handyman in every sense of the word, but he is also the only reliable and stable force in the Charmed Ones' home life. Indeed, on more than one occasion Leo's been the one to bring a dead Charmed One back to life—using his healing ability in combination with the raw strength of his sincere *intent* to turn back time and reverse events. Talk about an ultimate repair job. Incidentally, that's what healing is—a repair job. Even now that he's given up his Whitelighter powers, he's still the man with all the answers, the one who knows how to fix things even if he lacks the ability to do so directly.

When discussing metaphors, it's worth mentioning the notion of magical archetypes, as found in all storytelling traditions, in mythology and folklore. An archetype—defined as an original prototype of a certain kind of character or personality—is a familiar cultural representation throughout history. We all know and recognize general archetypes: the gruff detective, the clever thief, the saucy waitress, the smart-alecky kid, the naive ingénue, the holy fool, the whore with a heart of gold. And if we think of magical power archetypes, there's the shaman healer or witch doctor, the wise sage on a mountaintop, the wicked witch, the trickster, the magician, the mysterious priest, the dark overlord. All of them are faces of power, aspects of being, familiar to us since childhood, from stories and the media.

So why not consider a new power archetype to add to our imaginary lineup?

The handyman.

Because we can all use the help of one, now and then. And because we all admire a truly proficient handyman's—or handywoman's—prowess deep down in our heart of hearts. Even when we don't want to admit it.

None of us can fix every aspect of our lives. Sometimes, despite our best intentions, things go wrong. We yearn for the ability to undo what has been done, to start fresh and to control the details. So when we find someone who *can*, it's the most exciting and admirable and, yes, *attractive* thing in the world.

So this is the secret. This is how magic works its sneaky attraction upon the Charmed Ones and upon us. When it's flashy and sparkling and dangerous, it's only a crush. So is the lure of power or immortality or the promise of untold riches. It might take our breath away for a quick wild ride, but it leaves behind emotional garbage and debris in the form of loss and pain. When all the glamour-dust settles, it's the quiet, steady, even seemingly stodgy and unremarkable force that stays true, with all its healing, repairing, regenerative, all-capable wonder. It makes an impact and keeps us anchored, safe, together. We bask in the trusty handyman magic, and we are drawn to it.

Indeed, nothing's more attractive than the freedom of being able to do serious damage and outright destruction to your safest place, your personal anchor, without consequence, over and over again—and then possess the ability to make it all right.

Sort of takes you back to being three and carefree and playing in that sandbox. Imagine never having to worry about that leaky sink again. Or that empty place inside, that need-spot which nestles near the heart.

Because magic itself is the metaphor of life's perfect fix, the perfect solution. And it is so subtle that even a wise Wiccan witch may not know the full extent of its repercussions.

Consider this: The Charmed Ones recite a spell to rid the Manor of Evil ("Thank You For Not Morphing"):

When in the circle that is home,
Safety's gone and evils roam,
Rid all beings from these walls,
Save us sisters three,
Now heed our call.

As the spell is cast, truth about their father is revealed while the evil shape-shifters are vanquished. Yadda, yadda, spell succeeded on all levels, everyone thinks, and they go on with their lives after picking up the chunks and mopping up the mess.

But—just maybe—that was only one part of it. As in, that was just spell part A, and the true effects are still ongoing and far-reaching. Because later that same day a handyman knocks on their door.

Leo Wyatt is here, to repair the door to the attic, and repair their lives. Part of the magic? Spell part B? You decide.

Either way, you can be sure that from now on nothing will stay broken for long.

Vera Nazarian immigrated to the USA from the former USSR as a kid, sold her first story at seventeen and has been published in numerous anthologies and magazines, seen on Nebula Awards Ballots, honorably mentioned in *Year's Best* volumes and translated into seven languages.

A member of Science Fiction and Fantasy Writers of America, she made her novel debut with the critically acclaimed *Dreams of the Compass Rose* (Wildside Press, 2002), followed by *Lords of Rainbow* (Betancourt & Company, 2003). Look for her novella *The Clock King and the Queen of the Hourglass* with introduction by Charles de Lint from PS Publishing and her collection *Salt of the Air* with introduction by Gene Wolfe from Prime Books, 2005. Visit her Web site at www.veranazarian.com.

GOOD WITCHES NEED LOVE, TOO!

ALISON KENT

They're young, they're beautiful, they date hot guys...you'd think the Halliwells lived in a chick-lit kind of world. Alison Kent studied season one and found that each of the sisters approached her love story differently, but they all ended the same way: teary-eyed, undefeated and supported by their sisterhood.

WHETHER A WITCH by reputation or through inherited powers, every girl deserves a little love.

It could be argued, in fact, that witches may need even more than most women considering the constant uncertainty in their lives—uncertainty that is about more than filling a social calendar, hitting upcoming sample sales, making ends meet or balancing overtime with aerobics.

Seriously, what woman wouldn't want a strong, supportive man to turn to at the end of a long day spent battling warlocks and sorcerers, demons and ghosts?

Picture it. An intimate wine and candlelight dinner (or even burgers and fries by flashlight) over which to discuss the latest auction house acquisition or exclusive catering booking or shape-shifter annihilation. Follow that with a nice back rub or foot massage before cuddling up to a big male body and letting him, like Calgon, take you away.

Mm, mm, mm. All the stuff that makes romance fiction romance fiction. Boy meets girl, boy loses girl, boy wins girl—though, in the romance genre's current climate, the story arc is just as likely to be girl meets boy, girl loses boy, girl wins boy.

Having written romance now for a dozen plus years and followed the shifts in what the market will bear, as well as what readers expect in a contemporary heroine, the Halliwell sisters have for me been the perfect example of single female twenty-somethings seeking. Well, plus magical powers.

Whether struggling to find their place in the world, working to balance a demanding career with a personal life, or learning to accept the weight of their family heritage, the Halliwell sisters are no exception to the age-old quest of a woman seeking a mate.

Neither were the writers of *Charmed* shy in their employment of the romance genre's conventions, tenets and clichés when crafting the show's first season. Watching the original twenty-two episodes again, I was struck anew at how each sister exhibited characteristics of a female protagonist seeking love, companionship, intimacy and that *Jerry Maguire* completion—yet how each was drawn as an individual, approaching the dating game from a perspective unique to her own personality, her desires and her preferences when it came to the opposite sex.

That individuality, in fact, lent itself to plot lines and continuing story arcs that encompassed the broad spectrum of romance as a genre, from mainstream women's fiction to chick-lit to almost—just almost—the traditional romance novel with its happy ending. Yet, Charmed Ones or not, the sisters figured out quite quickly that their powers were good, as Prue said, "for everything but our love lives."

So why, in those early days (pre-Piper and Leo, pre-Prue's death, pre-Paige's appearance), did things continually go wrong on the Halliwells' road to romance? Were their failures to find—or accept—true love based solely on wrong choices in men? Were the sisters themselves simply not ready for what came their way? Or did their magical powers create an obstacle too big for romance to overcome?

Their belief in the power of love appeared in the first season's sixth episode ("The Wedding from Hell") when, after sending the demon goddess Hecate and her demonette posse back where they belonged and reuniting bride-to-be Allison with her fiancé Elliott, Piper wondered aloud if she, Prue and Phoebe would live happily ever after. Phoebe's answer? That if Allison and Elliott could do it, so could they. To that, Prue replied, "I guess true love does conquer all."

In the previous episode ("Dream Sorcerer"), after Prue told her sisters that since men wanted the unattainable, the three of them needed to stop trying to please the opposite sex and focus on what they wanted instead, Phoebe stated that she wanted "tons of fun, lots of heat and no strings attached," while Piper responded that no matter how *un-pc* it was, she preferred, "romance, long, slow kisses, late night talks, candlelight," ending with a sigh and a declaration that she "love[d] love."

During the same episode (and obviously having ignored Prue's directive), Piper agreed to go along with Phoebe in casting a reversible spell found in the Book of Shadows, one that would enable the sisters to attract lovers. Sitting at the low table in the attic, they read aloud one another's wish lists for what they want in a man.

First, Phoebe went over Piper's list, reciting, "You want a man who is single, smart, endowed...employed. A man who loves sleeping in on Sundays, sunset bike rides, cuddling by a roaring fire and late night talks. A man who loves love as much as you do. Wow, you're a romantic."

Piper admitted that she was, then read Phoebe's list. "You want the sexy silent type that finds you driving through town on the back of a Harley at three o'clock in the morning. A man who appreciates scented candles, body oils and Italian sheets." At that point, Phoebe took over, adding, "He's about hunger and lust and danger. And even though you know all this, even though you know he'll never meet your friends or share a holiday meal with your family, you still can't stay away."

We know, of course, that in season one none of the sisters would find and fall in love with a man possessing all of the above characteristics, or live happily ever after with him when they did. They would find, instead, many men possessing but one or two admirable qualities, and many more possessing traits of a more otherworldly, if not evil, nature.

Phoebe, the youngest sibling, was cast from the beginning as the wild child, the free spirit, the bad girl who after losing her job and being up to her eyeballs in debt, returned in the series' first episode from New York to San Francisco. She also returned to Piper's open arms and cold looks from Prue and was immediately forced into a defensive mode, denying the unspoken accusation from her oldest sister that she ever touched Prue's ex fiancé, Roger ("that Armani-wearing, Chardonnay-slugging trust-funder").

Further into the season, after Piper had shown an interest in handyman Leo Wyatt ("The Truth is Out There...and It Hurts"), Phoebe, while under Prue's truth spell, admitted that she was only after Leo because Piper was. And when the question was finally out in the open in "The Fourth Sister," her sisters told her that she was definitely a "boyfriend thief." Phoebe even dated Rex Buckland, Prue's boss at the Buckland Auction House, before finding out he was a warlock.

Phoebe's tendency to find her dates a little too close to home didn't sit well with her sisters. Prue preferred to keep her work and personal lives separate. And Piper found herself playing peacemaker between her older and younger sisters.

Set up early as a girl intent on a good time, Phoebe went out with Alec, "some hottie she hit on" in Piper's restaurant, as well as "tall, dark, brooding, very New York" Stefan, a world-famous photographer who invited her up to see his etchings...er, photographs, both in "I've Got You Under My Skin." At the end of the episode, after Stefan, a.k.a. the demon Javna, had been vanquished, Phoebe admitted that she needed to be more careful in her choice of dates—though at least she was now seeking out men on her own rather than borrowing from her sisters.

Of course when she and Piper cast the spell to attract a lover in "Dream Sorcerer" and Phoebe met Hans (who actually did arrive in her life on a motorcycle), she threw caution to the wind and had "safe sex, a lot of safe sex"—only to eventually feel smothered by this lover who she had attracted for all the wrong reasons. They jumped into bed based on nothing more than a physical attraction, never exploring beneath the surface of her "man wish-list."

Hans, in fact, not understanding the root of his obsession with Phoebe, eventually turned on her. And romance readers were hardly surprised. The couple's bond wasn't based on mutual interests, shared passions, similar outlooks and smoldering heat, but on magic. And as much as the genre's readers know romance *is* magic, they also know it's magic of the unexplainable—not the supernatural—kind.

Phoebe's most serious love interest in the first season, however, was her ex-boyfriend—the man from her days spent living in New York, the man she wanted to give a second chance now that he was in San Francisco, but the man who ended up being the same one she left behind, one who was always looking for an easy way out.

Seeing Clay again in "Feats of Clay" was a turning point for Phoebe. When Clay reminded her that in New York she needed three jobs to afford her social calendar, she let him know that things had changed. That she had changed. And as viewers, we'd seen it happen. She had become less the wild one than she was upon her return to San Francisco, seemingly intent on settling into her role as the youngest of the Halliwell sisters.

Even though Phoebe couldn't help but wonder if Clay was the one, even though he charmed her by telling her how much he missed "the day to day of us," she didn't deny Piper's observation that she wouldn't be the first Halliwell to misjudge a man. Neither did she counter her sister's belief that she wanted to give Clay a chance because she always sees the good in people.

Even after Clay told her that next time they crossed paths, he hoped he would be the man she always thinks she sees, she finally learned her lesson about inappropriate men and moved forward with her life, taking an active role in her future, admitting she was still looking for adventure and knowing that meant she wasn't ready to settle down.

During the rest of the first season, Phoebe was more focused on renewing her relationship with her sisters and finding herself and steady employment than on men. Even when she met blind Brent in "Out Of Sight," she kept their relationship strictly to the business of saving the boys kidnapped by the grimlocks. In this regard, Phoebe closely resembled a heroine found in a chick-lit novel, or in a *bildungsroman* (a German term indicating a novel of personal growth). Relationship experiments gone awry, she turned her attention to becoming a dependable member of the Halliwell family.

Still, Phoebe quite clearly still believed in love, playing matchmaker between Piper and Josh, encouraging a hemming-and-hawing Piper to let Leo know of her feelings for him and helping Piper over her fear of always falling for the wrong guy.

Phoebe did the same repeatedly for Prue regarding her on-again/off-again relationship with Inspector Andy Trudeau, giving Andy Prue's cell number despite Prue's "Cop. Witch. It's not a love connection" protestation and telling Prue that all she and Andy needed was one hot night to get back on track. When Prue confessed to Phoebe that she believed their secret made it impossible for any of them to have a relationship or a normal life, Phoebe reminded her eldest sister that they had lives and deserved to live and love like everyone else.

Having arrived in San Francisco unexpectedly, Phoebe came a long way in that first season, gaining the respect of both Piper and Prue as a woman capable of holding up her end of their magical triumvirate, as well as settling in and finding her place as their younger sister. As far as Phoebe's romances went, she seemed to have learned her lesson about keeping her magic fingers out of her love life.

Piper, the middle sister, ever the nurturer, the lover of love, the good girl who is a cross between Emeril and Martha Stewart and admittedly hates to be single, spent the first season continually falling for inappropriate men: as Prue said in "Love Hurts," "a warlock, a ghost, a geographically undesirable handyman and a very dorky grad student."

In the series' first episode, she was dating Jeremy Burns, a reporter for the *San Francisco Chronicle* whom she met in the hospital cafeteria the day Grams was admitted. Jeremy handed the bawling Piper a napkin—with his phone number on it. ("How romantic," was Phoebe's remark.)

Jeremy seemed perfect. He held down a good job and no doubt the accompanying benefits. He was complimentary of Piper's cooking and paid attention to her interests. He could flirt and banter like the best romance hero. (Opening his fortune cookie in the first episode, he read, "Soon you will be on top—" before Piper took it from him and finished the thought, "—of the world.")

He wanted to show her beautiful views of the city—the bay, the bridge—and took her to the top of the old Boeing building for a surprise. *How romantic*, we thought. The perfect boyfriend. Except he was a warlock intent on stealing the sisters' powers. After he tried to kill Piper and failed, she returned the favor and didn't. Their relationship ended, uh, explosively.

Remember Mark Chao from "Dead Man Dating"? He and Piper had a perfectly simpatico relationship that held great romantic promise…had Mark been alive. Unable to communicate with the non-magical living, Mark told Piper that if his body wasn't found, a funeral held and a proper burial completed before Hell's gatekeeper, Yama, captured his soul, he would be taken to Hell forever.

He and Piper then spent the hour working to help the ever-present Inspectors Trudeau and Morris solve Mark's murder—i.e., the story's external plot. The internal plot epitomized the perfect progression of a romance as Mark and Piper got to know one another. He explained how he and his mother had relied on each other after his father had died, and how she had taught him everything she knew about cooking.

Once Piper told Mark that she was a chef, the two flirted about Peking duck. Mark admitted that he enjoyed cooking enough that he could have seen himself as a chef had he not gone into molecular biology. Later, at his apartment, he gave her a box containing his family's recipes that he obviously no longer had use for.

They also discovered a shared love for Camus, Piper flipping open a book she pulled from Mark's shelf to read, "I love this world as a dead world, and as always there comes an hour when one is weary of prisons, and all one craves for is a warm face—the warmth and wonder of a living heart." Sigh. If only Mark hadn't been dead. (A paranormal romance author could have done great things with this plot!) As Piper said at the end, "Leave it to me to fall for a dead guy."

When she and Phoebe cast the spell to attract a lover, Piper dated the perfect Jack Manford—though the perfection, she realized, was because of the spell, not because of any chemistry between them. When Phoebe argued that maybe the spell allowed Jack to say and feel what he would have said anyway, Piper responded that, "Love is a magic between two people that cannot be explained and cannot be conjured."

Smart girl, that Piper. At least until she reverted and based her decision not to date Lucas DeVane in "From Fear To Eternity" on superstition, having met him on Friday the thirteenth—the same day she met Jeremy. Later, when pursued by Josh in "When Bad Warlocks Turn Good," she decided to trust her instincts and lay low. She'd had enough of inappropriate men.

That said, Piper was enough of a romantic that in the episode "Feats of Clay," she took on the role of matchmaker, playing Cupid at the risk of her own job by putting a spell on Doug, a bartender at [quake], that enabled him to have the confidence he needed to propose to his long-time-yet-recently ex girlfriend Shelly.

Unfortunately, the spell backfired, and Piper realized that true love has to take its natural course. She told Phoebe that there was not a thing wrong with a great guy like Doug, even if he was a little "boring on the surface" and "easy to overlook," since "the wrong guys are usually the most interesting. Until you get your hopes up and let your guard down and they reveal their true selves."

When Leo first appeared in "Thank You For Not Morphing," it was as the handyman the sisters had called to fix their attic door. He made his second appearance several episodes later and was by then a fixture in Piper's life.

She first tested out the attraction while under Prue's truth spell and then finally asked him out, making the leap into a relationship. In the same episode, once they'd made love, Leo told her he might have to leave. The upturn in the relationship reversed immediately, ramping up the conflict between them and the stakes of the romantic plot line. When he returned several episodes later in "Secrets And Guys," Phoebe was the first to discover his true identity as a Whitelighter, a guardian angel for good witches. Unfortunately, Whitelighters were forbidden from falling in love with said witches.

This created even more conflict on Piper and Leo's road to romance—as did the fact that she found him "geographically undesirable." She preferred not to get involved with a guy she couldn't see regularly—or so she used as an excuse instead of letting him break her heart. Yet when she finally broke up permanently with Josh, it was because she knew it was unfair to ask him to remain with her in San Francisco and turn down a job offer in Beverly Hills when her thoughts were still with Leo.

Leo's return in "Love Hurts" signaled the end of the Piper and Leo relationship for the first season. Though each admitted their love for the other after Piper saved Leo's life, they recognized their Whitelighter/good witch circumstances would not allow for their romance to blossom.

At the end of this story arc, the crisis was not followed by a satisfying *romantic* resolution—though it did end in such a way that would work in women's fiction, as it was an emotionally satisfying conclusion.

When Leo admitted that he could become human again, Piper refused to allow him to do so. Instead, she made the sacrifice and let him go, knowing that his work was more important than their being together. She had saved the love of her life. They were still in love. And nothing would change that.

Prue's primary romantic interest in the first season was the most traditional in many ways, and the ups and downs of the relationship made it the most mainstream. Inspector Andy Trudeau filled two romance conventions—that of the alpha male protector and that of the best-friend-turned-lover.

As a child, Andy had been a big part of Prue's life. We even saw the two of them as children ("That '70s Episode") when the Halliwell sisters cast a spell that returned them to the past to stop their mother from making a pact with a demon. During that episode, little Andy ran into Halliwell Manor dressed as a cowboy (another romance novel convention), guns drawn as he chased Piper and Prue. In the same episode, Phoebe admitted to her sisters that she used to listen to Andy and Prue through the heating vent that ran from the kitchen to the house's second story when Prue would sneak him up to her bedroom during their dating days in high school.

With a shared romantic history, the sexual tension between Andy and Prue was already established the minute they reconnected in the hospital emergency room after Phoebe's bicycle accident during the pilot. Their first conversation established that both had kept tabs on one another. She knew he had been in Portland. He knew she had been engaged to Roger. The viewer was given a quick history of Andy as a third generation law officer, and of the Halliwell sisters as recently reconnecting and returning to the home in which they grew up.

Having the introductory niceties out of the way quickly (no long, drawn-out past history conversations necessary here), the Prue and Andy story arc began at the end of the season's first episode when Andy stopped by to invite Prue out to dinner, asking her when she hesitated if she was afraid of "having too good a time, stirring up old memories, rekindling the old flame."

The romance novel convention of the old flame as hero enables the storyteller to bypass a lot of the awkward moments that naturally occur between two strangers getting to know one another amidst the rush of sexually charged hormones. It also allows for the characters to reach a deeper emotional connection that much sooner.

The beginning of the second episode found Prue sneaking out of Andy's bed. Once she was home with her sisters, we discovered that the couple had slept together at the end of the date, their first since high school, even though Prue had wanted to take things slowly. As amazing as things were between her and Andy, she wished it hadn't happened.

Andy called her later and tried to allay her misgivings. He told her he hadn't meant for what happened to happen. Aware as we were that they had known each other a long time, it wasn't hard to believe they were unable to help themselves. He wanted to talk, but Prue put him off. And the viewers got the first inkling that all would not be well in this reunion romance.

When they went out to lunch later in the episode, Andy told her that he wasn't sorry they made love. Prue, however, was—not because she didn't enjoy it but, not having seen him in seven years, picking back up where they left off seemed as if they were rushing things. She didn't want to rush, what with her life having grown so complicated. "We had sex. Doesn't mean we have to elope," Andy protested.

He then suggested they pretend like their night in bed never happened—that they count it as part of their old relationship, enabling them to slow down and start over, because they'd been given a second chance that he didn't want to blow. All Prue could do was agree to think it over. Her internal conflict had come into play (will she or won't she tell him that she's a witch?), tossing up a roadblock she would have to overcome before allowing herself the relationship.

The subtext of their past, however, continued to play close to the surface. During the episode "Thank You for not Morphing," when the Halliwell sisters' father reappears after a twenty-year absence, Prue listed for Andy several things she wished she could tell her father that he missed out on by not being around—one of those items being her prom. At the reminder, Andy replied, "Didn't we miss that, too?" Yet he encouraged her to talk to her father. He even told her he'd drop her off at the restaurant where Piper and Phoebe were dining with Victor.

Andy was there for Prue. A shoulder for her to lean on. An ear for her to bend. For her birthday, he wanted to take her away for a spa weekend. To be with her. Away. Together... again. Andy's potential as a romance hero was classic. He was thoughtful, sexy, fun to be with—he was one of a few good men. But Prue's secret didn't allow her the luxury of making the leap into commitment. She had to think about it. And when she blew up after finding out that Andy was divorced, he challenged her on the very secret she was keeping from him.

Yet he continued to court her. He called to do no more than hear her voice in "Dream Sorcerer." When in that same episode she was injured in a car accident, he showed up at her bedside with cheeseburgers, fries and a single red rose. They argued over videos for an at-home date, then argued over the constant interruptions to the dates they were never able to finish. Their bond continued to deepen as they shared their frustrations—Andy's that they never had time together, and Prue's that she couldn't share the truth. That frustration finally culminated in Andy walking out after Prue broke the same date three times.

He told her that he loved her and went on to say that it was obvious one of them was more interested in the relationship than the other. He admitted being hurt by her lack of trust and stressed that he'd done all he knew how to do to assure her that he was there for her, but he no longer knew if he could deal with her continually putting him off.

When Prue cast her truth spell in order to find out how he would feel were he to discover the truth of her identity as a witch, he told her he honestly didn't know if it was a truth he could accept. When pressed, he told her it wasn't a future he'd envisioned having, and Prue broke it off entirely. Once their relationship was over, Andy could no longer overlook Prue as a suspect in several unsolved and ongoing cases. Even his partner, Inspector Morris, wondered if Andy's personal feelings for Prue hadn't been getting in the way of his seeing her "secret life of crime."

When called to help the innocent young witch Max, Prue visited with the distraught father of the missing boy, listening while he told her how his recently deceased wife kept her identity as a witch from him. His feelings mirrored much of what Prue had heard from Andy. Max's father said that such a family secret would have been easier to accept had he known it sooner. When Prue countered that perhaps the man's wife was afraid he wouldn't accept her and love her, we heard the echo of her own insecurities about her relationship with Andy.

We also saw the truth and the depth of Andy's feelings when he thought Prue had died in "Which Prue Is It Anyway?" Though they were no longer dating, he was devastated to think he had lost her. Once Andy finally learned of Prue's powers, he was still not certain how he felt—though he wasn't the least bit happy to find out she had based their break-up on his response while under her truth spell.

Later, however, he told her that, magic or no, a minute, month or year, nothing would change. One day, he wanted a normal life—a two-car garage and a screaming kid, a white picket fence but no demons. And so came the end of their relationship... or so we thought. When he turned in his badge instead of revealing the truth about the Halliwell sisters to the department's Internal Affairs division, we saw that he was unable to write Prue out of his life entirely, sacrificing his career rather than giving away her secret.

The most telling events in Prue and Andy's relationship occurred during the first season's final episode, "Déjà Vu All Over Again." The demon posing as Inspector Rodriguez was out to prove himself by killing the three Halliwell sisters. Rodriguez was mentored by Tempus, the devil's sorcerer who could manipulate time and did so, resetting the day each time Rodriguez failed to succeed in his mission. The first time the day occurred, Phoebe was struck with a premonition of Andy's death. Prue went to warn him, telling him she didn't want anything to happen because of how much she still cared for him.

When the day arrived for the second time and Prue went to Andy, she told him that she loved him—a fact he admitted not knowing. A fact that left him shaken. The third time the day rolled around, she told him she would die if anything happened to him and they admitted their love to each other. It was the fantasy of being given a second or third chance to make things right, even while destiny meant they wouldn't be allowed to be together, that made the episode so emotionally compelling. And the sacrifice Andy made in the end, giving his life for Prue, spoke volumes about their love.

At the end of the first season, though none of the Halliwell sisters had found a soul mate (at least not one existing on a worldly plane, or one who was alive), they had come to realize there was more to life than the hot sex and temporary relationships they'd experienced diving into the dating pool. They'd each come away with an understanding of the challenges involved when mixing romance and witchcraft, challenges made all the more difficult by the secret they kept.

More importantly, the three had settled into their roles as sibling supporters, protectors, nurturers and friends. They'd shared the truth of their lot with family members from the past who'd taught them about themselves and about their powers. Through love lost, love found, love sacrificed and love denied, the sisters recognized that the greatest power of all was, indeed, love.

Saving the world may not have been their career choice, but they had accepted it as their calling—even if it meant true romance would have to wait. And with love on their side, how could they fail?

Alison Kent was a born reader, but was married with children before she decided she wanted to be a writer when she grew up. She found a home at Harlequin when she accepted an invitation issued by her editor live on the "Isn't It Romantic?" episode of CBS *48 Hours*. She now writes for both Harlequin Blaze and Kensington Brava, penning stories she believes in—fantasies that show readers the way love was meant to be. She lives in Texas with her hero, four vagabond kids and a dog named Smith. And she actually manages to write in the midst of all that madness.

"WITCH-LIT"—A SEASON OF ROMANCE

CATHERINE SPANGLER

Season four will always be for many of us the season that approached greatness. Phoebe as Queen of Hell alone was worth the price of admission. Catherine Spangler thinks she knows why this year was such a bright one: Taken as a whole, it was a great romance novel.

AS I WAS RE-WATCHING a number of *Charmed* episodes, I was struck by a startling realization (similar, I'm sure, to being hit with one of Piper's scatter spells). The stunning, magical revelation: The fourth season of *Charmed* had all the elements of a contemporary romance novel. Yep—romance, enhanced by the Power of Three.

The other seasons of *Charmed* have not followed this genre pattern so closely, although they had romantic elements, including Piper and Leo's courtship and marriage, various boyfriends for Prue and Paige and the on-again/off-again romance between Phoebe and Cole. The episodes in other seasons have tended to be more situational and plot-driven, with the focus on the paranormal elements that ultimately define *Charmed*. But season four was the TV equivalent of a romance novel.

I can just hear the "intellectual" viewers, those who watch (and read) fantasy and science fiction, those who are fans of horror, perhaps a few mystery and suspense thriller fans—and who knows, maybe some western fans (after all, *Charmed* has good guys and bad guys and shoot-'em-ups in the form of fireball battles)—protesting my statement. I can guess exactly what a number of these viewers, the ones with preconceived ideas about romance, are saying: "I don't read *those* kinds of books, or watch shows about *that*." (Yeah, yeah, I hear it all the time.) They're screaming their denial, possibly even holding up crosses and garlic to ward off this ideology (trust me, I've seen this, too), aghast at the thought that *Charmed* could parallel a romance novel. They're insisting *Charmed* is a paranormal show about magic and witches and Whitelighters and Avatars and demons and good versus evil—that it is *not* a romantic series.

"Ha! You're wrong!" I say, gleefully taking on the challenge of defining current-day romance as it applies to fiction and translates to screen and television. Yes, *Charmed* has all of the cool elements above, but that doesn't mean the fourth season wasn't primarily a romance. Who would know better than a romance writer (*moi*!) what elements make up a romance? So my quest is to bewitch you *Charmer*s into accepting my claim. (And be warned—never underestimate the determination of a woman who fiercely believes in the magical power of love!)

The New Romance—Chick-Lit

To understand how a sophisticated, magic-based show like *Charmed* compares to a romance requires a look at today's romance. Entering the twenty-first century, romances have veered away from the outdated stereotypical image of women as helpless and dependent on men for fulfillment and happiness. Contemporary romances are innovative and creative, with strong, autonomous heroines. In addition, there's the new romance offshoot called chick-lit. Chick-lit has become the ultimate expression of today's heroine, a.k.a. the contemporary woman: sexy, sassy, carving her own way, without needing a man to define her or to assure her happiness. She is in charge of her own destiny. Chick-lit focuses on a woman finding her place in today's society, and often includes romantic/sexual relationships (which is why chick-lit is considered an alternative version of romance). HBO's *Sex in the City* is an excellent example of the TV equivalent of chick-lit.

The New Paranormal Pop Culture—"Witch-Lit"

TV pop culture has also changed with the times. In response to current culture trends, television offerings have become more diverse and more realistic (look at all the reality shows now out there). This includes the supernatural venue, where characters are now more believable, more "real" to the viewer than ever. Today's supernatural heroines may fight ever more fantastic monsters and demons, but in between battles their lives are a lot like their viewers'. The writers of *Charmed*, headed up by the talented Brad Kern and Constance Burge, were at the forefront of this trend and created hip, sexy, romantic stories that are the witchy equivalent of romantic chick-lit—or, as I like to refer to them, "witch-lit."

The witches in *Charmed* are strong, determined, smart and ingenious. And they can take care of themselves—with or without a man (or warlock, wizard or Whitelighter)—thank you very much!

The Charming Facts about Romance and "Witch-Lit"

Has everyone laid down their crucifixes and garlic cloves? Hopefully you're beginning to see how a magical show like *Charmed* can also be a romance. To complete the spell, let's look at the elements that are common to virtually every modern romance:

1. *Romances are character-driven, with believable and sympathetic characters.*

Virtually every romance is character-driven. And while the characters don't have to be perfect (a common romance myth), they must be believable and real—and unlike other genres, they must be sympathetic. This means the characters must have redeeming qualities (including a code of honor), must have some worthiness and be deserving of love. The reader/viewer must be able to root for them.

Granted, almost every television show and movie focuses heavily on the characters. If the viewer doesn't identify with the characters, or at least care about what happens to them, then that viewer won't continue watching the show. Even so, the plot and situations often take center stage, or are at least as strong and compelling as the characters. This is particularly true of most fantasy, SF, action-adventure, mystery, horror and even situational comedy shows. The unfolding of the plot is the main focal point of the show/movie. What's a mystery without a dead body or a missing valuable and clues for the protagonist to follow? What's a fantasy without a quest? Or science fiction without galactic social issues or amazing technology and weapons? Those are plot points, not character development.

The main characters of *Charmed*—in season four, Piper, Phoebe,

Paige, Leo and Cole—practically leap out of the television and into our lives. Although they are not perfect, they are believable and sympathetic. They are people with whom we can identify. They *were* the fourth season of *Charmed*, essential to its storyline, and could not readily be exchanged for other characters without losing the momentum and power of the episodes.

Piper is the stability and foundation of the group. She's calm, loving, non-judgmental, the emotional heart of the family. She's Mother Earth (probable astrological sign Taurus), the Halliwells' version of the matriarch who grounds families everywhere. We know her—she's our mother, grandmother, favorite aunt, Cinderella's fairy godmother.

Phoebe is the adventurer of the group. She's fiercely independent, needing to blaze her own trails, headstrong and loyal to a fault. She has trouble separating her emotions from situations and reacts impulsively (probable astrological sign Aries). We recognize her as the infant, a baby discovering (sometimes painfully) the world in which she lives. She's our child, our little sister, an adorable imp tossing her Lucky Charms onto the floor, impossible to resist even as we want to scold her.

Paige is the dreamer of the group. Despite her youth and lack of experience as a witch, she has a spiritual maturity that indicates she is indeed an old soul. She feels deeply, is compassionate and has very strong intuition, in which she is continually learning to trust. We see in her the wise seer, the caring guidance counselor, the peacemaker during strife (probable astrological sign Pisces), even as we see an idealistic young woman who's somehow untouched by the evil in the world.

Leo is a gentle, patient soul who strives to keep balance and harmony for everyone (probable astrological sign Libra). He's our calm, patient grandfather, teaching us how to fish or whittle a piece of wood, or our big brother helping us with our homework. Leo is a perfect complement to Piper's Earth Mother role.

No way can we forget Cole, with his dark, brooding good looks, his deep, secretive nature and his propensity for violence and evil, even as he demonstrates he can overcome the darkness at times, rising like a phoenix from the ashes. He's the consummate bad boy we love to hate, even as we eagerly await his appearance, anxious to see what he'll do next. For the female viewers, he's the boy who took our virginity in the back seat of a car, who broke our hearts and who is a poor marriage bet. He's probably a Scorpio, not at all a good match for Aries Phoebe, but oh, what fireworks these two created together!

By season four, we'd come to know these people—they were real to us, we cared about what happened to them—and, with the possible exception of Cole (who created ambivalent feelings in most of us), we wanted them to achieve happiness and fulfillment.

2. *Romances have conflict and character growth.*

With the current emphasis now on realistic and believable people, it's acceptable, even expected, that characters be flawed. While some genres might allow these imperfect characters to remain static, the romance genre—because it is character-driven—demands they experience personal growth.

The best way to bring about change and growth is through conflict, which is an essential element for creating a good story in *every* genre. The conflict is what challenges the characters, gives them something to overcome and forces them to realize their strengths and weaknesses.

Charmed is no exception to this pattern. The show's conflicts are inextricably intertwined with the growth of its characters.

Phoebe's love for Cole often blinded her to the truth and was responsible for most of her challenges and growth throughout season four. Despite her love, she had her doubts, raised when she came face to face with Cole's demonic past in "Black As Cole." But she clung to her love for him... until her insecurities rose to the surface, giving her premarital cold feet. She cast a spell to decide if she should marry Cole (with some unsettling results) in "The Three Faces Of Phoebe." Later, she "fell from grace" when she allowed evil to overtake her and chose to be Queen of the Underworld, with Cole by her side. But ultimately, she made the painful choice of good over evil, when she helped her sisters vanquish Cole in "Long Live the Queen." (No one said the growth would be painless.)

Cole experienced his own growth as he battled the evil inside him. He faced the Source overtaking his body in "Marry-Go-Round." The battle continued as he had the opportunity to destroy Paige in "Bite Me," but resisted. Yet he couldn't quite overcome the lure of evil, as evidenced when he took Phoebe with him into the underworld and prepared to rule as the Source, then tried to destroy Piper and Paige.

Piper, Paige and Leo also had their own imperfections and challenges. Piper has a tendency toward stubbornness and putting on blinders when she doesn't want to believe something. She didn't take Paige's weird feelings about a creepy house seriously, which landed Phoebe in the clutches of a demon, in "Size Matters." Then again, Piper downplayed Paige's conviction that Cole was still evil in several episodes, most notably "The Fifth Halliwell." She also feels too deeply, her inability to deal with Prue's death making her vulnerable to the Furies in "Hell Hath No Fury."

Paige struggled to mature, both as a woman and as a witch. She stole the Book of Shadows and used it to cast spells for her own gain in "Hell Hath No Fury." She made a serious blunder while mixing potions and ended up switching bodies with Phoebe in "Enter the Demon." But she stepped up to the plate as season four progressed, admitting to her mistakes and taking her rightful place beside Piper and Phoebe in the fight against evil.

Even Leo had his insecurities. He experienced guilt for his actions on the battlefield in WWII, but learned there are two sides to every situation, in "Saving Private Leo."

3. *Romances focus on relationships.*

Going one step further, in the romantic venue the main focus is not just on the characters, but on relationships between those characters, most particularly the hero and heroine. While many romances contain sensual or sexual scenes, the focus is on the development of the relationship, not the sex (another common romance myth).

Charmed has multiple heroes and heroines, but the relationship between Phoebe and Cole was at the center of the fourth season.

Their off-and-on relationship had been ongoing since Cole's appearance as a district attorney in "The Honeymoon's Over," but it crystallized in the fourth season. In "Black As Cole" Cole asked her to marry him. Phoebe rebuffed his proposal even as she assured him that she loved him, but by "Marry-Go-Round" Phoebe had changed her mind and, although she still had doubts, she and Cole were married.

Their roller-coaster relationship continued, with love and passion and blind optimism lifting it to the high points and Cole's gradual succumbing to the darkness of the Source creating the lows. Yet even after Phoebe was forced to accept the truth and help vanquish him in "Long Live The Queen," the relationship continued, as it was discovered that Cole still existed in "Witch Way Now?"

There was also the relationship between the sisters themselves, with all the ups and downs any family experiences. Piper, Phoebe and Paige are intensely supportive of one another. Theirs is a true sisterhood, bound by love and respect.

4. *Romances are about emotion.*

I can just hear some of you groaning. Oh no! Not that, not...*emotion*! Yes—emotion. Remember that most romances are character-driven. If the reader or viewer doesn't bond emotionally with the characters, there's no desire to remain in the story world (or, in the case of *Charmed*, no reason not to pick up the remote and channel surf for something more gripping). The emotional involvement keeps us watching, makes us care about these characters. We identify with them, even inhabit them as we participate in their reality.

Charmed is layered with intricate levels of emotion, especially in season four. Foremost were Phoebe's myriad emotions about Cole. She loved him deeply, and once she put aside her doubts and decided to take a leap of faith, her love became unconditional, her belief in him unshakable. She defended him fiercely, refusing to consider the possibility that her husband could harbor evil. But then—when the Source had completely overtaken Cole, when he was on the verge of killing her sisters—Phoebe was forced to face the wrenching pain of the truth.

One of the most emotional scenes in the fourth season was in "Long Live The Queen" when Piper and Paige were helpless and Cole was about to annihilate them. With tears streaming down her face, Phoebe approached him, picking up the last crystal needed to complete a containing circle around him. She stepped inside the circle, and Cole, thinking she had come to join forces with him against her sisters, welcomed her. We (the viewers) already knew that Phoebe couldn't stand by while Cole destroyed her sisters, no matter how much she loved him, and we were wrung into emotional knots right along with her. She kissed Cole lovingly—an obvious, painful goodbye that he hadn't yet recognized—and then stepped back to place the final crystal in the circle's perimeter, trapping Cole there.

There was another emotional wrench, as Cole finally realized what was going on and cried out to Phoebe. The shock on his face—and his pain at her betrayal—tore at us. The tears still streaming, Phoebe joined her sisters. As they recited the spell to vanquish Cole, she wept even harder, barely able to say the words that would destroy her husband, her love, forever. But then we saw her resolve, her commitment to good over evil, her moral integrity, as she did what she had to do, finishing the spell. She watched as Cole was destroyed, screaming out his anguish. It was an amazing, powerful scene.

As if that wasn't enough, there was a final heartfelt scene in the same episode. Phoebe, inconsolable in her grief over losing Cole, lay in bed, sobbing. Piper and Paige, uncertain how to comfort her but knowing she needed their love and support, climbed into the bed with her. Piper cuddled behind Phoebe, while Paige curled up in front of her, wrapping Phoebe in the love of her sisters both physically and spiritually. The scene was so vivid; we could actually feel the love and the caring. Phoebe continued to cry, her sisters sharing her pain, as the scene faded out... ending an unforgettable episode. Pass the tissues, please!

This was only one of many episodes brimming with emotion. There were the ones that dealt with Prue's death, "Charmed Again I & II," where Piper's overwhelming grief put her at the mercy of the Furies. We saw continuing evidence of Piper's deeply emotional nature as she tried to become pregnant and learned she may never be able to have children in "We're Off To See The Wizard."

"Saving Private Leo" gave us rare insight into Leo as he struggled with horrendous guilt over the choices he faced as a young medic in WWII, choices that resulted in the death of his two best friends. He didn't want to attend an event honoring war veterans, but Piper convinced him to go. Once there, the veterans crowded around him, thinking he was his own grandson, and told him what a hero his grandfather (Leo) was. A lady passing by saw Leo surrounded by the older men and asked Piper, "Who is that?" Piper, with tears in her eyes, lovingly answered, "My hero." (Where did I put those tissues?)

Through the episodes, we shared Paige's guilt about her parents' deaths in "A Paige of the Past" as well as her frustrations as she tried to learn the magic craft in "Hell Hath No Fury" and fought to be taken seriously in "The Fifth Halliwell." We couldn't help but identify with her struggles to find her place in the world.

And of course the love the sisters shared for one another, their commitment to protecting innocents and honoring good over evil were the overriding ties that wove all the episodes together.

5. *Romances are about empowerment.*

Empowerment is the one defining element of every current-day romance. It is the universal theme that runs through these stories, their heart and soul. Romances go beyond the physical love between a man and a woman, beyond the spiritual love of that relationship, to the *empowerment of love.* Think of the love of a mother for her child, of God for His/Her creations, of a soldier for his or her country, of the love between a man and a woman. What could be more powerful? While the focus in a romance is generally on female empowerment, men aren't excluded from the transformation.

In *Charmed*'s fourth season, this empowerment was vividly illustrated by Phoebe's love of Cole, by her absolute belief in him, her determination to stand by him and later by becoming his queen of darkness. She was willing to lay everything on the line for the man she loved, and her love stretched like a golden safety net around Cole, helping him to resist the Evil Source, which claimed him in "The Three Faces of Phoebe." Even as the Source's hold on Cole strengthened, Phoebe's love for him (and his love for her) kept alive that faint spark of humanity still within him. For her, he held on, even sparing her meddling sisters.

Even in a romance, empowerment doesn't come solely from romantic love. The modern heroine is strong, self-sufficient and powerful in her own right. Piper, Phoebe and Paige have strong magical abilities that empower them. Piper can freeze people and objects and blow things up. Phoebe is empathic and proficient in martial arts. Paige can move things with her mind and orb to other places. Yet true feminine power doesn't lie in physical abilities, but in the magic of the heart. Piper, Phoebe and Paige embrace the motto of "harm none," and their love for each other, along with their dedication to protecting innocents, gives rise to the Power of Three. When they draw on this power, they are virtually invincible. For where there is love, how can evil truly exist?

In the fourth season of *Charmed*, it was ultimately Phoebe's love for her sisters, and her love for doing what is right (her higher calling), that led her to help vanquish Cole. And Piper and Paige's nurturing love gave Phoebe the will to keep going, despite the devastation of losing Cole.

6. *Romances have a positive ending.*

Another common romance myth is that the hero and heroine always end up together and live happily ever after. Since today's heroine no longer needs a man to define her happiness, this simply isn't so. Granted, while an upbeat ending is a requirement for today's romances, not all end in marriage, or even with the hero and heroine together—especially not in chick-lit, where the heroine is her own woman and may or may not choose to share her life with someone else. The same applies for witch-lit and our independent, self-empowered witches.

At the close of the fourth season of *Charmed*, not only was Phoebe beginning to heal from the loss of Cole, but Cole had resurfaced, lurking in the Wastelands. While Phoebe and Cole did not end up together as the fifth season got underway, we knew they still loved each other, and there was a possibility they would work things out.

At the end of the fourth season, Piper learned she was pregnant and would finally have the baby she'd been longing for. And Paige found she had proven herself and accepted her rightful place with her sisters.

The season finished with us believing everything was going to work out for Piper, Phoebe, Paige and Leo—offering satisfying closure and fulfilling the final requirement of a romance.

The Magic of Love

Now that our spell is concluded, I think you'll agree that the fourth season of *Charmed* definitely embraced all the tenets of a romance. The characters—sympathetic and realistic people—drove the story, as the episodes explored the relationships between these characters while encompassing conflict, personal growth, emotion and empowerment.

As for the positive ending, the overriding theme in *Charmed* is one of hope. The show's message is ultimately optimistic and uplifting, leaving us confident that whatever evil the Charmed Ones face, the Power of Three will always win out, and the good guys (or gals, in this case) will don their white hats and ride away into the sunset (or is that another genre?).

There's one final thing—the magic of love. The enchanting, mystical power of *Charmed* is almost tangible, and its magical love will continue to linger in our lives... long after we turn off the television....

And live happily ever after.

Catherine Spangler is the author of the award-winning Shielder series, futuristic romances that are literally out of this world. The latest book in the series, *Shadow Fires*, was a 2005 RWA RITA finalist for best paranormal book. Coming next is a dark and edgy paranormal Sentinel series, set on current-day earth. Catherine grew up in Alabama and now resides in Texas with her husband and a menagerie of animals. You can visit her Web site at www.catherinespangler.com.

THEIR VIEWERS

WE LIKE TO WATCH

I don't remember why I first began to watch *Charmed*, I just remember not being able to stop. Different viewers are drawn by different things, but there is one attraction they all cite: the Power of Three. There's something about that sisterhood....

CHARMING THE TWEENER

VALERIE TAYLOR
WITH HELP FROM JANE FINOCHARO

A friend of mine, Valerie Taylor, began to watch the show with her very smart nine-year-old daughter after I said, "You have to see this." When I asked her how that was working out, her story of watching *Charmed* with Jane was so charming, I made her write it down.

A YEAR OR SO AGO, my friend Jenny Crusie recommended a show she was watching called *Charmed*.

Jenny's a pop culture maven and has made some great TV recommendations in the past—*Buffy the Vampire Slayer* and *Gilmore Girls*, among others—so when my local cable station started up with the first episode of *Charmed* in daily reruns, I decided to give it a look-see.

"It's camp," Jenny told me. "Jane might like it, too."

Jane is my daughter, then nine years old and entering her "tweenerhood," that period between true childishness and becoming a teenager.

Jane did like it, and so did I. We TiVoed it each evening religiously and watched it together the following afternoon when she got home from school. I spent significant portions of the years since the birth of my first child—hours of my life I'll never get back—clenching my jaw to keep from yawning through eyecrossingly vapid episodes of *Blue's Clues*, *That's So Raven* and all the stuff that came in between. It was really quite a thrill to find myself curled up with my daughter on the couch watching something we were both actually enjoying.

And as if that weren't enough to make me like the show, *Charmed* had a lot going for it from a mom's point of view. Strong women triumphing over scary things. Siblings realizing they were stronger together than apart. Extended family overcoming differences. Women refusing to change their basic selves in order to keep a man. The transformational power of love. Demons getting zapped. This was great stuff.

But there were also a few things not to like. For one thing, *Charmed* is full of storylines and plot elements that, while they work on several levels and therefore are part of what makes the show appeal to both of us, contain complicated enough symbolism or complex enough moralities that they sometimes made me wonder a bit uneasily what Jane might be taking away from them. Sophisticated sexual situations, for another really big thing. And, of course, lots and lots of violence, often in the course of events like abductions, blindings and feedings on live victims, generally culminating in often-grotesque death.

The violence was what struck me first. In the very first episode, "Something Wicca This Way Comes," Piper's boyfriend Jeremy (unbeknownst to her a warlock) tried to kill her with a knife—an athame, in *Charmed*'s pseudo-Wiccan parlance, though at that point Piper had probably never even heard the word—and later sprouted thorns from his entire face and body before the sisters finally exploded him into tiny bits. It all seemed pretty scary to me, but it was cartoonish enough that it didn't seem to bother Jane at all. That turned out to be the case for the entire series. Other than the occasional, "Eeew, gross!" when the blood and gore were really over the top, Jane was unfazed. So I made my peace with the violence early on.

Then there was the sexual content. These are not just sexually active women. These are women who are downright exuberant about their sex lives. They enjoy men, and they quite frankly want regular sex and miss it when they don't get it. They joke about getting it—or not getting enough of it—among themselves and openly go after attractive men.

Which is not necessarily a problem. I'm no prude, and in general sex in pop culture bothers me less than violence. It's my feeling that forbidding sex before marriage encourages intemperate early marriages between very young adults who don't have the experience to realize that the fact they want desperately to have sex with someone has very little to do with whether or not they should try to build a life with that person. I had lots of sex before I was married, and I'm really glad I didn't marry Major Boyfriends One or Two—each of whom I thought I loved permanently and either of whom I might have married had I been dedicated to the proposition of taking my virginity to my marriage bed. So I have no argument with adult women engaging in sex without a lifetime commitment.

But I do think it's a really bad idea to present promiscuity to tweeners (or teenagers, for that matter) as healthy and normal. So when we first encountered the sexual sophistication of *Charmed*, I was a little concerned.

So was Jane. "Mom, should I be watching this?" she asked the first time a scene opened with a couple in bed together, clearly to my adult eyes pre- or post-coital.

"Um, let's just skip this scene," I told her.

She flipped past it, and that's how we handled it from then on. I let her manage the remote, figuring she was the best person to decide what she felt comfortable with. Sometimes she flipped past stuff that seemed pretty innocuous to me. Other times she watched stuff I thought would have been embarrassing to her.

And over time what we both saw was that these women aren't promiscuous. They're serially monogamous. They are faithful to their boyfriends, and they expect their boyfriends to be faithful to them. Relationships end and it's not the end of the world—or at least, by the end of the episode the world is back where it belongs. They cry, they mope, they eat too much ice cream and do other neurotic things—mostly temporarily—and then they move on. They want eventually to get married and to raise children with their husbands. Divorce is not something to be approached lightly. It all actually seemed pretty healthy to me.

Now that I've defended their virtue, I do have to admit it doesn't help that they all—well, all but Piper—dress like they do it for nickels down at the Greyhound station. Jane picked up on the clothing issue right away. "Mom, is she wearing *that* to *work*?" Hard to fathom how a nine-year-old understands more about what is even minimally appropriate for showing up in the morning at an auction house, a social services agency or a newspaper than the wardrobe department of a television production company. When Phoebe, having exchanged karma with Mata Hari in season six's "Used Karma," dressed "like a stripper" according to Paige—who in my opinion has very little room to make such comparisons—Jane didn't get the distinction. I came in late to that episode, and Jane explained what was happening by saying, "I think Phoebe's supposed to look different," as we watched Phoebe tear veils from her bikini-like costume and drape them around her boyfriend's neck. Prue, Phoebe, Paige (but especially Phoebe)—they all dress like a sixteen-year-old's idea of what she should wear to get served in a luxury hotel bar. Piper, who actually works in a bar and could possibly be considered appropriately dressed for work in a halter top with criss-cross strapping and low-rise jeans with a thong showing, comes off looking nearly dowdy in comparison. Jane's not-so-complimentary explanation of that phenomenon? "Piper's a mom." I didn't bother to dignify that by pointing out that apart from the memorable "Coyote Piper" episode in season three—which forever changed the music video that plays in my head when I hear the song "Unbelievable"—Piper had dressed that way long before she became a mom.

We first encountered the sexual nature of *Charmed* early in the first season. Prue ran into her old high school boyfriend, Andy Trudeau, in the first episode. The next episode, "I've Got You Under My Skin," included a scene that opened with Prue in Andy's bedroom. It was obviously—again, to my eyes—the morning after. He was asleep in his bed and she was tiptoeing around getting dressed. She snuck out without awakening him and went home, where Piper asked if the date went badly. Prue sheepishly admitted that, on the contrary, it had gone quite well. "You know. Dinner. Movie. Sex."

Piper responded with a mock accusation of sluttishness. "Excuse me? On your first date? You sleaze."

Prue deflected this with defensiveness but no regret. "It wasn't exactly our first date, Piper."

"High school doesn't count."

We were left to wonder whether the high school relationship included sex, but that implication at least I'm sure was way over Jane's head.

This was the first indication I had that this actually might be a very adult show. Violence aside, it was the first time I really wondered if maybe watching with my daughter wasn't A Great Moment In Parenting History. Blowing up thorn-sprouting demons was one thing. No one could take that seriously, and Jane clearly hadn't. But sexually oriented banter between women who are comfortable enough with each other to discuss their sex lives unblushingly? This felt uncomfortably close to reality, and certainly—or so I assumed—would require some explanation. But how do you explain such joking to a person who has only recently learned about menstrual cycles?

Turns out you don't.

Jane neither questioned it nor appeared to be even considering skipping it. I wondered whether she was taking it in for future processing or if it was going over her head. "Little pitchers have big ears," was what my mother used to say sotto-voce to her friends when I was pretending to read or play in the next room, meanwhile avidly listening to them discuss the neighborhood gossip. I don't really remember much about all that gossip I heard, so I'm guessing—or hoping—that it didn't affect me much. At any rate, Jane doesn't skip such scenes. She seems to believe that listening to women talk about sex is completely different from seeing a woman in bed with a man. And I can't really argue with her there.

In an informal and nonscientific analysis of the sexuality of *Charmed*, I calculated the average number of overt sexual situations or references in a random sampling of episodes from season one—which can be assumed to be the original vision for the show—and compared it to season five, by which time it can, in my opinion, safely be assumed that the producers were (as rumored) aware that they had a large following among tweener and teenage girls. There was a definite difference—on average, eighteen hits for the first season episodes versus five for the fifth season. Was this intentional? Who knows? The sisters certainly didn't seem to be dressing any differently from season to season, at any rate.

So with the overt sexuality more or less accommodated by the judicious use of the TiVo remote, the remaining trouble spots were the ones inherent in the complicated storylines and plot developments. Perversely, these trouble spots have turned out to be one of the most rewarding things about watching *Charmed* together. I've gotten an opportunity to talk to my daughter about subjects that I wouldn't otherwise know how—or when—to bring up.

I've felt a lot like I feel when I'm driving along on some errand with Jane in the back seat asking questions. I'm not the only mom to spend much of the drive time between school and the dentist pondering questions that demand thoughtful responses. It's no mere coincidence that this is a favorite time for kids to ask these questions. It might feel easier to us if we could discuss these things while peering into their little faces, but it obviously isn't easier for them. The whole point, from Jane's point of view, is that with my attention focused on the road rather than on her, she's more comfortable asking things like, "Mom, what's 'gay' mean?"

"Gay is when a man falls in love with another man, or a woman falls in love with another woman."

"Oh."

In my experience, "Oh," should be interpreted as, "Okay, that's enough information for now. I'll think about it for a while and get back to you if I have further questions."

I'm always thrilled when we have these over-the-seatback discussions. I know that because they're instigated by Jane, they're timed perfectly. Because I let her control the direction of the conversation, I know

I've provided exactly the right amount of information. Conversations like these always leave me feeling like a pretty decent parent.

And so it is with *Charmed*. An embarrassment of riches in difficult questions springs to Jane's mind while we watch, clearly generated in her pointy little head by all the complex and sometimes morally ambiguous storylines and plot turns she's seeing. Jane's capable of sophisticated thinking, but her understanding of adult relationships is, as with most kids her age, not sophisticated. Sometimes her questions are clearly in response to seeing something new and puzzling.

"Why would Cole try to *make* Phoebe stay with him, mom?" she asked me once when, in season five's "The Importance of Being Phoebe," Cole had kidnapped Phoebe. "That's just going to make her hate him more."

"Yeah, but he wants so badly for her to love him that he's convinced himself he can force her to," I told her. "He's wrong, of course."

"Oh."

Other times she comes up with questions dealing with topics she has clearly wondered about before and given some thought to. For instance, in season six's "Valhalley of the Dolls," when Piper asked Leo to stay away from the Manor because having him around was just too hard for her, Jane's first reaction was, "But Wyatt needs his father, doesn't he?"

"He sure does, Jane. Piper's being selfish. She's not trying to be, and I know she's in pain, but she's not thinking about Wyatt." Jane has friends and cousins whose parents are divorced, so it seemed like a great time to talk about what was happening in those families—and any worries that it might happen in her family—under the guise of discussing *Charmed*. "Sometimes when two people who used to be married aren't getting along, they forget how important it is for kids to still spend lots of time with both parents."

She didn't say, "Oh," so I figured there might be more to come pretty quick. Sure enough, she thought about it for a few minutes and then, "I know you and Dad would never get divorced, but if you did, you would never do that, would you?"

"Right, Dad and I aren't getting divorced. But if we ever did, I would never say you couldn't see your dad because it was too hard for me. And your dad would never, ever do that either."

"I didn't think so."

But it's nice to know for sure, isn't it?

Other discussions center on the relationship between the sisters and their men. Unlike early television witch Samantha Stephens in *Bewitched*, these women refuse to give up their magic for the sake of a man. They're still hiding it from the world at large—some things will never change—but when a man can't handle it, it's the man who is jettisoned, not the magic.

Jane noticed that the sisters often don't have much luck persuading non-magical men to accept them as is. Instead, they have to find men who are already capable of appreciating their powers: either other magical men or men who have for other reasons accepted magic as a part of their worldview. Even that doesn't always work out. Piper finds Leo and then loses him and then finds him again. Phoebe finds Cole and then loses him. Paige finds Richard and then Kyle Brody and loses them both.

In season six's "Used Karma," after she had dated him for over a year—since season five's "Baby's First Demon"—and just as she was steeling herself to tell him about her powers (prompted by the fact she was planning to move to Paris with him), Phoebe's boyfriend Jason discovered she was a witch. He didn't handle it well at first.

"Just like Andy," said Jane. Jane liked the wimpy Leo and even the evil, kidnapping Cole better because they loved Piper and Phoebe no matter what.

I told Jane about Samantha Stephens and her never-ending struggle to keep from using magic because it made her husband feel threatened. My post-feminist daughter, who never donned a man-tailored suit complete with opaque stockings and floppy silk bow at the throat, thought this was nuts.

"Why did she marry him?" she wondered.

"Well, I guess she fell in love with him."

"Why would she fall in love with a man who didn't like magic, when she's magic?"

Good question.

What I've found watching *Charmed*—and other shows that include themes aimed at least partially at an older audience—is that my daughter, at this age, is still very willing to talk to me about all manner of topics. More importantly, she's still willing to listen to me. And so my occasional anxiety over whether or not we're getting into some of this stuff a little too early has been overcome by my feeling that opening these subjects in a way that makes her comfortable is a really good thing. In a few years, Jane may feel embarrassed or in some other way less comfortable talking to me about things like premarital sex and how men and women should relate. I'm glad we're opening these discussions now, while boys are still icky and Mom still knows a thing or two.

Thanks, *Charmed*.

Valerie Taylor is a mom and writer whose novels include *The Mommy School* and *How to Marry the World's Best Dad*. Jane Finocharo is a fifth-grader and budding pop culture maven. They live in Cincinnati with their family and their TiVo.

THE CHARM OF CHARMED

LAURA RESNICK

To get an analytical viewpoint on *Charmed*, I corralled a levelheaded, some might even say cynical, friend of mine, Laura Resnick, and made her watch the first season on DVD. "So what is it that makes this show so watchable?" I asked her when she was finished. "The sisterhood? The magic? The hot guys?" "Nope," she said. Read on.

I'M NOT ORGANIZED ENOUGH to be a fan of many TV shows. A fan is someone who knows who the show's characters are, what their relationships are and how those relationships change over time. A fan is able to follow the ongoing storylines and the shifting parameters of a show's premise. A fan knows that the reason the actress playing a major character is no longer in the opening credits is because last season her character died or left town (perhaps to start a spin-off series).

A *fan*, in other words, is someone who watches a show regularly. Some fans watch religiously, others are more casual in their habits; but, by and large, a fan is a person who catches quite a few episodes of a show.

This requires a *tremendous* amount of organization.

For one thing, you have to know what day of the week a show is aired. As a direct corollary to this, you also need to know what day *today* is on any given day of the week.

Right there, I start running into problems.

Like Phoebe early on, my lifestyle allows me to be at home all day. And it's remarkable how hard it is to keep track of the days of the week when you don't spend several days *of* each week going to a place where everyone keeps *reminding* you what day of the week it is. (You know: "It's Monday, so we have a staff meeting today"; "It's Wednesday, so we're halfway to the weekend"; "It's Friday, so we get paid today!") Without these little reminders that people who regularly go to work take for granted, I have to consult my computer to find out what day of the week it is—if, for some reason, I'm suddenly seized by a burning desire to know.

The next organizational burden to befall anyone who wants to be a fan of a TV show is that you have to find out what *time* a show airs. Having done so, you then have to keep an eye on the clock that day; and you have to do this on that *same* day *every week*.

You see how complicated this is getting?

Like Prue, the "strong" one, I work full-time. (I just happen to work at home.) So you might reasonably suppose I keep track of the hours each day, as most working people do. But you'd be mistaken! I'm a writer. In fact, I'm a *fantasy* writer. This means that I spend most of each working day lost in other realms, struggling with mysterious forces, confronting towering evil and saving the world. I don't freeze time the way Piper does, but time does frequently *seem* to freeze while I'm working. Only much later, as I emerge from another day of battling the blank page, do I discover that rather than standing still, time actually progressed in its usual manner, it's now much later than I thought and I owe apologies to various people who may have been expecting me at dinner, at yoga class or at an appointment of some kind.

Consequently, even if I've managed to find out what day and time a show is on, and figured out that it's on *today* at a certain time... I usually miss it anyhow.

This, in a nutshell, is why I've never become a fan of *Charmed*. I'm just not organized enough.

I have not been unaware of the show's existence. I sometimes see ads for it. I occasionally stumble across the middle of an episode of *Charmed* while flipping channels. Friends of mine (some of them contributors to this anthology) mention the show to me now and then, suggesting I'd like it if I could get organized enough to watch a few episodes of it.

So I know what you're thinking: Why don't I just get TiVo to save *Charmed* for me?

Hah! I don't have TiVo.

And I know what you're thinking *now*: Okay, no TiVo, but good grief, is this chick so inept she can't even program her VCR to record a few episodes of *Charmed*?

In fact, I do have that capability. When armed with a large cup of strong coffee, some chocolate and the VCR owner's Manual, I can pre-set the machine's timer to record a program for me.

However, in order to pre-set the VCR to record *Charmed*, I'd have to find out what day of the week *Charmed* airs, what time it airs and what channel airs it. And this is a *big* challenge.

If you could see my cable channel guide, you'd understand the problem immediately. There are twenty-four hours per day of television programs listed in this thing, all day every day for an entire month, and the listings appear to be for well over one hundred channels. In other words, there are tens of thousands of entries here. For goodness sake, not only can I not find *Charmed* in this guide—I also can't find the State of the Union address, the Superbowl game or a nightly news broadcast in it!

Additionally, there are several kinds of cable-viewing packages available in my city. Each kind seems to come with its own unique numbering system. Consequently, even when I do find a program listed in my cable guide, I can't tell which of the channels listed for it is the one *I* should watch.

My God, man! When burdened with a system *this* confusing, how it is possible that many Americans are reputedly watching up to eight hours of television per day? Amazing! I can only attribute those statistics to the staunch determination and strength of character that distinguish us as a nation.

Thus it was that when Jenny invited me to contribute to this book, I was forced to explain that I couldn't participate, because I had never seen an episode of *Charmed*. It wasn't that I'd never felt any interest in a female-centered fantasy show that several of my friends had assured me I would enjoy; in fact, it sounded like just my sort of thing. But my organizational skills had never been up to the task of tracking down *Charmed*, let alone tracking it down enough times to become a fan—or to become capable of writing about it.

This, of course, is what DVDs are for.

As of this writing, the complete set of season one DVDs for *Charmed* has recently been released. So, after delivering an overdue book, sleeping for twelve hours and then performing some much-needed acts of personal hygiene, I borrowed the *Charmed* DVDs and watched all of season one over the course of the next ten evenings, with a view to, er, *organizing* my thoughts well enough to write about my reaction to the show's first year.

I've still never managed to find *Charmed* during a regular broadcast. So I currently know the story of the Charmed Ones only up through the final episode of season one, "Déjà Vu All Over Again," in which Detective Andy Trudeau died to save the three sisters from a time-looping demon who was trying to kill them.

But speaking as a newcomer, I'd say the show has two obvious strengths: first, the relationship among the three sisters, and second, the humor.

Without these two factors, the show wouldn't work. That undoubtedly seems a self-evident statement in terms of the sisters; *Charmed* is built entirely on their relationship. The comfort and conflict of their familial bond is the primary emotional component of the show, and the triumvirate of power that the sisters share—the Power of Three—is the central fantasy premise, the unique feature that makes them the Charmed Ones, the witches whose delicately balanced combination of supernatural abilities is sought, feared, envied and challenged by their various fantastical nemeses. So I wouldn't argue with any premise that the single most important factor in *Charmed* is the relationship among the sisters.

However, I think the show's humor is so important that, while it may run second to the sibling rapport, *Charmed* wouldn't work without it. This is because, at least in season one, the humor, in a necessary and effective way, props up or fills in for aspects of the series that are weak.

It's an enjoyable show—a *Charm*ing one, if I may say so without getting whapped by the smelly wet salmon of pun-punishment—and I look forward to watching the season two DVDs as soon as they're released. But most of the show's charm resides in the same two elements I've cited as its strengths. And it does have many weaknesses, ones which would prevent it from working effectively as a more "straight-faced" show.

I can't address the series' accuracy (or inaccuracy?) in terms of witches, witchcraft or Wicca, as these are areas in which I've done relatively little reading and can claim zero expertise. However, my overall reaction to season one is that the fantasy basis of *Charmed*, its portrayal of a supernatural world, while often fun, is not particularly strong or well crafted.

For example, sure, I'd love to find a thick, mysterious, ancient tome in my attic that contains the solution to every supernatural problem I'll ever encounter. But in addition to being a heavily contrived story device, the Book of Shadows is such a handy, all-encompassing problem-solver that it makes the outcome of almost every episode seem predictable and anti-climactic. We realize fairly early in the series that most *Charmed* installments follow a similar pattern: The sisters encounter a supernatural problem, and they page through the Book of Shadows until they find an explanation for it and a handy spell or set of instructions for solving it. By the end of season one, this particular fantasy-based plot path already feels too well worn. Even allowing for the fact that we know when watching *any* weekly TV show that things have to turn out well enough for most of our main characters to return for a new adventure in the next episode, we can nonetheless too easily foresee the likely *Charmed* solution to a wide variety of supernatural problems the moment they're introduced each week: Look in the book.

Additionally, the script material that comes from the book consists mostly of simplistic singsong rhymes and generic-sounding spells. Having just sat through twenty-two episodes, I don't recall any spine-tingling, frightening, provocative or emotionally moving text emerging from the Book of Shadows, despite its prominent place in the series.

The show also stumbles over weak links in its fantasy premises in episodes that do *not* rely on the Book of Shadows to solve the plot problem. For example, in "From Fear To Eternity," Prue was able to vanquish the evil Barbas upon overcoming her greatest fear (drowning) by relying on the power of love (for her sisters). While drowning, she was led to this revelation by her deceased mother, who came to her in the form of a vision or spirit visitation. Which was fine, since we willingly suspend our disbelief and embrace such possibilities when watching a fantasy show. But such premises need *internal logic* within the structure of the show's fantasy world. And there wasn't any for this incident. There was no previous episode where Prue experienced such a visitation, meaning there was no established premise for the incident. There was also no episode-based premise for her experiencing such a visitation on *this* occasion. And there was no explanation of (or inquiry into) why she didn't keep experiencing such visitations after this episode.

The villains weren't a particularly powerful aspect of the show, either. Except for the delightfully oily Rex Buckland and Hannah Webster, colleagues of Prue's at the auction house who were gradually exposed as supernatural villains over the course of several episodes before being vanquished in "Wicca Envy," the villains were mostly single-episode characters.

Some of them were quite memorable, usually because they played on common fears or well-established tropes, such as the Dream Sorcerer, the Wendigo and the sewer-dwelling, child-stealing grimlocks. In most cases, though, the villains weren't around long enough—or were not distinctive enough—to make a very strong impression. They were more like sketches of characters than characters. And a rather large number of them had seemingly interchangeable motives: they wanted to kill the sisters for being powerful or they wanted to acquire the sisters' power—as in "Something Wicca This Way Comes," "Thank You For Not Morphing," "The Fourth Sister," "The Witch Is Back," "Wicca Envy," "Which Prue Is It, Anyway?" "That '70s Episode," and "Déjà Vu All Over Again."

Another aspect of the show that often lacked weight was the sisters' relationships with men. Phoebe dated several stud muffins in season one who were all generically good-looking and not very interesting. Piper's love life was such a busy revolving door (four "loves" in one season) that I couldn't feel sad about Leo's departure in "Love Hurts." He'd already returned from two previous departures, after all, and Piper's pattern so far suggested that she'd soon find someone else if Leo actually *stayed* away this time. However, there were a lot of strong elements to Prue's love story with Andy, and this was one sister whose relationship with a man held my attention throughout season one.

In any case, if the strong, believable and often complicated relationship among the three sisters is the motor that drives *Charmed* forward, the humor could be likened to the wheels that roll right over the show's various weaknesses and leave them behind like road dust.

I thought that far and away the least effective episodes of season one were those with the least humor. For example, "Secrets and Guys," in which Prue helped a boy witch who'd been kidnapped, left me cold. Without enough humor to buoy the episode, not only did I get restless while watching it, but I was annoyed by the kind of inconsistencies in the fantasy elements that I shrugged off in funnier episodes—such as moments in "Secrets and Guys" where Prue could have solved a story problem by using her power and there was no explanation for why she didn't do so. Another example was "When Bad Warlocks Go Good." I found my mind wandering during what seemed like too many longish info-dumps in the dialogue of this mostly not-funny episode, and I thought it was a self-evidently bad decision to turn loose a being who'd come as close as aspiring-priest Brendan Rowe did to committing human sacrifice. After all, if news headlines in this country have taught us anything in recent years, it's that being ordained doesn't prevent a dangerous individual from harming the helpless.

Meanwhile, episodes which were much more humorous held my attention, made me eager to keep watching the show and effectively minimized or masked story weaknesses. "The Truth Is Out There…and It Hurts," in which Prue cast a spell that forced everyone to speak truthfully for twenty-four hours, was funny enough to keep me from dwelling on the paradox problems of a time travel story. Phoebe's ruthless use of the truth spell to interrogate a cop in this episode was particularly amusing and was a much more creative solution to that particular plot problem (the need for information) than leafing through the Book of Shadows. The subplot where Phoebe tried to use her power as a marketable job skill in "Dead Man Dating" led from one funny scene to another, culminating in her trying to save the life of an innocent who, quite understandably, thought she was either insane or a money-grubbing charlatan. Instead of Phoebe's gift being once again just a handy plot device, the humor in this episode opened the door to understanding how bizarre life becomes when one possesses such a gift, and how simultaneously dramatic and absurd the results of exercising it may be.

Overall, the humor in *Charmed* usually took one of two forms: verbal or situational. These often overlapped or were combined, of course. The frequent sarcasm, ribbing and dry commentary which are such a central feature of the sisters' communication with each other is part of what makes their relationship feel so real—and so durable. These are sisters who know each other extremely well, who can be annoyed with and critical of each other without it being a threat to their relationship, and who ultimately accept each other, warts and all. And although wit isn't essential for me to become interested in a character, I am nonetheless typically much more drawn to a character with a strong sense of humor.

One of the most appealing and effective uses of situational humor in *Charmed* is the comedic consequences of the sisters having supernatural powers. After all, the very first time anyone drives a car with power steering and power brakes rarely goes smoothly, and the acquisition of a new computer is usually followed by a week or two of hair-tearing. So the difficulty the sisters had in controlling *their* new powers was not only enjoyably funny, it was also very familiar to us, and this familiarity made their supernatural powers also seem more *real* to us, more believable. In "I've Got You Under My Skin," the sisters flew into a panic, fearing discovery, when Piper accidentally froze Andy while he was in her restaurant. In "Something Wicca This Way Comes," Prue's attempts to appear calm were belied by the way her power wreaked havoc on nearby objects when she was angry. In "Dream Sorcerer," Phoebe and Piper's attempt to improve their love lives through magic backfired wildly, producing various single-woman's worst-case scenarios with the opposite sex. A spell intended to increase Prue's power instead produced Prue clones—who revealed aspects of her personality that she normally preferred to repress in "Which Prue Is It, Anyway?"

In short, without the humor which is used so often and so effectively throughout *Charmed*, the sisters' relationship would be less interesting than it is, and the weakness of the show's fantasy elements would be much more apparent. The humor doesn't only serve to distract us from less well-crafted elements of *Charmed*; it also makes those elements more well rounded, more believable. And making the fantastical somehow more real to us, turning something supernatural into a metaphor we identify with personally, is one of the hardest and yet most essential tasks of fantasy. If season one is any indication, *Charmed*, through its use of humor, is very capable of doing just that.

> Laura Resnick's fantasy novels include *Disappearing Nightly*, *The White Dragon* and *The Destroyer Goddess*. The author of numerous short stories, essays and articles, she has also written more than a dozen romance novels under the pseudonym Laura Leone. She is currently waiting for the next season of *Charmed* to be released on DVD.

SEDUCING THE CHARMED VIRGIN

C. J. BARRY

C. J. Barry approached *Charmed* like a research project, determined to take random samplings and analyze its appeal with a clear and rational mind. Then the sisters had to blast Cole for the good of humanity, and Phoebe sobbed, and so did C. J. . . .

IT'S TRUE. I had never watched an episode of *Charmed* before. Honest. I'm a writer. I take care of my family, I have a day job and at night, I write. Somehow in the past seven years, I have managed to miss this show that reruns daily. Not even a magical glimmer that it existed.

So naturally when I was invited to write an essay, I jumped on it. There simply aren't a lot of virgin opportunities left for a forty-three-year-old woman with kids. Besides, how difficult could it be to wrap my writer brain around a TV show?

But I wondered, why an anthology about *Charmed*? What was the attraction? What was that magic spark that made this series worthy? We virgins are a cautious lot. After all, that's why we're virgins in the first place. I'm not giving up my vestal status without serious persuasion.

So before venturing into the unknown, I attacked this project like any other—analytically and objectively with research and hands-on experience.

Phase One: Research

Google pulled up 147,000 hits on "*Charmed* TV sisters." Yikes. *I hope my brain is up to this*, I thought. I hit the first few pages and discovered that *Charmed* is about three Halliwell sisters—the Charmed Ones—witches with supernatural powers who fight evil and save innocents. Being one of three sisters myself, I was intrigued by the sisterhood. Of course, my sisters and I aren't quite as photogenic as the TV versions. Don't tell them I said that.

Cast of Characters

Piper Halliwell: Levelheaded and super cool under pressure. Able to blow things up and freeze time, a power I envy, especially at deadline. And she's beautiful.

Phoebe Halliwell: An empath who gets random premonitions, writes magic spells and, on occasion, levitates. Her powers seem a bit on the quiet side, but she makes up for it in spunk and kickboxing skills. And she's gorgeous.

Prue Halliwell: Starred in seasons one to three before being replaced by Paige. She wielded telekinetic and astral projection powers. And she was stunning.

Paige Matthews: Long-lost half-sister, conveniently discovered after Prue is killed, thereby keeping the Power of Three intact. Possesses her own telekinetic and teleportation abilities. And she's, well, you know.

In addition, Piper's lover/hubby/ex Leo Wyatt is a Whitelighter. He's cute as a button—*and* has healing powers. Phoebe has apparently been busy with several men depending on the show's year, the biggest and baddest being a demon-turned-lover-turned-demon (aren't they all, really?) named Cole Turner, a.k.a. Belthazor, a.k.a. the Source. Finally, there's a token mortal in the mix named Inspector Darryl Morris who keeps those pesky humans at bay.

The Fans

Let's just say, there are a whole lot of them. One report I found said approximately 5.3 million viewers an episode. 5.3 *million*. Holy smokes.

Then I hit the WB Web site to the *Charmed* page. By the time I'd drilled down in to all the ancillary pages, I realized that this show is a veritable empire.

- **Magazine**: Six issues a year chock full of everyone's favorite witches.
- **E-cards**: Send them to your favorite *Charmed* fan.
- **Online game**: I spent a good hour playing drop the magic potion bottle.
- **Downloads**: All the posters, desktops, calendars and skins you could want. I had to chuckle at the "locker poster." There's a hint of a demographic if I ever saw one.
- **Music**: I didn't think I'd recognize anyone on this list, which speaks of my own demographic. But to my surprise, there are a lot of my choice artists here. Some oldies, some newbies—a real eclectic mix. At least I knew, when I started watching, that I'd like the songs.
- **Shop**: More merchandise than you can shake a magic wand at. The music, DVDs (first season) and books.
- **Message Board**: This was my most interesting stop. 166 pages of messages that ranged from "Which witch is the hottest?" to "Are there any guys who watch the show?" to my personal favorite, "How old is everyone who watches *Charmed*?" The average age was around seventeen. Perhaps the real question should have been "How old is everyone who posts to the *Charmed* message board?" There was a great deal of discussion over Prue and her untimely demise from the show. I was tempted to post something along the lines of "What's so great about Prue?" but I didn't want to bring down the servers.

As any good PR person knows, it's all about the demographics. Yes, there might be 5.3 million seventeen-year-olds out there that tune in on Sunday nights, but I suspected the actual viewership was more widespread than that. So who *really* watched this show? As it turned out, most of my friends, family, co-workers—even my mom! Had every person in the universe heard of this show except me?

At work, I asked one woman about it and the gal in the next cubicle heard me. Before I knew it, I was surrounded by fans of the show all talking at once:

"I like the world of witches and magic." —forty-eight-year-old female

"Alyssa Milano's bare midriff." —thirty-one-year-old male

"The sisters are great. I was pissed when Shannen Doherty was killed off and replaced." —thirty-six-year-old female

"They give witches a good name. For a change." —forty-two-year-old female

"It is cool to see three young women kick demon butt each week!" —thirty-five-year-old female

I've worked with these people for twenty-two years. Who knew? The amazing thing was watching everyone's eyes light up when they talked about the show. It was like Christmas for grown-ups.

Okay, okay, I admit that I was curious. I was even more determined to uncover the appeal of *Charmed*. And so, the virgin went forth.

Phase Two: Viewing

I checked the TV listings. Whoa, the show played two to three times a day on TNT. That's a lot. Was it that good? Did it have cheap syndication rights? What would make anyone want to watch a show three times a day, or, at least, what would make some TV exec think they would? And it's billed as a supernatural drama. A drama? Hmm....

"A Paige from the Past" (4-10)

Paige travels back in time to find out whether or not she caused her adoptive parents' deaths in a fiery crash. In the meantime, Piper is busy chasing down ghosts who have possessed Phoebe and Cole to go on a mad matrimonial crime spree.

Guilt-ridden after watching a car explosion, Paige was persuaded to face her past and popped through a magic door to emerge, braces and all, in her bedroom. Of course, the whole time I was thinking, "She's only, like, twenty, so just how far back in time are we talking here? Five years?" If it were me, I'd go back to 1986 and buy Microsoft stock.

I was still chuckling over that when her father, who would die later that day, showed up and along with him the inevitable parent-teenager growing pains.

While watching Paige struggle to convince her parents that she is/was a good person amidst the added tribulations of being a teen, I stopped laughing. I had been there once. Granted, it was a long time ago, but I still carry the guilt of tormenting my parents at that age. When her parents told her that they knew she wasn't a screw-up, and that their biggest fear was that she was lost and wouldn't find her way, I started tearing up. And by the time they were dead (again), and she was back home troubled that they would never know the good person she'd turned out to be thanks to them, I was sobbing.

What is wrong with this picture? I wasn't ready for that. Nothing in the research told me that there would be tears. *No fair.*

CHARM SPEAK

Demons: Your basic ghouls, goblins, seers, trolls, ghosts, Darklighters, Furies, grimlocks and other evil villain types. Team: Evil.

Vanquish: To banish said demon to the Netherworld, never to return unless some other demon unleashes it by accident or for his/her own nefarious gain. Obviously the Netherworld is not as secure as it should be.

WHAT DID WE LEARN TODAY?

Never say never: As in, "We'll never see *that* demon again." Don't count on it. Demons are kinda like bad pennies that way, and when you least expect it, POOF, there they are again to utter dreadful one-liners.

Best line
PHOEBE: Can you take me back to meet John Lennon?

Second-best line
PAIGE: They'll never know what good parents they were. (Sniff.)

"Once Upon A Time" (3-3)

Broken-hearted and bitter, Piper renounces her evil-bashing ways while her sisters must find their inner child in order to battle nasty trolls.

This episode starred Shannen Doherty as the older sister and pre-hubby Leo, who's been put off-limits by the powers that be (i.e., the Elders). But the real stars here were the fairies and the trolls and the idea of innocence lost. It was a kind of a preschool good versus evil plot. I laughed over the troll/fairy lines as well as Prue and Phoebe each getting in touch with her inner child, dodging doorways and trying to drag an on-strike Piper along.

And then there was Cole as his demon half, Belthazor. Maybe it's a bad-boy complex but, even with shades of Darth Maul, I think he's hot. Now I understand why he kept switching back to a demon—probably from all the female viewer fan mail.

It was good light stuff until Piper had to go and give up true love with Leo for the betterment of mankind. Then I dug out my tissues again.

CHARM SPEAK

Whitelighters: Magic fingers, ladies. That's all I have to say about that.

Elders: A bunch of old guys who like to mess with the world for kicks. Team: Good.

WHAT DID WE LEARN TODAY?

Do a background check on every guy you date: Let's say you meet a really cute guy, and then one night under the stars he reveals that he's a demon. Wouldn't that just tick you off? Save yourself the trouble and look for evil ancestors before you pledge eternal love.

Best line
PRUE: Do you think the trolls know about doorbells?

Second-best line
PIPER: The first troll I see is in really big trouble. Let's go.

"All Halliwell's Eve" (3-4)

On Halloween, the three sisters are pulled back to the 1600s to save their infant ancestor from an evil witch. Confused yet? Keep reading.

It was Halloween and the sisters were dressed as—what else?—witches! I particularly liked Piper's Glinda costume and hoped that she would do it justice. I always felt it was pretty catty of Glinda to not tell Dorothy about the red shoes, forcing her to face flying monkeys and melt evil witches instead, but that's another anthology.

When the two Uncle Fester–wannabe demons showed up at the front door, the sisters were sucked through a time portal, costumes and all. Where to? 1670 Virginia, of course. Where else would three witches get time-traveled to on Halloween? Okay, I thought it should have been Salem too, but nobody asked me.

Surprise! Cole was evil again and sporting long hair even. I was happy! Who can resist a man with the Underworld at his fingertips?

Unfortunately, the Charmed Ones had lost their powers because they didn't exist yet. But if they didn't exist, then how could they remember who they were? And if they weren't there to save the baby in the first place, then how did they get here in our time? You see why I don't write time travels. They make me crazy. Anyway, the sisters had to learn "real" witchcraft to save themselves and their future ancestor.

So out came the cornhusk dolls, carved pumpkins, pointy hats and broomsticks. I'm no expert on Wicca, but I really enjoyed this segment and was impressed by how they tied it into our modern Halloween elements. After they were captured, the girls were executed by hanging instead of burning at the stake. That much I know to be true. Hooray for historical accuracy!

They saved the baby by using their newfound skill set, which included Phoebe riding a broomstick across a full moon and fulfilling every witch's worst stereotype. Even so, I loved this one. A scattering of history, a smattering of legend and Hallowed lore. Fun and educational at the same time. You don't see that every day on cable.

CHARM SPEAK

Book of Shadows: An old book that contains the answers to those difficult witch questions. More coveted than the Internet.

Vision: A premonition, usually something that proves helpful later on in the story.

WHAT DID WE LEARN TODAY?

Install a security camera at your front door: Nothing will ruin a perfectly good day like opening the door to find a demon hell-bent on killing you.

Best line
PHOEBE: Eternally Elvira, yecch.

Second-best line
PHOEBE: Don't tell me we've time traveled again. I hate time traveling. (I hear ya.)

"Long Live the Queen" (4-20)

Although Phoebe accepts the Evil Queen crown, she finds herself torn between her love for Cole and her old demon-bashing ways.

Ah true love, you never know where it will take you. In this episode, it took Phoebe to the cradle of Evildom—the Underworld. It was worth the price of admission alone to watch a pregnancy-induced, hormone-rampaging Phoebe terrorize demons. Don't we all feel that way during pregnancy? But she actually got to vent hers. It is good to be Queen.

But the real story was the lure of the Dark Side. Face it, it's more fun to be bad. You never see villains complaining that they're unhappy or bored, and you can't tell me that Phoebe wasn't having a ball zapping demons and pain-in-the-butt bosses. Eventually her good side prevailed, but it was fun while it lasted.

The best character this entire episode was Cole. How can you not love a guy who juggles mutinous demons, an unstable pregnant wife, a really obnoxious Seer and a psychopathic human side?

At the base of it all was the old classic: Good versus Evil. Would love be stronger than evil? In Cole's case, it was a constant internal battle that would put Jekyll and Hyde to shame. Of all the characters, he was the most complicated, vacillating between good and evil, unable to make the jump to either side. Ultimately, Phoebe was able to make a choice where Cole could not, one that even Cole understood. I don't know many men who would profess their undying love while being torched like a demon-kabob. But there was no other option. Love and Evil don't mix well. As the Seer noted, "It is not in the nature of Good to compromise."

The real killer though, was the final scene. No words. Just Piper and Paige comforting a heartbroken Phoebe. Sisters don't need words when it comes to pain. They've seen every emotion possible. It's part of the sister gig; we understand and embrace that.

I cried my eyes out. And then I called my sisters.

CHARM SPEAK

The Source: As in, Of All Evil. Very bad dude. Captain of the Evil Team.

Innocents: You and me. The little people.

WHAT DID WE LEARN TODAY?

Use your powers for good: No one likes a bad witch. So if you are suddenly given dark supernatural powers, be nice to the rest of us.

Best Line
PIPER: Uh, Phoebe, you're evil. You're like the queen of all evil, literally.

Second-best Line
COLE: I will always love you. (Sigh.)

"Witchness Protection" (7-10)

Fast-forward a whole bunch of years. Piper and Leo are married with kids and experiencing that whole family insanity thing. (Just wait until soccer kicks in.) Leo ruins the family photo to save a half-dressed Seer that doesn't look like any demon I've ever seen, and then things get a little crazy after that. The Seer is trying to switch teams, which is apparently frowned upon by the demon code.

The Seer and Phoebe hit it off on the fashion level, bringing the lighter moments to the episode. And then Q showed up! I wondered whatever happened to him. He's an Elder now. The uber-evil Zankou was loose and sucking up other demons' abilities like nobody's business. You ever notice that it's really hard to take an evil guy seriously when he's insanely good-looking? Brody (no idea who he is) and Paige got hot and heavy, causing Paige to turn against her sisters. The three of them can battle demons without blinking an eye, but a lover never fails to screw everything up.

Leo had become an Avatar, whatever that is. But were they good or bad? Oooo, forget that; he didn't tell Piper he was an Avatar. Bad hubby move, Leo. There's not a demon alive (or dead) more dangerous than a scorned wife.

Shortly thereafter, the Seer got fried, but not before leaving a cryptic vision with Phoebe. Hmmm, is it my imagination or did the line "Not since the Avatar" sound a little…oh. I don't know…ambiguous to anyone besides me? Peace on Earth? Hello! We *all* know that's not going to work.

But where does that leave our sisters? If they don't join forces, they will never know if they missed the one shot at peace for themselves and the rest of us. On the other hand, if they unite with the Avatars and defeat the demons and the Elders, and *then* the Avatars turn out to be psychos, the Charmed Ones will end up having to find a way to defeat the Avatars solo since the other factions have been removed.

At the end of the episode, they called the mysterious Avatars to hear them out. I blame this misguided decision on demon fatigue. However, one thing I've noticed about the sisters is that they are smarter than your average demon. I don't worry about them too much.

Unless of course, this is the end of the series. I mean, what would the sisters do if every demon were vanquished? Their lives would be boring—just like reality. Ack! We can't have that. There are already enough bad reality shows on the air. Okay, everyone root for the Avatars to be evil, and we'll watch next week to see what happens.

Er, I'm *not* hooked, I swear.
The show is on Sunday night, right?

CHARM SPEAK

Underworld: Where the evil dudes and dudettes hang out. Imagine the parties.

Avatars: A bunch of young guys who like to mess with the world for kicks. Team: Unknown.

WHAT DID WE LEARN TODAY?

It's a complete waste of time to clean house: Because some demon is going to show up and make a big mess anyway. Spray some air freshener, and you'll be good to go.

Best Line
SEER: Grimlocks... emphasis on the "grim"... hate me.

Second-best Line
PHOEBE: Paige! Demon! No active power! Do something!

Phase Three: My Final Answer

Well, I did my homework. I listened to fans, watched a whole bunch of episodes and took copious notes to find the secret behind the show's amazing success. What was that magic that held viewers spellbound? I am no *Charmed* expert, but I think I figured it out.

While somersaulting through several seasons, I decided that although the core of this series is supposed to be the fight between Good and Evil, the one constant that ran through every episode was the love of the three sisters. No matter what they transformed into or who they were possessed by or how many times they died, they never gave up on each other. And the demons they saved each other from weren't necessarily the corporal variety they could simply blow to kingdom come.

Instead of being my usual analytical self, I found myself crying, laughing and rooting for them. Between the body-hopping, power-swapping and demon-stomping, I grew to care about the characters. And although Good has prevailed so far, it hasn't been without sacrifice. I'd like nothing better than to see them win and have peace, but that's not how life works. Their lives may be more dramatic than ours, but we all hurt the same. We all have demons. They might not show up at the front door, but they exist and the challenge is to vanquish them. Every week, we get to watch the sisters do just that—with courage, attitude and each other. And that was what finally seduced me.

Okay, maybe that's not why everyone else watches this show, but it's my reason and it's just as good as the others I heard. And in the end, the reason doesn't really matter.

Suffice to say, I am no longer a *Charmed* virgin. I'm captivated. I'm smitten. And like everyone else, I'm just plain *charmed*.

C. J. Barry is an award-winning author whose love of the paranormal began young, with science fiction novels and her brother's comic books. An earthbound wife and mother of two, C. J. lives with her family and cat in a small town in Upstate New York where she works as an Information Technology Manager. She is a member of the Romance Writers of America, the Fantasy, Futuristic & Paranormal chapter and president of the Central New York Romance Writers. For more information, visit her Web site at www.cjbarry.com.

CAST BIOGRAPHIES

Shannen Doherty is Prue Halliwell

Born April 12, 1971, in Memphis, Tennessee, showbiz veteran Shannen Doherty includes Jenny Wilder on *Little House on the Prairie* and Brenda Walsh on *Beverly Hills 90210* among her almost three dozen film and television credits.

During her tenure on *Charmed*, she directed several episodes ("Be Careful What You Witch For" in season two and season three's "The Good, the Bad, and the Cursed" and "All Hell Breaks Loose") and choreographed Piper's dance sequence in "Coyote Piper," in addition to playing eldest Halliwell sister Prue. The multitalented actress with the famously fiery temper also has business savvy—despite having left *Charmed* after the third season, she still owns 5% of the show.

Holly Marie Combs is Piper Halliwell

California native Holly Marie Combs was born in San Diego on December 3, 1973. Future demon-vanquisher Holly and her mother Lauralei moved to New York when Holly was in elementary school, and within two years Holly was doing print work and appearing in television commercials. She landed her first big role, Kimberly Brock on David E. Kelley's *Picket Fences*, when she was eighteen and followed that success with her role as Piper Halliwell on *Charmed*.

Like the character she plays, Holly devotes her time and energy to worthy causes—she is involved with Thursday's Child, a charity helping at-risk teens and has also been a spokesperson for the treatment and cure of breast cancer. Holly also, like Piper, knows the importance of family. She and her mother were very close—Holly was an only child and Lauralei a single mother—and her work on *Charmed* has generated another family: her own. In 2004, her longtime relationship with *Charmed* key grip David Donoho resulted in the birth of a son, Finley Arthur Donoho.

Alyssa Milano is Phoebe Halliwell

Thanks to an enterprising aspiring-dancer babysitter who took her along on an audition, Brooklyn-born Alyssa Milano snagged her first role at the age of seven, in the first natural touring company of *Annie*. From there she won high-profile roles on *Who's the Boss?* (as Tony Danza's adorably precocious daughter Samantha Micelli), *Melrose Place* (as Jennifer Mancini) and finally as Phoebe Halliwell on *Charmed*.

Extracurricular activities have included television advertising campaigns for Candie's and 1-800-COLLECT, serving as the facial inspiration for Ariel in Disney's *The Little Mermaid* and fighting to protect actors' rights on the Web. Thanks to her involvement in charity work, Alyssa has also been appointed a National Ambassador for Unicef.

Rose McGowan is Paige Matthews

Wild child Rose McGowan, born September 5, 1973, spent her childhood traveling through Europe and emancipated herself from her parents at the age of fifteen. A regular in independent movie circles, Rose has been cast in projects as diverse as *Encino Man*, *The Doom Generation* and the dark comedy *Jawbreaker* before her addition to *Charmed* as Paige Matthews, the long-lost fourth Halliwell sister.

Rose is the former fiancé of Marilyn Manson and sang backing vocals on the track "Posthuman" on the band's album *Mechanical Animals*—great practice for Paige Matthews' song in season five's "Sense and Sense Ability." She has also lived with depression most of her life and, in accordance with her *Charmed* character's social worker past, has said that she might someday like to start a counseling program for teenage girls since she herself had such a difficult adolescence.

Brian Krause is Leo Wyatt

Brian Krause, nicknamed Blue Flamer on the *Charmed* set, was born in El Toro, California, on February 1, 1969, and has been acting since the age of sixteen. He dabbled in sports medicine and a semi-professional soccer career before landing his first feature film role in *Return to the Blue Lagoon*. That role was quickly followed by other theatrical releases, including Stephen King's *Sleepwalkers* and *The Liars' Club*.

He also guest-starred in several television shows such as *Walker, Texas Ranger* and had a recurring role in *Another World* before becoming a series regular on *Charmed*. When not protecting the Halliwell sisters from otherworldly harm as Leo Wyatt, he enjoys playing golf, auto racing and playing Scrabble with his friends and family. He has also worked with the Olive Crest Foundation, which aids foster children.

Dorian Gregory is Inspector Darryl Morris

Washington, D.C., native Dorian Gregory was born January 26, 1971. After starring as parapsychologist Diamont Teague on the weekly show *Baywatch Nights*, he began to land guest appearances on shows such as *Pacific Blue*, *Murder She Wrote* and *Living Single*.

In 1998, he was cast in *Charmed* as Inspector Darryl Morris, the watchful police officer and invaluable friend to the Halliwell sisters. In addition to his role on *Charmed*, he finds time to do film work and also co-hosted *The Other Half*, a syndicated talk show. Like his charitable co-stars and his *Charmed* persona, he also feels an obligation to the greater good. He is active in the Jeopardy Program, which aids youths at risk in Los Angeles, and also serves as the national spokesperson for the American Diabetes Association.

Julian McMahon is Cole Turner

Julian McMahon was born July 27, 1968, in Sydney to the former Prime Minister of Australia. Though he started out studying law at the University of Sydney, he soon switched to a modeling career, and his work in commercials propelled him to popularity and a role on an Australian soap opera before he began performing on stage in both musicals and plays.

He then began acting in America and landed his role on *Charmed* as the half-demon Cole Turner. Though his character is no longer with *Charmed*, Julian can now be seen playing Dr. Christian Troy in the critically acclaimed FX series *Nip/Tuck*. In his spare time, he enjoys surfing, biking, cooking and collecting classic books.